The Memphis Guide is an important addition to the resource material available about Memphis. It has brought together in one reference, fragments of material which were heretofore present but unaccounted for. I think it has depth and scope while at the same time serving as a quick reference. It should be a valuable tool to Memphians and visitors alike.

> Fred L. Davis
> President, Fred L. Davis Insurance Agency

...covers the spectrum—from the arts and architecture to sounds and scenes, a little history and a lot of useful information. A real help for Memphians and newcomers alike.

> C. T. Bingham, Jr.
> Executive Vice President, Memphis Area Chamber of Commerce

*Take time to read **The Memphis Guide**—the definitive source book for both Memphians and visitors. Even those who thought they knew it all will be pleasantly surprised. Discover interesting places, little known facts and enjoy a great tour of Memphis at its best!*

> Jeanne C. Arthur
> President, Memphis in M_

D1088519

Virginia McLean's ***The Memphis Guide*** finally provides what Memphis has so long needed—a thorough, highly readable guide to places of interest in the city. The book is carefully researched, well written, and conveniently organized. It will be found informative and enjoyable by natives of the City and will be indispensable to newcomers and visitors.

> Mrs. Charles F. (Kay B.) Newman
> President, Memphis Heritage, Inc.

"The Memphis Guide"

by

Virginia Overton McLean

Redbird Press
P.O. Box 11441
Memphis, Tn. 38111

Library of Congress Catalog Card Number: 81-90083.

ISBN O-9606046-0-X.

First Edition, First Printing — March 1982.

Edited by Elaine Shannon.
Cover design by Catharine Roberts.
Art design and layout by Susan Patton Robinson.
Typography by Jean Roberts Typesetting.
Printing by Harris Press.

CONTENTS

MAPS

ACKNOWLEDGMENTS

So many people, from strangers who took the time to answer questions to close friends who helped proofread, have encouraged and helped me with this project. I appreciate it so much and want to list everyone. Because of space limitations that's impossible; I must just say — thank you.

I want to give special thanks to Elaine Shannon who edited the book, to Catharine Roberts who designed the cover, to Susan Patton Robinson who has done the art work and pasteup, to Linda Sharp who typed the copy, to Jean Roberts who typeset the book, and to Neill Harris who has handled the printing and binding.

To the photographers and photo collections who have so graciously and generously allowed me to use their photographs, — William Eggleston, Larry Kuzniewski and "Memphis Magazine", Alan Copeland, Erwin Williamson, Knox Phillips, the Kemmons Wilson family, Mrs. Paul Cooper and the Medical Auxiliary's Health Sciences Collection, Ruth Wyckoff Hunt and the Mississippi Valley Collection at Memphis State University Libraries, the Frank Collection in the Mississippi Valley Collection at Memphis State University Libraries, the Memphis Room of the Memphis/Shelby County Public Library and Information Center, the Association for the Preservation of Tennessee Antiquities, the Memphis Cotton Carnival Association, Federal Express Corp., and the Library of Congress — I can't thank you enough.

I also want to thank Jim Dickinson, Peggy Jemison, Ellen Rolfes, Lisa and Bayard Snowden, Kim Spencer, Jeanne Arthur, Josephine Isabel, and Mathilde and Hite McLean — without your help and enthusiasm *The Memphis Guide* would not be.

To my Ultimate Guide—I sing praises for the joy I've had in exploring this city and in putting together this book. "To Him be the glory for ever and ever." (II Timothy 3:18)

FOREWORD

The great meandering Mississippi, wide and flat, flowing serenely past the high bluffs, or swollen, raging and powerful, a torrent of spring flood-waters; a multitude of lush green oaks, elms, and tulip poplar trees, thousand upon thousand lining every avenue and corridor, a gentle green carpet seen from the air, and in April, punctuated with the pink and white and lilac of azalea, dogwood and wisteria; the enticing aroma of pit barbecue wafting through the city tempting every palate; the sounds— river music, jazz, ragtime, rhythm and blues—the Memphis Sound, the sound of Elvis; the luxurious and historic Peabody Hotel; warm and friendly citizens, hospitality. This is Memphis—these are some of the things which linger in the mind.

Memphis has a history rich with traditions, and cultural roots all its own. From its founding in 1819 as a rivertown, through the days when hardwood lumber, mules, and cotton — always cotton, were kings, to the thriving metropolitan area of today, Memphis has preserved and incorporated these traditions and that which came before into itself. A modern city, a sprawling commercial center, a major medical center boasting the world's largest private hospital, a distribution center — the sixth largest in the United States, a city of corporate birth and success — Holiday Inn and Federal Express, Memphis is a vital, vibrant urban center which has not forgotten its rural roots.

In a city as old and large and diverse as Memphis, a guide is always helpful. A guide, preferably native, can point out the local sites, provide a bit of background and history to local customs, traditions, and institutions and even recommend shops and services which may be unknown to the newcomer. For you, the resident, newcomer, or casual visitor, this book provides just such a guide to investigate one of America's great cities. Not only is the author a native Memphian, but she is well traveled throughout the United States and Europe and has lived in several other cities in the U.S. She has anticipated a visitor's or newcomer's questions, needs, and interests.

Cities are complex, dynamic, and multifaceted. Activity, opportunities, entertainments, and services are never ending and always changing. This book will help you explore this thing called a city, and, we hope, to discover, appreciate, and enjoy what is special and unique about Memphis. You couldn't have a better guide.

—Richard K. Kearns
Director of the Preservation Foundation of Palm Beach Inc.
and a Fellow of the National Trust for Historic Preservation

SAMPLE FORMAT

NAME OF ATTRACTION
Address, Memphis zip code. Telephone (area code 901, unless otherwise noted).

Hours: *Opening and closing times.*

Tours: *Whether guides, brochures, or informational slide shows are available. Are guided tours regularly scheduled or by appointment? Length of time tour takes. Minimum and maximum number of people allowed. Age restrictions and suggestions.*

Cost: *How much is the admission? Are there group discounts, free hours?*

Lunch: *Information given when facilities are available.*

MATA: *Bus routes that go closest to the attraction. When omitted there is no service. If you have questions, call MATA* at 523-2521.*

Other: *Gift shops, programs, special events, and unusual suggestions or requests are listed here.*

E&H: *Information especially for the elderly or handicapped. Wheelchair accessibility, excessive walking, or anything that might hinder or help you visit. Special facilities and programs for the blind and deaf are indicated where available. See also: Useful Information/Especially for the Elderly and Especially for the Handicapped.*

ABBREVIATIONS

🚲   : Indicates those activities of interest to children under 6.

NRHP: Indicates buildings and areas included in the National Register of Historic Places.

Asterisk (*): Indicates that the same place or event appears elsewhere in the book with more details. Check the Index for page number.

c.: Indicates century.

Days of week: M, Tu, W, Th, F, Sat, Sun.

NOTE

Things change fast and inflation rapidly is raising costs. There are bound to be changes since *The Memphis Guide* went to press. If you're going to a special place or need to know exact rates or hours, please phone in advance.

If you have any suggestions for omissions, admissions, corrections, or elaborations, please let me know:

> Virginia Overton McLean
> c/o Redbird Press
> P.O. Box 11441
> Memphis, Tennessee 38111

Transportation

Train crossing the Frisco Bridge at Memphis about 1900.

BY AIRPLANE

MEMPHIS INTERNATIONAL AIRPORT
off Interstate 240, between Airways and Democrat. 345-7777.

Hours: Open 365 days and nights a year.

Tours: By appointment. 10am M-F. Allow 45 minutes. Children must be at least 5 years old. Groups of 10-25 preferred. Shows the concourses, boarding, and baggage areas. You'll also learn about airport security.

Cost: Free.

Lunch: Restaurants and coffee shops, both cafeteria and waitress style.

MATA: Bus #20 (ex Sun) runs to and from downtown about once an hour ONLY DURING RUSH HOUR. A sign in the baggage claim area gives the schedule. The fare is 80¢, express service/85¢ and senior citizens/35¢. There is no Sunday and no night service. For information phone 523-2521.

Other transportation from airport to city: 1) Airport Limousine Service—Leaves from baggage claim area approximately every 20 minutes going to most major motels, hotels, and downtown. The cost is $4.25 per person. Airport limousine service is also available to such stops as Millington Naval Air Base and hospitals throughout the city, again for $4.25 per person. For further information phone 346-1300. 2) Individual Motel and Hotel Courtesy Cars—Map in baggage claim area gives hotel and motel locations and provides a phone for reservations. The individual hotel or motel will tell you of possible courtesy car service. 3) Taxi—Available just outside the baggage claim area. Minimum charge/$3.75. Fares to downtown and the city's eastern section range from $7 to $11. Best to negotiate the fee in advance. 4) Car Rental—Avis (345-3514), Budget (345-2420), Hertz (345-5680), and National (345-0070) have facilities at the airport. See also Transportation/By Car/Rental. 5) Private Limousine—See Transportation/By Car/Rental or the yellow pages of the phone book under limousine service. Approximate fare, $25.

Other: Traveling military personnel with questions, go to the USO Military Acceptance Center on the main floor of the airport.

E&H: 1) Building is wheelchair accessible. 2) Passenger use of wheelchairs may be arranged by contacting the individual airline. 3) Children, senior citizens, and handicapped persons who need help making transfers contact Traveler's Aid Society, Rm. 1025, 46 N. 3rd, 38103, 525-5466. Open 8:30am-4:30pm M-F; service fee, $5.

In 1910, only seven years after the Wright brothers flew the first plane, Memphis aviation buffs sponsored a national aviation meeting. In the 1920s the Aero Club leased land for an airport and encouraged Vernon and Phoebe Omlie to open a flying service in Memphis. She was the first licensed woman pilot in the U.S. In 1929 the first municipal airport was dedicated. Commercial service began when Mid-South Airways offered three round-trip flights a week to Chicago. Daily commercial service came in April of 1930 with service to St. Louis, Jackson, Miss., and New Orleans.

Today Memphis International Airport is one of seven inland ports of origin for foreign flights and serves nine airlines. It is home for the package airline Federal Express*. There are more than 200 flights a day serving more than two million passengers a year.

AIRPLANE CHARTERS

Several services in the Memphis area charter airplanes for sightseeing flights over the city. Rates are based on plane size, and/or time in the air. They vary, so it is best to phone around. An hour flight for three people ranges from approximately $24 to $190. Make arrangements in advance.

Paul Crowder Aircraft Sales and Service
2339 W. State Line Rd. 393-4388

Executive Charter of Memphis
Memphis International Airport 345-5691

Hagler Aero Service
3870 Fite Rd., Millington 872-2261

Southern Institute of Aviation Inc.
Memphis International Airport 345-5410

Southland Flyers Inc.
2742 Winchester Rd. 346-1760

Transit Air Charter of Arkansas Inc.
Municipal Airport of West Memphis, Ark. 735-3407

Whirlybird Helicopters Inc.
5275 Cole Rd. 767-3310

Keith Wilson Helicopters
2731 N. 2nd 358-2674

BY BOAT

Memphians have a special identity with the Mississippi River*. The city began to grow up in the early 1800s as a river town. At first it was a port for cargo going down river to market in New Orleans. When the steamboat was developed to travel against the current, up stream as well as down, Memphis became a center of trade and commerce for Mississippi, Arkansas, and Tennessee. Because of frequent flooding, the area's farmers depended on boats to carry crops to the Memphis market and from there to New Orleans, the east coast, and Europe.

Today Memphis is the third largest port on the Mississippi River. Seven common carrier barge lines move about 14 million tons of river cargo through the Port of Memphis annually. The Memphis Port Commission will give tours to prospective business users, though the small staff is unable to offer public sightseeing or school tours.

Three passenger boating services are available: the Delta Queen run, the Memphis Queen excursion line, and a private yacht club.

DELTA QUEEN STEAMSHIP CO.

511 Main Street, Cincinnati, Ohio 45202. 1-800-543-1949. The Delta Queen and the Mississippi Queen are the only two overnight passenger steamboats still cruising the Mississippi. Trips originate in New Orleans and St. Louis, each boat stopping in Memphis five or six times a year. The Delta Queen is 55 years old and carries 188 passengers; the Mississippi Queen was built in 1976 and carries 375 passengers. Average daily cost per person, per day, double occupancy/$110. For reservations and information contact your travel agent or the steamship company directly.

MEMPHIS QUEEN EXCURSION BOATS

Foot of Monroe at River. 527-5694.

Tours: 2:30pm daily Apr-Nov, 4:30pm Sat & Sun Apr-Oct, 10:30am M-Sat June-Aug, 6:30pm daily June-Labor Day, 2:30pm weather and passenger load permitting (primarily Sat & Sun) Dec & March. Closed Jan & Feb.

Cost: Adults/$5, children age 4-12/$2.50, children under 3/free.

Lunch: Snack bar on the boat sells hot dogs, soft drinks, popcorn, and beer.

MATA: Nearest stop, Front and Monroe. Showboat Bus or any bus that runs downtown.

Other: 1) Charters may be arranged. The Belle Carol, a paddlewheeler, handles 65 passengers and charters for two or more hours $50 per hour or $3 per person, whichever is greater. The Memphis Queen, the paddlewheel steamer that handles regular cruises, has a 300 person capacity and rents for two hours for 150 people for $450 plus $2 for each additional person. The Showboat, a barge, handles 600 and rents for $600 for the first 150 people plus $2.50 for each additional person. 2) Arrangements may be made for catering on board.

E&H: The boat is accessible to wheelchairs, but please arrive early and avoid rainy, slippery days.

The trip covers ten miles and stops on a sand bar so you can ooze your toes in the Mississippi mud. Purchase a captain's hat in the souvenir shop on board and dream of the paddlewheels'* glory days, or just sit back and enjoy the scenery. Captain Meanley tells the story of the changing river as you cruise. Fun for all ages!

MEMPHIS YACHT CLUB

Mississippi River at Court Ave, P.O. Box 3099, 38103. 525-3808. The Memphis Yacht Club is a private club where travelers on the river can dock for repairs and service on equipment, rent tie-up space for overnight or longer, visit the snack bar, and get information about the river and city. Fees vary with service. Tie-up space, about 20¢ per foot per night. Club open 24 hours a day.

BY BUS

INTERSTATE BUS SERVICE

Two bus terminals, Greyhound and Trailways, are in downtown Memphis. They serve six bus companies which have regularly scheduled highway trips from Memphis. Bridge Transit Corp. offers local service between Memphis and West Memphis.

Bridge Transit Corp.

581 S. 2nd Str. 526-8358. Bridge Transit Corp., operated by Yellow Cab Co., offers bus service between Memphis and West Memphis, Ark. Their black, orange, and white buses leave from a MATA bus stop near Union and 3rd Str. 5:30-8am and 3-4pm M-F. They go out Crump Blvd. and through West Memphis. Their final destination is the mall in West Memphis. Fee, adults/$1, children under 12/75¢. When the West Memphis race track is open, buses run to and from the dog races* about every thirty minutes. Fee, $1.50. Phone for further information.

Greyhound Bus Lines

203 Union Ave. 523-7676 (nationwide fare and schedule information).

MATA: *One block east of 2nd Str, the main southbound route for downtown buses. If you're carrying suitcases you may want to take buses #20, 34 (ex Sat), or 56 which stop directly in front of the terminal.*

The main Greyhound Terminal is on Union near 3rd Str. Suburban stops are made in Frayser at Frayser Rexall Drugs (3068 Thomas), in east Memphis at the Royal Oaks Motel* (4941 Summer), in southeast Memphis at the Greyhound Suburban Bus Station (2805 Winchester Rd.), and in West Memphis, Ark. at the Greyhound Terminal (404 E. Broadway).

Three other bus companies, Dunlap, Great Southern, and Gulf Transport, operate out of the Greyhound Terminal. Information on their service is handled by Greyhound.

The history of Greyhound is a Memphis success story. Fred Smith put a bus together, sold tickets, and drove the bus to start Dixie Bus Lines. The company became Dixie Greyhound and later Greyhound. Smith's son, Fred Smith, built his own transportation empire in the 1970s— Federal Express Corp.*

Trailways Bus System
235 Union Ave. 523-0200 (fare and schedule information).

MATA: #20, 34 (ex Sat), 56.

The main Trailways terminal is at Union and 4th Str. with an east Memphis stop at the Royal Oaks Motel* (4941 Summer). A passenger may depart at other locations along the route as agreed upon by the driver, but the baggage compartment will not be opened at such stops. River Bus Line, serving Arkansas, operates out of the Trailways terminal.

LOCAL BUS SERVICE

MATA
701 N. Main 38101. 523-2521 (information)—Memorize this one. It's an invaluable help.

MATA stands for Metropolitan Area Transit Authority which is a municipally owned system of air-conditioned buses serving the city and concentrated population areas outside the city limits.

MATA routes, going from downtown to individual points of interest, are listed throughout this book when connections are possible. Unfortunately several spots are unreachable by bus. You must transfer several times to get to other spots. For free route maps and schedules, write or phone the Authority.

The phone information service—523-2521—operates 6am-8pm M-F, 7am-8pm Sat, and 8:30am-5pm Sun. Be ready to tell them where you are and where you want to go. Most MATA buses run from 6am-6:15pm M-Sat. On most routes there is no night, Sun, or holiday service. (Routes #2,4,5,8,16,39,52,56,57 run until 9pm and on Sun.) At writing, MATA is facing a financial crisis; service cuts and increased fares seem imminent.

MATA stops are clearly marked along bus routes. Look for the green or blue rectangular MATA coach stop signs attached to poles at mid-block or street corner locations. Downtown's two major bus stops are at Front & Jefferson Strs. and at 2nd Str. & Madison Ave. Most MATA buses run through downtown, circling the mall, going north on Front, east on Linden, south on 2nd, and west on Exchange. Downtown sights served by buses on this route are indicated by MATA: Downtown buses.

Fares: At writing, most adult MATA fares are 85¢ and exact change is required. Each transfer costs 10¢ extra. Express service, Blue Blazer and Green Rocket, is available on some routes and costs 95¢. To save money, buy books of tickets from MATA. For outlets phone 523-2521. A 40-ride ticket book costs $32.

Children under 5 may ride free if accompanied by an adult. With an I.D. card senior citizens (65 +), the blind, and the handicapped may ride for 40¢. Students under 18 with an MATA I.D. card may ride on all but express buses for 50¢ (city) and 55¢ (county) 6am-6pm M-F. Contact your school or MATA for information on how to get a card.

Showboat Bus: Ten buses that look like paddlewheel riverboats link 38 downtown and mid-town attractions. It's a great way for visitors to see some of the sights and a treat for children. The route is marked on the fold-out map at the back of this book. Take a ride. There are many stops along the route and nine major "landings", the Holiday Inn-Rivermont*, Beale Street*, Handy Park*, Hotel Peabody*, Mud Island*/ Civic Center*, Medical Center*, Overton Square*, Memphis Zoological Gardens* in Overton Park*, and Mid-South Fairgrounds/Libertyland*. You'll pass: the Orpheum Theatre*, many riverfront parks*, the Memphis Queen* riverboat landing, Cotton Row*, Cook Convention Center*, Shelby County Court House*, several historic downtown churches*, Magevney House*, Victorian Village*, University of Tennessee Center for Health Sciences*, Forrest Park*, Christian Brothers College*, Memphis Memorial Stadium*, the Coliseum, Memphis Academy of Arts*, and Brooks Art Gallery*.

Showboat buses run every 20 minutes, 4:30am-midnight M-Sat, 5:45am-midnight Sun. The fare is the same as for regular MATA service. Hopes are that merchants along the way may offer free tickets; or maybe there will be an unlimited stops/day pass you can buy. This is unsettled at writing.

Hustle Bus: Another special, the Hustle Bus, runs between downtown and the Medical Center*—from Mid-America Mall out Monroe to 3rd to Madison and through the Medical Center. Buses run every ten minutes 6:30am-7pm M-F. The fare is 25¢.

Special buses run to sporting and other public events. These buses leave from shopping centers and go directly to the event. For information phone 523-2521.

An interesting and inexpensive way to see Memphis is just to go for a bus ride. Bus #50 Central/Walnut Grove or Central/Yates goes from downtown east along Linden through the Vance-Pontotoc* neighborhood, out Peabody through the Central Garden* neighborhood, past E. H. Crump's* house, and out Central, Poplar, Walnut Grove, and Shady Grove through some of the city's most beautiful residential areas. Buses run all day seven days a week. Or take Bus #41 from downtown east through residential areas, major shopping areas, and rural areas, to the small town of Collierville, Tn. It runs twice in the morning and twice in the afternoon. A one-way ride takes an hour and costs $1.30. In case you want to get off at an earlier stop, the fare within the city limits is 95¢, to Germantown* $1.05, to Forest Hill $1.10, and to Bailey Station Rd. $1.25.

CHARTER BUS SERVICE

City and highway charters are priced competitively, so shop around.

City

Five bus companies are licensed to operate buses that may be chartered for transportation within the city. They are Bridge Transit Corp. (526-8358), MATA (528-2891), River Bus Line (357-2293), Star Lite Bus Service (529-8482), and Tri-State Transit (362-6117). City charters are sold by the hour, usually with a five hour minimum.

Highway

Seven bus companies offer "highway charters" which is chartered bus service that leaves the city limits. They are Bridge Transit Corp. (526-8358), 4 Seasons Tours Inc. (726-4433), Greyhound Bus Lines (523-2137), River Bus Line (357-2293), Star Lite Bus Service (529-8482), Trailways Bus System (529-9482), and Tri-State Transit (362-6117). Highway charters are sold by the mile.

Miscellaneous

The Variety Club at 889 Union in the Sheraton Motor Inn (525-2220) provides a 26 seat bus to non-profit organizations. There is no charge except for gasoline. Groups must provide their own drivers. Reserve in advance.

Sterling Realty (767-4280) owns a 35 seat London double-decker bus. It's available to all groups. A driver is provided. Fees are negotiable but run around $20 per hour. Sterling sometimes provides free service to non-profit organizations.

TOUR COMPANIES

Cottonland Tours

Peabody Hotel lobby, 149 Union, 529-8687. 5645 Murray, 767-8979. Lots of interesting anecdotes are part of the four regularly scheduled tours that leave from Cottonland's office in the Peabody Hotel daily year-round unless otherwise indicated. Free van pick-up from city motels is offered. City tours leave at 9:30am, 2pm, and 6pm (the latter June-Aug only), last three hours, and cost adults/$9, children under 12/$6. Elvis Presley tours leave at 9:30am and 2pm, last three hours, and cost adults/$9, children under 12/$6. Mississippi Riverboat tours leave at 2pm Mar-Dec weather permitting, last three hours, and cost adults/$10, children under 12/$7.50. Nightclub tours include dinner at Blues Alley* and all the domestic beer you can drink, are for those 19 and older, leave at 6:30pm, last three to four hours, and cost $20. Cottonland accepts AE, MC, Visa.

Cottonland also offers customized tours and tour guides. They can give sign or foreign language tours and will organize out-of-town trips to such spots as Holly Springs* and Vicksburg*, Miss, Reelfoot Lake* and Shiloh*, Tn, and Land Between the Lakes in Kentucky.

Gray Line Tours

3755 Elvis Presley Blvd. 527-2508. Take a Gray Line Sightseeing Tour, offered daily, and leave the talking to your guide. Regularly scheduled city tours and Elvis tours leave from 3755 Elvis Presley Blvd., across from Graceland*, at 10am and 2pm daily. If you phone in advance, a van will pick you up and take you to the tour bus for no extra charge (all areas except Macon Rd. and Frayser). Fee, adults/$7.50 or $9 with entry to Sun Studio*, children ages 3-11/$5, and children under 3/free. A city riverboat tour, offering a ride on the Memphis Queen riverboat* and a half hour motor tour of Memphis, leaves at 2pm daily and costs, adults/$10, children 4-12/$7.50, those under 4/free. Each of the three daytime tours lasts about 2½ hours. A nightlife tour is offered from May through Sept nightly except M. It costs $20, lasts five hours, starts at 6:30pm, and is limited to those over 18. They'll pick you up at your motel. Phone for reservations. No credit cards are accepted—only cash and traveller's cheques.

Gray Line also arranges special tours for groups of 25 or more. They have planned tours to Libertyland*, Victorian Village*, and ante-bellum homes*; a ladies shopping tour; and a golf and tennis tour. They also offer special tours for the physically handicapped.

Inside Memphis Inc.

2454 MacKinnon 38138. 682-9203. Three imaginative innovative women started this service about four years ago. They'll plan customized tours, programs, and conventions for any group of 30 or more or for executives interested in learning about Memphis. You pick the thrust of the tour: gardens, history,.... There is a minimum fee for guides of $75 for the first three hours plus....

Rivertown Tours

2035 Madison Ave., 38104. 725-9341. Rivertown plans customized tours for any size group. You pick the thrust: cotton, especially for students, black heritage,.... They'll provide guides and transportation or just guides. Rates for guides are $75 for the first three hours, and $15 for each additional hour.

For information on foreign language translators and guides see Useful Information/ Especially for Travelers and Newcomers.

BY CAR

Around 1894 Samuel Carnes was scaring mules and pedestrians with what is believed to have been the first car in Memphis. Carnes, who lived in South Memphis* at Linden and Wellington, began his career as a bookkeeper for the cotton house of Hill, Fontaine & Co. The adventurous Carnes pioneered many technological frontiers. He ran the original Memphis electric light company and brought the telephone to Memphis. He was also president of the Scimitar Publishing Co.

Since the turn of the century Memphis has sprawled, first to the east and then to the south and north. We've become increasingly dependent on automobiles.

For those of you not familiar with the local traffic ordinances, the city speed limit, unless otherwise marked, is 35 m.p.h. In the county the speed limit is 45 m.p.h., in school zones 15 m.p.h., and on the expressway 55 m.p.h. A right turn on red is permitted unless there is a sign specifically prohibiting it; horn honking is illegal, except as a danger signal. Parking meters are enforced between 8am and 6pm on all days except Sunday, New Year's Day, July 4th, Thanksgiving, and Christmas.

You can buy city road maps for about $2 at the Convention and Visitors Bureau of Memphis (12 S. Main, 526-1919), at Walgreen Drug Stores, at area bookstores, and at local service stations. Some service stations give them away free.

If you need information on hazardous road conditions or emergency help contact the Tennessee Highway Patrol, 6348 Summer, 38134, 386-3831. They're open daily, 24 hours.

CAR RENTAL

In addition to the standard car rental agencies (see yellow pages under Automobile Renting & Leasing for these), there are two other services available locally: used car rentals and chauffeured limousine and van service. To rent a used car, vintage 1966-1973, contact Rent-A-Relic at 596 N. Graham & I-40 (452-0397). Their prices are usually less than for late-model cars.

You can hire chauffeured limousine service at Elegante Limousine Service of Memphis (743-5353), Executive Limousine Service (942-4513), and Yellow Cab Co. (526-8358). Rates are about $20 per hour with a three hour minimum. If you want to go to Nashville for dinner or to a football game in Oxford, you will be charged by the mile.

TAXI

In Memphis you don't hail a cab on the street corner, you phone for one. The cabs are metered and rates are set by law: 85¢ for the first 1/7 mile, 10¢ for each additional 1/7 mile, 20¢ for each additional person, and a 25¢ gas surcharge. There is no minimum charge on trips except a $3.75 minimum on those from the airport. Several carriers provide service to all parts of the city: Friendly Cab Co. (276-4451), Little John Taxi Service (525-7733), Orange Mound Cab Co. (324-1936), United Taxi Co. (525-0521), Veteran's Cab Co. (525-3535), West Memphis Transportation Co. (526-8358), and Yellow Cab Co. (526-2121).

BY CARRIAGE

RIVER CITY CARRIAGE CO.
527-2313. A horse drawn carriage ride—what a great afternoon for children, or the perfect spot for you and your sweetie some starlit night!

You can hire carriages during warm weather and the Christmas season downtown and in Overton Square*. Downtown there are two services. Hour long historic tours leave from a ticket/gift shop at Beale and Wagner Strs. For a quick ride, hail the horse drawn shuttle service that clops between hotels, restaurants, and shops. A ride from the Peabody Hotel* to the Orpheum* is about $1 per person. In Overton Square buy tickets at the popcorn wagon for 10-minute rides around the Square, 30-minute rides around the Square and neighborhood, and hour rides through the Square and Overton Park*.

Unfortunately no schedules or rates have been firmly established. Your best bet is to phone ahead, select your ride, negotiate the fee, and reserve a carriage for a specific time. Rides usually cost from $3 to $7 per person. Rental arrangements for special occasions like weddings have fees based on the occasion, location, and length of time.

BY TRAIN

The railroads have been a big factor in the city's growth. The Memphis & Charleston Railroad, completed in 1857, linked the Mississippi River and the Atlantic Ocean. During the Civil War, this was the only east-west railroad across the Confederacy. By 1884 the Louisville, New Orleans, & Texas, now known as the Illinois Central Gulf, was completed from Memphis to Vicksburg, and the Delta* opened to year-round travel. Memphis became a world cotton and lumber market.

The first bridge to span the Mississippi River at Memphis was a railroad bridge, the Frisco. Opened in 1892, the span became an important gateway to the West for Eastern traders.

Train stations marked the city's skyline, first the Poplar Street Depot* circa 1890 and then Union Station in 1912, both now demolished. In 1914, almost a year before the completion of Grand Central Station in New York, Memphis' Central Station at Main and Calhoun opened. Much fanfare and more than 20,000 opening day visitors saluted the "grand" eight story ten track station. The Illinois Central, the Yazoo and Mississippi Valley, the Frisco Railroad, and the Rock Island Line served the station, and 60 trains could move in and out daily.

Today Memphis is still a railroad freight center. It is the nation's third largest east-west rail crossroads. Six railroads move about 90 trains in and out of the city each day. But passenger train service has dwindled. Only one northbound and one southbound Amtrak train pass through Central Station daily.

AMTRAK
545 S. Main. 1-800-874-2800 (toll free).

MATA: Going south buses #12, 45, 16, 39, 35 (ex Sat), 17. Going north, any bus.

An Amtrak train, the City of New Orleans, leaves Memphis at 3:05am going south, arriving in Jackson, Miss. at 7:08am and in New Orleans at 10:35am. Northbound the train leaves Memphis at 11:55pm and arrives in Chicago at 10:45am the next day.

SENTIMENTAL JOURNEY
Old Engine No. 4501 is pulled from retirement and steams southeastward to Corinth*, Miss. for one weekend each May. The 10-hour round-trip travels the historic Memphis & Charleston Railroad route departing Buntyn* Station, Southern at Semmes, at 8am. The train stops in Germantown* and Collierville and reaches Corinth at noon for a two-hour visit. Then back to Memphis by 6pm. Round-trip tickets are about $25 from Hobbies of Memphis (4515 Poplar) or Hobbies of Balmoral (6070 Quince). Proceeds go to Le Bonheur Children's Hospital*.

FOR THE ELDERLY & HANDICAPPED

In addition to taxi* and limousine service* there are several sources of transportation to medical and legal appointments, the grocery, bank,.... Be sure to reserve in advance.

Churches—several have senior citizen programs and offer transportation. Check with individual churches; see the yellow pages of the phone book for a complete list.

Easter Seals—452-2181. By van with lift to medical facilities only. Qualifying handicapped and seniors only. Long waiting list.

MATA* Handilift—528-2886. Vans with lift. Fee, comparable with regular bus service. Offered 8:30am-4:30pm. Phone for information and application forms.

MIFA* Escort Service—527-0061. By car or van.

The Mississippi River & Its Parks

Riverboats at Memphis 1910.

THE RIVER/HISTORY OF MEMPHIS

Ole Man River churns some 2500 miles from Minnesota, past Memphis, to the Gulf of Mexico. The river first heads north, then bends and heads south. It drains the largest river basin in the northern hemisphere. In the world, only three river basins are larger—the Amazon, Congo, and Nile. Indians who lived along its banks gave the river different names in their own languages. The name that stuck came from the Chippewas in Minnesota. They called the river Mechesebe, meaning the great water. European settlers came to spell it Mississippi.

The Missouri River joins the Mississippi at St. Louis, and the Ohio River meets it at Cairo. From this point south, plant and wild-life change, and the river becomes muddy looking with silt. This lower "muddy" Mississippi and the history of Memphis, once only a 5,000 acre tract of riverfront property, are inseparable.

The Indians and early white men were attracted to the site by the strategically important river bluff. The town began to grow around a flatboat port. With the development of steamboats, it became a center of trade and commerce. Development came by river, so too disaster: Federal troops during the Civil war and yellow fever epidemics in the 1870s. After 1890, levees helped control flooding, and bridges spanned the river. The South and West were developing, and Memphis became a commercial center for Tennessee, Mississippi, and Arkansas farmers, businessmen, and financiers.

EARLY HISTORY

The bank of the river rises abruptly in four places along the lower Mississippi; it is on the fourth and most southern of these bluffs that Memphis is located. The river used to overflow its banks every year, but the four bluffs were usually safe from major flooding.

The bluff location was strategically important for control of the river. The Indians, French, Spanish, English, and Americans all wanted to hold the high land.

Until 1500 Indians lived at the present site of Chucalissa Indian Museum*. Later, Indians lived in northern Mississippi and followed trails across their hunting territory to the Chickasaw bluff, their main river landing.

Hernando de Soto is believed the first European to come here. In 1541 DeSoto, searching for gold, crossed the river somewhere near Memphis. He met with Chisca, chief of the Chickasaws, and convinced the Indians he was the child of the sun. When he died of fever near the river in 1542, his body was hidden in a hollow oak log and floated into the river. In 1673 white men came again; French explorers Louis Joliet and Jacques Marquette led a canoe expedition down the Mississippi searching for a route to the Pacific Ocean. In 1682 René Robert Cavelier, sieur de la Salle, a Frenchman, passed through the area.

In the early 1700s France and England struggled for control of the river. The Chickasaw Indians took the side of the English; the Choctaws allied with the French. The French built Fort Assumption on a site within what is now Memphis, but abandoned the fort in 1740. At the end of the Seven Years War in 1763, the Treaty of Paris gave the territory east of the Mississippi to England.

In 1783, at the close of the Revolutionary War, the new American nation gained possession from England of the land east of the Mississippi.

During the American Revolution, Spain had begun to eye the river valley. A schism developed among the Chickasaw Indians who controlled the land. Gayoso, Spain's representative, bought the bluff from one faction and built Ft. San Fernando de Barrancas* in north Memphis. The American explorer William Clark, here in 1793, and his Indian agents made friends with the other Chickasaw faction. The U.S. sent arms and men to protest the sale to Spain, and in 1797 the Spanish burned their fort and withdrew to the west side of the river. The U.S. placed Ft. Adams near the Spanish fort site. Ft. Adams was renamed Ft. Pike in 1800 and Ft. Pickering in 1801. (In 1862 Ft. Pickering was relocated to the south, running from the foot of Vance to below modern DeSoto Park*.)

American settlers moved west of the Appalachian mountains, and in 1796 Tennessee became the 16th state to join the Union. The settlers' titles to land ownership in western Tennessee were clouded by Indian claims to the land. In 1818 the Tennessee state legislature petitioned Congress to appoint a commission to purchase the Chickasaw Indians' western Tennessee hunting grounds. General Andrew Jackson, later President, and Governor Isaac Shelby of Kentucky headed the negotiations which culminated in the signing of the Chickasaw Purchase, Oct. 19, 1818. According to the treaty the Indians were to be paid $20,000 annually for 15 years for the land.

In 1794 John Overton, a middle Tennessee lawyer and real estate speculator, had bought a 5,000 acre tract of bluff land from North Carolinian John Rice. When the Indians yielded their rights, John Overton and his partners, Andrew Jackson and James Winchester, had the land surveyed and in 1819 laid out plans for Memphis. The three owners continued to live in middle Tennessee but sent Winchester's son Marcus to Memphis as their real estate representative.

The Chickasaws retained rights to their 5-million acre heartland in northern Mississippi, but in 1830 the U.S. Congress passed the Indian Removal Act which forced all Indians living east of the Mississippi River to exchange their tribal holdings for an equivalent amount of western territory. The state of Mississippi passed legislation in 1830 abolishing the tribe and authorizing the arrest of Chickasaw leaders. Between 1831 and 1834, many Chickasaws moved west. By 1836 those remaining were being driven out at gunpoint. In 1838 the last large group of Chickasaws were put aboard four steamboats in Memphis bound for Ft. Smith on the Arkansas River.

MEMPHIS AS A CENTER OF TRADE

Memphis is a river city. She grew up as a rough river port in the early 1820s-40s. Flatboats, built as westerners imagine Noah's Ark, rough wooden crafts with sloped roofs, floated downstream loaded with goods. When they reached New Orleans, the boats were scrapped, and the men returned north by land trails. It was by flatboat that Davy Crockett* first came to Memphis in 1823. His boat snagged and broke apart. Crockett who had been asleep, escaped the wreck, swam ashore naked, and was clothed by Marcus Winchester. They became friends and Winchester eventually encouraged Crockett to run for political office. The rugged frontiersman served two terms, 1827 through 1831, as U.S. Congressman from the district which included Memphis and Shelby County. He became a vigorous opponent of President Andrew Jackson's Indian policy and was defeated for re-election in 1831 and again in 1835. Discouraged, he left Memphis in 1835 for Texas where he died at the Alamo, a hero in the war with Mexico.

In the early 1800s steamboats which could make the return trip upstream were developed. Memphis flourished as river traffic expanded.

The New Orleans, an experimental steamboat, made the first trip down the Mississippi in 1811. In 1816 Henry Miller Shreve of Shreveport, La., launched his steamboat, the Washington. Earlier steamboats had been designed for deeper waters. Shreve's engine had higher pressure to push against the strong Mississippi currents, and its shallow hull could slip through the river's low points. The prototype for later riverboats, the Washington had a second deck and paddle wheels on its sides.

The lower Mississippi prospered with the booming river commerce. The river was the cotton planters' road to the world. By the 1830s New Orleans' banking capital exceeded New York City's and its port competed with New York's. Upriver, steam packets, either stern-wheeler or side-wheeler riverboats propelled by steam and carrying cargo, passengers, and mail on fixed routes, moved in and out of the port of Memphis. The port was becoming a major distribution center for the South.

The Lee family, whose homes, the 1st Lee House* and Lee House*, remain on Adams Street, began steamboating in the early 1800s on the Cumberland River. In 1866, James Lee Sr. formed the famous Lee Line of riverboats with Memphis as its home port. A son, James Lee Jr., joined his father's empire in 1877, and until 1926, the Lee Line served about 1,400 miles on the Mississippi and Ohio Rivers and their tributaries.

Over the years, vessels and paddle wheels grew bigger, and engines became more powerful. Boats gilded with ornamentation made traveling an opulent affair. Chefs were hired from famous restaurants. There were maids and butlers to assist cabin passengers. Some boats even printed their own newspapers. Owners and crews took great pride in the boats and loved to race them. Steamboat racing was at the height of its popularity in 1870 when the Robert E. Lee beat the Natchez from New Orleans to St. Louis. The Robert E. Lee made the course in three days, 18 hours, and 14 minutes.

But racing and the dangers of navigating the swift, unpredictable river brought great disasters as well. Memphis was the scene of the first and worst. In 1830 the Helen McGregor exploded while docking and more than 50 people were killed. Their bodies were flung into the streets of the city between Poplar and Madison. In 1865 the Sultana was wrecked as she carried 2,400 Union soldiers home. More than 1,500 of them died.

By the 1880s "river palaces" with their paddle wheels were slowly retiring leaving romantic memories of riverboat gamblers, roustabouts, explosions, disasters, races, and minstrel shows. The last Lee packet, the Harry Lee was sold in 1930.

Steam packets, which carried cargo on board, were replaced by tows which pushed cargo loaded barges in front of them. Towboats and barges now ply the nine foot deep, 300 foot wide river channel, maintained by the U.S. Corps of Engineers. It is an inexpensive way to ship bulky, heavy cargo such as grain, petroleum, machinery, and coal. Ashburn Park* on the river honors the father of towboats, T. Q. Ashburn.

CIVIL WAR

The Civil War spread to Memphis by river. In 1860 Memphians were pro-Union, but after Lincoln's call for troops, the city favored secession. Memphis contributed 50 companies, from 83 to 103 men each, to the Confederacy.

In May of 1862 after the Battle of Shiloh*, Confederate troops under Gen. Pierre Gustave Toutant de Beauregard evacuated Corinth, Mississippi, and Confederate soldiers withdrew from Memphis. On June 5 the Federal fleet anchored just above Memphis. That night cotton crops in Memphis' port were burned to avoid their capture by Federal troops. On June 6 in the hour long Battle of Memphis, seven of eight Confederate vessels were captured, sunk, or burned. Federal gunboats used steel rams for the first time. Mayor John Park surrendered the city to the Union; the city itself escaped destruction.

During the war Memphis was a center for contraband trade between the North and South. The South sold its cotton for medicines and material. Lincoln is said to have allowed the trading, fearing that if trade were cut off, the upper river valley and cotton-hungry Europe might enter the war on the side of the Confederacy.

During the war both Gen. Ulysses S. Grant and Gen. William Tecumseh Sherman occupied Memphis. Sherman had command of Memphis for five months in 1862 before marching through Georgia to the sea. The site of his quarters during this time is marked on Tennessee Street between Nettleton and Butler Streets.

Nathan Bedford Forrest, considered one of history's best cavalry commanders, was the local Confederate hero. Forrest served in the Confederate Army under General Bragg until he broke away and formed his own 3,500 man unit, Forrest's Raiders. Based in Oxford, Miss., this cavalry unit practiced hit and run guerilla type warfare. On one occasion in August of 1864, Forrest daringly sent troops around the Federal lines into Memphis to tempt Union forces to withdraw their support from Sherman's supply line to Atlanta. As Forrest had planned, the Federal troops withdrew to defend the city. It is said that the German General Staff, before the blitzkrieg, and the Israeli Commandos studied his military tactics.

Forrest was born in northern Mississippi, the eldest of a poor blacksmith's 11 children. His father died when Forrest was 16, and Forrest went to work trading horses for his uncle in Hernando. Horse trading led to slave trading, and in 1850, Forrest moved to Memphis. He became one of the largest and richest slave traders in the South at a time when some slave traders made annual profits of $50,000 or more, astronomical sums in those days. In 1858 he was elected city alderman and in 1859 retired to Mississippi to become a planter.

When the Civil War broke out Forrest volunteered as a private and raised a cavalry unit of which he was lieutenant colonel. He was promoted to brigadier general in 1862, major general in 1863, and lieutenant general in 1865.

After the war, Forrest was a leader in the Ku Klux Klan, but when he saw the Klan heading toward violence, he worked for its dissolution. He lived in Memphis and for several years was president of the Selma, Marion, and Memphis Railroad. He died in 1877, and he and his wife are buried in Forrest Park on the north side of Union Avenue between Dunlap and Manassas Streets. The park's statue of Forrest is by Charles Henry Niehaus.

YELLOW FEVER—THE 1870s

Disaster, in the form of yellow fever, came by river too. Two epidemics in the 1870s practically depopulated the city. In 1873, 25,000 of the city's 40,000 inhabitants fled. Of the 15,000 remaining, 5,000 became ill and 2,000 died. In 1878, when the fever again came upriver by boat from New Orleans, only 19,000 people remained in Memphis. Fourteen thousand of these were blacks who believed they were immune to the fever. This time 5,150 people died. At one point the daily death rate reached 295. The only institutions that kept functioning were the newspapers, telegraph, railroads, steamboats, druggists, undertakers, doctors, and the Catholic clergy.

At the time no one knew what caused yellow fever. The fever itself lasted 24 hours. Four or five days later the person was either well or dead. It was not until 1900 that Major Walter Reed proved that yellow fever was transmitted by mosquito bite.

The city improved sanitary conditions but many people who had fled did not return. The character of the city changed for the worse. Northern investment capital needed to rebuild after the war went elsewhere.

Carpetbagger-dominated government plunged the city into debt. The growing deficit, the yellow fever epidemics, and unsuccessful municipal projects eventually forced the city to default on its bonds. On January 31, 1879, the state legislature repealed the city's municipal charter, made it a taxing district of the state, and placed its affairs under a governing council. It was not until 1893 that home rule was restored to Memphis.

1890 - 1980

By the 1890s Memphis, the bawdy vigorous river town, was growing again. In 1892, the Frisco Bridge was opened with much fanfare. A railroad bridge, it was the first bridge south of St. Louis to cross the Mississippi. Built between 1883 and 1892, the 791 foot span was the largest cantilever truss bridge in the U.S. The bridge made Memphis a focal point for trade between the industrial East and the emerging Southwest. The Harahan Bridge for cars and trains was completed in 1916. The Memphis-Arkansas Bridge opened in 1949. Modern DeSoto Bridge, part of the interstate highway system, opened in 1973.

The area suffered destructive floods in 1903, 1912, 1913, 1922, 1927, 1961, and 1973. Work by the U.S. Army Corps of Engineers*, over time, has reduced the land's exposure to rampaging waters. They began an aggressive flood control program in 1917, but it was not until after 1937 that enough large levees were built to control flood waters around Memphis. Since 1936, the Corps has built about 1,700 miles of levees and flood walls along the lower river. As the levees were built, farmlands were reclaimed and agricultural trade in Memphis expanded.

Riverboats loaded and unloaded cargo along the bluff, the city's western front, but by 1930 much of the bluff had become a parking lot and the docking facilities began to serve tour boats and small craft. Commercial and industrial traffic, now by barge, is centered on President's Island and along the Wolf River channel. Today Memphis' port is the third largest inland port on the river, handling about 14 million tons annually. Each day about 50 barges pass through.

President's Island, which was connected to the mainland by an earthen embankment after World War II, has been developed as a 900-acre industrial park. It is located across Jack Carley Causeway off I-55 South/Riverside Drive. For a look take a roundtrip ride on MATA #15 from 2nd and Court Square about 3:15 or 4:15 pm M-F.

For source information see Historic Sites/Sources.

RIVERFRONT PARKS

Parks lining the riverfront commemorate the city's and river's history. Visits to these would be a good way for children to learn the city's history. You might want to picnic or just rest and look at the river in the following:

MUD ISLAND
Entrance: 125 N. Front at Washington Str.

MATA: Downtown buses and Showboat Bus.

In the early 1900s the U.S. gunboat Aphrodite was anchored in the river here. An eddy was created and sediment lodged to form Mud Island. Today the island is being developed as a river museum, scheduled to open summer of 1982.

A monorail transit system and pedestrian bridge will connect the island to the city near the Civic Center*, Front and Washington Strs.

The entrance to the island will be a four-story building, two floors of which will house the Mississippi River Museum. The museum will tell the story of the lower Mississippi River, from Paducah and Carruthersville to the Gulf of Mexico. Exhibits will show the river's impact on wild life and vegetation and will illustrate the history, music, and culture of the river valley. There will be Memphis music* exhibits and even a refurbished riverboat to wander through. The ground floor of the entrance building will have gift and specialty shops.

On the west side of the island will be the "river walk", a 2,000 foot long scale model of the lower river. The walk will end at a paddleboat lake representing the Gulf of Mexico. The seven flags that have flown over the site of Memphis—Spain's, France's, Britain's, the United States', North Carolina's, Tennessee's, and the Confederate States'—wave over the island.

Mud Island also promises an amphitheatre, a 76-boat public marina, a yacht club building, two large play fields, a shady picnic area, and an observation platform on the southern end so visitors can watch river traffic. A restaurant offering gourmet cuisine, a New Orleans-style cafe, and regional snack bars are planned.

Hours have not been set at this writing. Fees tentatively are 50¢ to get on the island, 25¢ for a one-way ride on the monorail, $4.25/adults & $2.25/children (ages 4-15) to visit the museum, and $5/adults & $3/children for admission to special performances in the amphitheatre. After 5pm those with amphitheatre tickets will not be charged island admission.

CHUCALISSA INDIAN MUSEUM AND VILLAGE (NRHP)

1987 Indian Village Dr. 38109, five miles west of U.S. 61 off Mitchell Rd. 785-3160.

Hours: 9am-5pm Tu-Sat, 1-5pm Sun. Closed M, Thanksgiving Day, and during the Christmas/New Year season.

Tours: For organized groups, given by Choctaw guides or other museum staff. Arrange two weeks in advance. Other visitors who want an escorted tour, ask at the reception desk; a guide will be assigned if available. All visitors can see a 15-minute free slide show. A 25¢-guidebook is sold at the reception desk.

Cost: Under 6/free, senior citizens & those 6-11/25¢, 12 and over/$1. Free admission 10-11am Sat.

Lunch: Bring your own, and picnic at tables and grills on the grounds.

MATA: Nearest stop, Mitchell Rd, at least a two mile hike from the entrance. If you want to brave it, take a #45 (ex Sun) from downtown or a #37 (ex Sun) from Florida and Belz. By car drive south from Memphis on U.S. 61 to Mitchell Rd. Follow the signs for about eight miles to the museum.

Other: 1) Indian games, dance, and craftwork demonstrations occasionally during the summer. 2) Indian pottery, beadwork, baskets, and mats for sale. 3) Free films on Indian customs in museum auditorium, 2pm every other Sun. 4) Archaeology and museum courses offered here by Memphis State University Department of Anthropology. 5) Identification of archaeological specimen and investigation of possible area archaeological sites by staff. 6) Staff talks and craft demonstrations on American Indian life and customs for area school classes. Interested teachers, phone to arrange. Best for children 10+. 7) Staff lectures on Chucalissa, Mid-South archaeology, and Indian customs on a limited basis. 8) Camping facilities available in adjoining T.O. Fuller State Park*.

E&H: 90% of the exhibits are wheelchair accessible.

It is unknown which tribes lived on this site, but there is evidence that from 1000-1500 A.D. there were several different Indian settlements here. These early Indians were members of the temple-mound culture. They were capable farmers, craftsmen, and artists and lived in large permanent towns of thatch-roofed houses grouped around a town square. They raised their crops in the river bottom below the village and made their own tools and implements.

At Chucalissa, a Choctaw word for abandoned houses, there is a reconstructed village of two mounds with nine dwellings. A museum houses exhibits on Mid-South Indians and archaeology and a slide show on traditional Indian customs of the region.

DESOTO PARK

On the river, off Riverside Drive, intersection of California and Delaware Strs. It's hard to reach, but the view is worth the effort. Take President's

Island exit off I-55 South. Veer north as the road forks and head for the river, not President's Island.

The park opened in 1887 and was originally called Jackson Mound Park after Andrew Jackson. There were band concerts and special celebrations from spring to fall.

In 1914 the ten-acre tract was bought by the Memphis Park Commission and renamed DeSoto Park after explorer Hernando de Soto*.

Children can slide down the ancient Indian mound. During the Civil War the mound was hollowed out by Federal troops and used for artillery placements that guarded the river.

Next to the park is the National Ornamental Metal Museum* on the grounds of the old Marine Hospital which was used to treat mariners with rare diseases. Six buildings were constructed from 1883 to 1939. The older structures are Italianate, the newer ones Georgian Revival.

CONFEDERATE PARK
On river bluff, west side of Front Str. between Court and Jefferson Strs.

MATA: Downtown Buses.

The park offered a commanding view of the river to Memphians who came in carriages to watch the Battle of Memphis*. The view from here is still exciting.

The site was used as a dump until the Park Commission rescued it in the early 1900s.

A statue of Jefferson Davis, President of the Confederacy, stands in the center of the park. Cannons in the park are from World War I.

JEFFERSON DAVIS PARK
On the river, just west of Confederate Park.

MATA: Downtown buses.

Jefferson Davis Park is named, of course, for the President of the Confederate States of America. Davis (1808-1889) also served as U.S. Secretary of War under Franklin Pierce and as both U.S. Representative and U.S. Senator from Mississippi. In the 1870s, Davis moved to Memphis and lived at 216 Court Street, two blocks east of Court Square. He served as president of the Carolina Life Insurance Company, offices at 42 Madison. Both of these buildings have been demolished. Davis retired to Beauvoir in Gulfport, Mississippi.

MARTYR PARK
Southwest of the Holiday Inn-Rivermont, where Georgia Str. meets the river.

MATA: Showboat Bus.

A memorial sculpture to those who died of yellow fever was dedicated in 1978.

TOM LEE PARK
On the river at Beale Str.

MATA: Showboat Bus.

A 30-foot obelisk honors the black laborer for whom the park is named. In 1925 Tom Lee saved the lives of 32 people who were aboard the U.S.S. Norman when she sank 20 miles below Memphis. Tom Lee, who could not swim, bravely carried the 32 surviving victims of the steamer to shore in a 24-foot in-board motor boat, the Zev. A dime-in-the-slot machine at the river's edge plays an account of the story.

ASHBURN PARK
On the river bluff, Riverside Drive at Georgia Str.

MATA: Showboat Bus.

This two-acre park offers an excellent view of the river. The park is named for Major T. Q. Ashburn of Ohio who introduced towboats to the Mississippi. The terminal for Ashburn's company, Federal Barge Lines, stood on the river bluff where the park is today.

MARTIN LUTHER KING, JR. RIVERSIDE PARK
Intersection of S. Parkway W. and Riverside Drive.

MATA: From downtown take any bus to Cleveland and then #31 to Trigg & Riverside; walk one block.

The park was designed in the early 1900s as part of the park and parkway system of a growing city. Originally known as Riverside Park, it was renamed Martin Luther King, Jr.* Riverside Park after Dr. King's assassination in Memphis in 1968. King was in Memphis to support the sanitation workers' strike.

The 388-acre park has a golf course, picnic areas, nature trails, and boat ramp access to McKellar Lake with marina facilities.

To learn about a ride on the river see Transportation/By Boat.

Historic Sites

Assn. for the Preservation of Tn. Antiquities.

Fontaine House, circa 1871, Victorian Village.

AUCTION/NORTH MAIN

MATA: #8 Chelsea runs from Front Str. through this area.

The original town of Memphis was centered in the Auction/North Main area, slightly north of today's downtown center. Wolf River flowed into the Mississippi River at the foot of Auction, and before 1909, Mud Island* did not exist. Today this Auction/North Main area is overshadowed by the Hernando DeSoto I-40 Bridge. Only a few historical markers and the remains of the old Pinch and Greenlaw neighborhoods make one aware of the area's historical significance.

Early in 1819, Memphis was laid out by John Overton, Andrew Jackson, and James Winchester, the proprietors of the land. Four squares were set aside for public use: Auction, Market, Exchange, and Court. Early settlers thought Court* too distant and seldom used it.

MARKET SQUARE, which ran a half block along the west side of 2nd between Market and Winchester, was the civic center of early Memphis. Today it is used for car parking. One block east, on the northeast corner of Main and Winchester, stood the city's first formal bank, Farmers and Merchants Bank, organized in 1834. The building collapsed in 1967.

EXCHANGE SQUARE was located between Poplar and Exchange where Cook Convention Center* now stands. The original Exchange Building was built on this site in 1847 by W. A. Bickford and housed a city hall, court rooms, and a medical college.

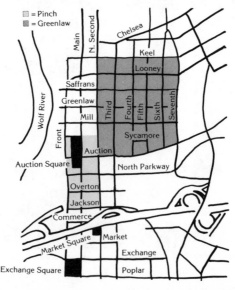

AUCTION SQUARE was located on Auction, bordered by Sycamore Str. to the north, Concord to the south, Front to the west, and Main to the east. It was a focal point for business in the city's early years and was the site of the first food market.

Some say the granite marker in the center of Auction Square was used for public slave auctioning, but according to historian Frederic Barcroft's *Slave Trading in the Old South,* there were probably never any public slave auctions on this site or anywhere else in Memphis. The city was a major slave trading center, but slaves were sold by individual dealers from their own establishments.

In early years slaves were brought to Memphis by water from Virginia, Kentucky, and Missouri. After 1857, when the railroad from Charleston, S.C. was completed, slave trade routes also ran to Memphis from the upper Carolinas, Georgia, and other parts of Tennessee. At that time more than a dozen local traders advertised in the newspapers. Although there were not a large number of slaves in Memphis, many buyers came to the city's markets from surrounding farmlands in Arkansas, southwest Tennessee, north and west Mississippi, and northeast Louisiana.

It was at approximately this same site, Auction east of Front, that the Spanish, in order to fortify Wolf River, had erected a garrison, **FORT SAN FERNANDO DE BARANCAS,** in 1795. The French, Spanish, and English had struggled for control of the territory since the late 17thc. (See The River/History.) In 1797 the Spanish burned their fort and withdrew to the west bank of the Mississippi River. Archaeologists are now excavating the area hoping to find some remains of Fort San Fernando. The fort was square, 200 feet by 200 feet, and was surrounded by a 12-foot high wooden stockade fence. There were block houses that stored food, arms, and ammunition, barracks for 132 men, a commander's house, and a powder magazine.

After the Spanish withdrawal, the Americans built **FORT ADAMS** on the Fort San Fernando site. A marker stands at Main, south of Auction. The fort was renamed **FORT PIKE** in 1800 and **FORT PICKERING** in 1801. Zachary Taylor, future President of the U.S., was commander of Fort Pickering in 1804. In 1862 Fort Pickering was relocated to the south, running from the foot of Vance Str. to below where DeSoto Park is now.

Moving through the Auction/North Main area, from south to north, historical markers indicate the locations of the following:

POPLAR STREET TRAIN DEPOT, circa 1890, west of present day Cook Convention Center at Poplar and Front. The stone retaining wall and iron fence are all that remain. It was from here that Casey Jones* left Memphis on his fateful journey April 30, 1900. Speed was vital to competitors for lucrative post office contracts. As Casey tried to make up lost time on the 188-mile Illinois Central run from Memphis to Canton, Miss., freight trains were sidetracked to allow his passenger/mail train to pass. Near Vaughan, Miss., a freight train, too long for the sidetrack, was left on the main rails. Casey saw collision was inevitable. The hero of song and legend lost his life as he stayed aboard and slowed his train down, saving the lives of all others aboard.

A monument on Main, north of Winchester, commemorates **ISAAC RAWLINGS,** the area's first permanent white settler and an early Memphis mayor and merchant. According to a 1961 article by James Roper in the "Tennessee Historical Quarterly", Rawlings was appointed in 1814 to be the Indian trading agent at Fort Pickering*. In 1817 he moved to the Arkansas River to set up a new trading post to serve the Cherokees. Returning to Memphis in 1821, Rawlings opened the town's second store. Rawlings was mayor of the new town from 1828 to 1835. He died in 1839 and was buried in Raleigh Cemetery*.

A marker on the southeast corner of Front & Jackson commemorates **MARCUS WINCHESTER'S STORE,** the town's first. It opened in 1819. Marcus, the son of James Winchester, was sent to Memphis by the early proprietors to act as their real estate agent. He was also the town's first mayor and postmaster.

An 1850's home on Front Str. at Overton Str. marks the site of **BELL TAVERN** and **PADDY MEAGHER'S STORE.** In the 1820s Paddy Meagher's Store sold, among other things, whiskey and tobacco. The store became known as the Bell Tavern because of a bell that stood in front. John Overton, Sam Houston, and Davy Crockett frequented the tavern.

An historical marker on Front, south of Auction, gives a brief history of **MEMPHIS NAVY YARD** in operation from about 1843-1853. The navy yard produced one warship, the Allegheny, at a cost of approximately $500,000. It was too slow to be of much service. On its first major trip to New York, it docked in Norfolk, Va. for repairs and was condemned. The present day Coast Guard building is just east of this site and is guarded by an iron fence, the remains of an early Shelby County jail.

The site of the city's **FIRST COTTON GIN** is marked on the north side of Auction, a block east of Front, just north of today's Colonial Park. The gin was built between 1819 and 1821. The building to the north of the marker once housed the Schlitz* brewery.

PINCH/NORTH MAIN COMMERCIAL DISTRICT (NRHP) took its name from "Pinch-Gut", a phrase used to describe early Irish settlers who moved here escaping the potato famine. The phrase referred to their stomachs pinched by tight belts. The area is bounded by Front, Jackson,

Auction, and an alley between Main and 2nd. Waves of immigrants have lived here. First came the Irish, then Italians, and later Russians. Stop for lunch at Abraham's Deli, 338 N. Main, a last vestige of the once thriving ethnic neighborhood. (See Sandwich restaurants.) Other historic sites are Anshei Mishne Synagogue, circa 1927, at 112 Jackson, now boarded up, and the city's first mikvah, a public bathing facility for Orthodox Jews, built in 1917 at 78 Overton. Drive north of Pinch to 258 Bethel, and you'll smell the fresh bread from Meyer's Bakery, for about 50 years the only place in the city selling kosher breads.

A few urban pioneers are beginning to rehabilitate the cast-iron columned buildings. Broom Corn at 426 N. Front has a large selection of decorator fabrics. (See Fabrics.)

In 1856 the streets were laid out in Memphis' first suburb, the 30-block **GREENLAW ADDITION.** Bayou Gayoso, today an underground drainage canal, separated the suburb from the rest of town. Greenlaw covered an area between Main and 7th from Mill to Auction. There is some rehabilitation in the area.

In the suburb laid out by William and John Greenlaw, prominent families lived in elegant, moderately sized, two-story homes. The Costen-Willey House* and part of the Chase-Walsh House* are all that remain of the original ante-bellum dwellings.

By the end of the Civil War more modest cottages were interspersed among the earlier homes. Settlers from the North and Midwest moved into the area. In 1870 Greenlaw was annexed by the city.

By the turn of the century various ethnic groups had moved into the area—Irish in the 1840s, followed by Germans in the 1860s, and Italians in the 1870s. Many of the immigrants had settled in the area of Pinch* and then spilled over into Greenlaw. By 1880-90 Russian and Polish Jews were living in the area. Many 1890-1910 Victorian homes remain with their irregular roof lines, shingles on the eaves, gingerbread trim, and porches. Among them are Mill House*, Love House*, and Sambucetti House*.

Blacks lived in the area in the 1890s. Records show that Dr. A. D. Byas, a black physician, lived here in 1908. His relative, Dr. James Byas, today practices medicine in this area on N. Main. W. C. Handy's Knights of Pythias Band was headquartered on N. 7th and the North Memphis Brass Band had its home at Auction and N. 7th.

For more information see the MIFA "Greenlaw Rediscovered" study by Peggy Jemison, Virginia Dunaway and Ray Kramer in the Memphis room* of the library.

For those interested in architecture:

Go north to 826 N. 2nd, **BURKLE HOUSE*.**

Go east to 253 Auction, the **ARTESIAN WATER COMPANY PUMP-ING STATION.** It was built in 1890 just after an artesian well was discovered in the city. A broken sewer line contaminated the water in 1919 and the station was abandoned.

Go east on Keel to Manassas where **PORTER LEATH (NRHP)** Children's Center, originally Leath Orphan Asylum, is located at 850 N. Manassas. The north wing dates from 1856, and the main building from about 1875. An example of Victorian Italianate style architecture, Porter-Leath has been in continuous use since its construction, as an orphanage until 1969 and today as a full social service center. The original exterior brick and trim has been restored.

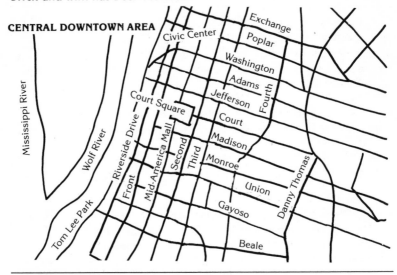

MID-AMERICA MALL/CENTRAL DOWNTOWN

MATA: *Most Memphis buses run along Front and 2nd parallel to the Mall. In this book they are referred to as Downtown buses.*

Mid-America Mall, said to be the longest pedestrian mall in the U.S., runs from Poplar to McCall (one block north of Beale), parallel to the Mississippi River, over what until 1976 was Memphis' Main Street. Today's mall with its fountains and trees is a far cry from Main Street of the 1800s where a team of oxen once drowned in a mudhole. During most of the city's history, this north-south street was the center of commerce with hotels, restaurants, theatres, shops, and places of entertainment. Downtown Memphis aged badly after World War II as racial tensions grew and middle class families moved to the suburbs. Today new condominiums and restaurants are signs of an urban resurgence. The Mall itself is a pleasant place to stroll with such abstract sculpture as Richard Hunt's "Memorial to Martin Luther King Jr." between Poplar and Exchange, Louis Pounders' "Apogee" at Jefferson, John Seyfried's "River" at Monroe, and John McIntire's "Muse" at Gayoso. Wander from north to south, and you'll learn a lot about Memphis history and architecture.

COOK CONVENTION CENTER and AUDITORIUM, north end of the mall, under the shadow of the I-40 Bridge, was completed in 1973 and can accommodate 45,000 people. It has conference rooms and exhibit and storage space. The Auditorium, opened in 1924, housed a produce market for many years. Today everything from circus to opera fills its 2,300 seat Music Hall and 4,300 seat Amphitheatre. The center is named for Everett R. Cook, WWI fighter pilot, Deputy Chief of Staff of the 8th and 12th Air Forces in WWII, and successful Memphis businessman.

City, county, state, and federal office buildings form the **CIVIC CENTER** which is on the mall just south of Poplar.

CITY HALL
125 N. Mid-America Mall. 785-3660.

Tours: *By appointment, arrange 3 months in advance. 9:30 - 11:30 am Tu & W Oct.-Apr. except Dec. Chaperones required for children. Groups of 1-30. About 1 hour.*
Cost: *Free.*
MATA: *Downtown buses.*
E&H: *Wheelchair accessible.*

Tours given by the city's Department of Youth Services include a brief history of Memphis and an explanation of the workings of city government. Sights include the Mayors' portraits, the City Council chambers, and sometimes the Mayor's office. City Council meetings at 1:30 pm Tu are free and open to the public.

SHELBY COUNTY ADMINISTRATION BUILDING
160 N. Mid-America Mall. 528-3588 (Shelby County Public Affairs Department - they make the arrangements).

Tours: *By appointment, arrange 3 months in advance. 9am-noon M-F. All ages and interest levels welcome but it's probably best for those 9 +. Groups of 1-40, optimum 20. Lasts about 2 hours.*
Cost: *Free.*
MATA: *Downtown buses.*
E&H: *Special wheelchair accessible routes will be taken, just let them know in advance.*

See how the county operates. Tour also includes the courthouse*. County Commission meetings in the lobby chambers are also free and open to the public.

Continuing south, you come to Adams. The section along Adams from Main to 4th has been designated the **ADAMS AVENUE HISTORIC DISTRICT.** It contains Victorian townhouses, Neoclassical government structures, and Gothic churches.

The **NORTH MEMPHIS SAVINGS BANK** at Main and Adams was built about 1901 to house the bank begun by John and Anthony Walsh. "Boss" Crump, the state's most colorful 20thc. political figure, later had his offices in this building.

Edward Hull Crump was born in Marshall County, Miss. in 1874 and came to Memphis in 1893. His political career began in 1901 when he was elected a delegate to the county Democratic Convention. In 1905 he was elected to the Memphis Board of Public Works, and in 1907 became Police Commissioner. In 1909 the commission form of government went into effect in Memphis with a board of five elected commissioners, one of whom would be mayor. The first mayor under this new system was the 36 year old, red-headed reformer of the public utilities, Crump. His campaign song in this election, "Mr. Crump don't 'low no easy riders here", was composed by W. C. Handy* and later became known as "Mémphis Blues". Crump was re-elected mayor twice. He was ousted from office in 1916, ostensibly for not enforcing prohibition, but according to many, for favoring a municipal power company.

Undiscouraged, Crump began building the political machine that made him feared and famous. His candidates began by taking county offices. By 1927 they controlled key state offices. "Boss" Crump hand-picked every Memphis mayor from 1927 until his death in 1954. Crump himself served in the U.S. Congress from 1931 to 1935 and was again elected mayor in 1939.

Along with fellow Memphian, U.S. Senator Kenneth McKellar, Crump dominated the state Democratic party for more than two decades. His power was not challenged successfully until a young Chattanooga lawyer, Estes Kefauver, was elected to the U.S. Senate over Crump's opposition.

Crump, who was also active in the mortgage-loan, investment, real estate, and insurance businesses, built his home in 1909 at 1962 Peabody Ave. **THE CRUMP HOUSE (NRHP)** remains a private residence.

Just to the east, near 2nd and Adams, are the old **MEMPHIS POLICE STATION** and **ENGINE HOUSE,** both designed by Shaw and Pfeil, circa 1910, and the **CRIMINAL COURTS BUILDING,** now the jail, built in 1924.

On Adams between 2nd and 3rd is the
SHELBY COUNTY COURT HOUSE, circa 1909
140 Adams. 527-3573 (Memphis and Shelby County Bar Assn.).

Hours: *8am-4:30pm M · F.*
Tour: *Court rooms are open to the public, but to arrange a tour contact the*
          County Public Affairs Office at 528-3588. Offered 9am-noon, M · F.
          Groups of 1-40. 2 hours. Also offered by Young Lawyers, Memphis and
          Shelby County Bar Assn. during law week each May.
Cost: *Free.*
Lunch: *Limited snack stand.*
MATA: *#53 (ex Sun).*
E&H: *Wheelchair entrances at 3rd and Adams and 2nd and Washington.*

The Court House was built about 1905 in the Beaux Arts style. It was designed by architects H. D. Hale and James Gamble Rogers. Rogers also designed most of the Gothic buildings on Yale University campus. Room 305 retains its original floors, massive mahoghany furniture, and chandeliers. The cage elevators and statue of Andrew Jackson are also noteworthy. The bronze statue of Jackson, done by John Frazee in 1859 for Court Square*, was moved here for protection from the weather.

See whether local attorneys are as dramatic as Perry Mason.

If it's lunchtime, you might want to try Diane's. (See American restaurants.) It's on top of the city's tallest building, the 38-floor **100 NORTH MAIN BUILDING.**

The upper stories of buildings at **63** and **55 NORTH MAIN** are good examples of turn of the century commercial buildings. Most of Main Street's existing buildings were built during the 1900-1917 building boom when the street was the center of Memphis' shopping activity.

The 21-story **COLUMBIA MUTUAL TOWER (NRHP),** 60 N. Main, has terra cotta ornamentation, popular in Memphis in the 1920s.

COURT SQUARE, 2.07 acres between 2nd and Main on Court, was one of the four original parks set aside for public use in 1819. The square was intended as the site of the courthouse, but early settlers considered it too far south and located their temporary courthouse in Market Square*. In the 1830s a log house then in Court Square served as Eugene Magevney's* first school.

The fountain with its sculpture of Hebe, the Grecian cupbearer to the gods, was dedicated in 1876 to mark the nation's centennial. It was a gift from fifty citizens whose names are on the surrounding wall. The sculpture is a copy of a work in Leningrad by the Italian sculptor Antonio Canova.

In the late 19thc., the park sank into disrepair. President Benjamin Harrison campaigned here in 1891 against Cleveland, Admiral Dewey visited in 1900, and President William McKinley came in 1901. In 1907 the present trees were planted. Today Court Square is the focal point of Mid-America Mall. An historical marker on the north side of the park says that inventor Thomas Edison once roomed in a house which stood at 126 N. Court and here invented a cockroach shocker.

Children will enjoy feeding the squirrels and pigeons.

The Moorish, towered castle on the northeast corner of Court Square, 130 Court, was built to house the **TENNESSEE CLUB,** an exclusive gentlemen's club founded in 1875. The building was built about 1895 and today is a law office.

The **WELCOME WAGON BUILDING,** 145 N. Court, circa 1907, housed the Commercial Appeal newspaper from 1907-1933. People gathered in Court Square to read the latest news as it was flashed across the front of the building.

On the southeast corner of Court Square, 9 N. 2nd, is the 20-story, 2nd Empire Commercial style **EXCHANGE BUILDING (NRHP).** It was built in 1909 to replace the 4-story, 1884, Memphis Cotton Exchange. The Exchange Building housed the Cotton Exchange* from 1910-1924.

The **PORTER BUILDING (NRHP),** 10 N. Main, the southwest corner of Court Square, was Memphis' first skyscraper and, according to architectural historian James Patrick, is the most historically significant piece of existing architecture in Memphis. Built in the Romanesque Revival style in 1894 for the Continental National Bank, it was the first skyscraper constructed south of the Ohio River. When architect E. C. Jones presented his plans, city officials were afraid a strong wind might blow the building down and had to be persuaded to award the builders a permit. There was a 10¢ charge for the thrill of riding the elevator up the building's 11-stories. The building was the highest structure in the world heated with hot water.

In the late 1890s the bank was liquidated, and the Porter family bought the building as a memorial to the deceased Dr. D. T. Porter. Dr. Porter, a pharmacist, had served on the boards of several banks and businesses and as a commissioner of the Taxing District of Shelby County.

The **KRESS STORE** with its polychromed facade, 9 N. Main, circa 1937, is Art Deco in style. In 1896 the first Kress store in the U.S. opened several blocks south of here and sold no item priced over 10¢. Thirty-one paintings from the Kress Art Collection were given to Brooks Memorial Gallery* in 1957 and are on display there now.

Continuing south on the mall, you come to Madison Avenue. To the west, the street deadends at the Beaux Arts **U.S. POST OFFICE AND CUS-TOM HOUSE,** 1 Front, circa 1885 (wings circa 1932).

During the first part of the 20thc. Madison Avenue was the city's financial center and was known as **BANKER'S ROW.** Still standing are **UNION PLANTERS BANK BUILDING,** circa 1920 at 67 Madison, **TEN-NESSEE TRUST BUILDING,** circa 1904 at 81 Madison, and **OLD FIRST NATIONAL BANK BUILDING,** circa 1909 at 127 Madison.

During the Civil War, the Tennessee legislature briefly met at the site of **UNION PLANTERS BANK'S MANHATTAN BRANCH,** 140 Madison, the northwest corner of Madison and 2nd.

Notice the Beaux Arts style commercial buildings, circa 1915, at **150-152 MADISON.**

The modern **FIRST TENNESSEE BANK BUILDING,** 165 Madison, continues the street's financial legacy. Plans are underway for a 51-panel mural on Tennessee history by artist Ted Faiers to hang behind teller's row in the main lobby.

Continue east on Madison to the old **SCIMITAR BUILDING,** 179 Madison, built in the early French Renaissance style by Napoleon Hill. The Scimitar newspaper was published here from 1902-1923.

Napoleon Hill lived across Madison at 8 N. 3rd where the 29-story **STERICK BUILDING (NRHP)** now stands. When completed in 1929, the Sterick Building was the tallest building in the city.

Architecture buffs wander farther east. See the contemporary **C&I BANK BUILDING,** 200 Madison, and **PRITCHARD BROTHERS PLUMBING BUILDING,** circa 1903, 433 Madison.

South of Madison on the mall, you come to the **COMMERCE TITLE BUILDING,** 12 S. Main. Built in the early 1900s, it now houses the Tourist and Convention Center and Memphis-in-May* offices.

The next street crossing the mall is Monroe. Just east of 4th on Monroe is the **H. T. BRUCE BUILDING,** 260 Monroe. This building has been oc-cupied for a long time by Arthur Fulmer, but in the early 1900s it was operated by H. T. Bruce as the largest mule barn in Memphis. His name is high on the front.

Mules were big business in Memphis. Originally pens were located along Jefferson, but before the Civil War they moved to the area along 3rd and remained there until WWI. As early as 1896 there were auctions in which 1,000 mules were sold in a day.

About 1911 many dealers moved to south Memphis, nearer the railroads, and Memphis replaced East St. Louis as the mule capitol of the world. It has been estimated that as many as 75,000 mules were traded in Memphis in a year, and that the trading brought $10 million a year into the flow of trade. The best year for sales is said to have been 1918 when purchasing agents from U.S. and European armies were buying.

As cotton plantations and coal mines mechanized, the use of mules practically disappeared. In 1961 the last mule barn was converted for cattle operations.

To the west on Monroe is the Shrine Building and the beginning of Cotton Row and the Gayoso-Peabody Historic Districts. The **SHRINE BUILDING (NRHP),** 66 Monroe, was built in 1923. The 13-story building shows how styles changed to tall building architecture. Primarily an office building, the top five floors housed the Al Chymia Shrine Temple. The famous Tivoli Roof Garden Restaurant was once on top. Today the building is being converted to apartments.

COTTON ROW HISTORIC DISTRICT (NRHP)
Along Front Street between Monroe on the north, Gayoso on the south, Center Lane Alley on the east, and Wagner Place on the west.

Cotton's impact on Memphis began in the early 1800s with the invention of the cotton gin. After Eli Whitney's gin made it possible to clean short-staple cotton, there was a rush west for land to produce this crop, first for foreign and later for domestic markets.

In the 1850s Memphis was beginning to rival New Orleans as a cotton market. The "white gold" was grown on the rich farmland along the Mississippi River and transported to the Memphis market over planked roads, by steamboat, and by the new railroads. In 1857, 26 buyers and 28 factors were listed in the city directory and by 1860, 400,000 bales of cotton valued at $16 million were handled annually in the city.

During the Civil War the Union embargo on trade from the south was poorly enforced. Gerald Capers in *Biography of a Rivertown* says Lincoln feared that a serious reduction in Southern trade with either the upper mid-west or Europe might force either or both of these trading partners into the war as allies of the Confederacy.

After the war and the emancipation of slaves, the cotton factor replaced the plantation owner as controller of production. Necessary heavy capital investment was borrowed from the factor, and the planter raised his crop on credit. All cotton produced was turned over to the factor who arranged for its sale for a brokerage fee. During the 1880s and 90s, these factors became the social elite, many serving as presidents and directors of local banks.

By 1871 cotton was being shipped directly from Memphis to Liverpool in three to four weeks. By 1887 Memphis boasted the world's largest inland spot cotton market and the largest producer of cottonseed oil in the world. Cotton Row, stretching along Front from Madison to Linden, was at its height.

Cotton is picked from the boll in the field and taken to a gin where seeds are removed and the cotton loosely packed in 500-pound bales. These bales are then compressed and either stored or shipped to mills where cloth is made.

Most of the cotton offices that still stand in Cotton Row were built between 1848 and 1928. During this time cotton was literally sold on the spot. Cotton merchants usually purchased the baled raw cotton from the farmer, classed it, and then sold it either directly to mills or to a shipper who accumulated large stocks of cotton and sold to major world textile centers. The merchant usually charged the farmer a commission or handling fee for performing this service.

In the brick buildings, ground floors were usually office space. The second floors were used for storage and sample rooms. The top floors, with skylights to capture the north light, were used for classing. Samples were classified as to grade, staple and color. There are 9 grades, 7 colors, and 17 staples—in all, nearly a thousand different classifications.

In the mid-1900s nearly half of all U.S. cotton crops were bought and sold on Memphis' Cotton Exchange, yet the cotton business as a whole was feeling the crunch of synthetic fabrics and world competition. Government subsidies and loan programs had been initiated to help the cotton farmers and traders. Trading in cotton future contracts had increased. Many small merchants were going out of business. Today large cotton traders like Dunavant Enterprises, Inc., Hohenberg Bros. Co., and L. T. Barringer & Co. trade in both the spot and futures cotton markets. In 1977 Dunavant Enterprises, Inc. alone handled ten percent of all cotton traded in the U.S.

To see Cotton Row walk north to south along Front. You'll pass:

MID-SOUTH GROWERS ASSN., 44 S. Front, constructed of reinforced concrete, circa 1936. Until 1977, it was the home of the Mid-South Growers Assn., a lobbying unit formed in 1931 to represent farmers. Today, apartments and Up Front, an avant garde art gallery, are in the building.

SHELBY COTTON CO.
48 S. Front. 526-3157.

Hours: 8:30am-6pm M · F, 9-4:30pm Sat.
Tours: By appointment. Groups of 1-20. All ages. 15 min.
Cost: Free.
MATA: Downtown buses.
Other: Souvenir shop.
E&H: Wheelchair accessible.

Robert Farrish, in the cotton business since the '40s, tells the story of cotton from the field to the gin, the warehouse, the factory, and finally the shirt on your back. You'll see cotton plants at various stages of growth, old-fashioned farm equipment, and cotton samples.

BLUES ALLEY, 60 S. Front, circa 1875. Built in the Italianate Victorian style, this building houses Blues Alley, a good spot to hear authentic Memphis music* and eat barbecued ribs. (See Nightspots/With Music.)

HOWARD'S ROW, a group of Victorian style buildings at 77-85 S. Front and 49 and 45-47 Union, were built by Wardlow Howard about 1848 and formed an early cotton trading center. The 45-47 Union building which houses John Malmo Advertising, Inc. is believed to have been a hospital during the Civil War. The Timpani Apartments, next door at 41-43 Union, are in a renovated cotton office, one of the first buildings redeveloped downtown. If it's lunchtime, have a sandwich* at Front Street Deli, 77 S. Front. Carter Seed Store, 85 S. Front, sells plants, seeds, and related items. It is the last of the Cotton Row seed stores.

COTTON EXCHANGE BUILDING
84 S. Front. 525-3361.

Tours: *You must be accompanied to see the Exchange. Phone for an appointment, usually possible 8:30am - 4pm F.*
Cost: *Free.*
MATA: *Downtown buses.*
E&H: *No ramp, but wheelchairs can enter through lobby door.*

The Exchange, organized in 1874, was located in the Exchange Building* on Court Square until the present building was completed in 1924.

Quotations from the New York futures market flash on an electronic board but a handshake still seals some business transactions. The Exchange has 175 members. In the early 1950s people were willing to pay $15,000-$17,000 for a membership. Today a seat can be had for less than $500.

On the tours, raw cotton marketing is explained but don't expect to see actual trading or cotton sampling. A trip to a cotton gin or warehouse in the fall would probably be more fun, especially for children.

MURDOCH'S INTERNATIONAL COTTON SCHOOL
84 S. Front. 526-0100.

Tours: *By appointment. Groups of 1-10. All ages.*
Cost: *Free.*
MATA: *Downtown buses.*
E&H: *Wheelchair accessible.*

One of the few cotton schools in the world, Murdoch's International Cotton School, is in the Exchange's building. W. L. Murdoch founded the school in 1920. Today, W. L. Murdoch, Jr., his son, runs it. Students learn how cotton is grown, marketed, and classed by color, texture and purity. Sixty-five percent of the students are from foreign countries.

JOSEPH N. OLIVER BUILDING, 101 S. Front, built in 1904 as the Memphis Cold Storage Warehouse, was the first cold storage operation in the South. The Front Street side houses The Butcher Shop, a steak restaurant; on the river side is The Pier Restaurant (See Happy Hours).

GAYOSO-PEABODY HISTORIC DISTRICT
Extends south from Monroe to McCall and east from Center Lane Alley to Hernando.

The Gayoso-Peabody district filled the needs and desires of the cotton men when cotton was king. There were hardware, drygoods, and grocery stores, hotels and rooming houses, and saloons and brothels for after-hours entertainment. The district was named for its once elegant hotels: the Gayoso, opened in 1842, and the Peabody, opened in 1869. Most of the buildings here were built between 1880 and 1927.

To see the area walk from north to south past:

The now boarded up **BUSINESS MEN'S CLUB BUILDING,** 79-81 Monroe, circa 1906. The club was formed in 1900 to attract investment capital to the city and became affiliated with the U.S. Chamber of Commerce in 1913.

LEMMON-GALE BUILDING, 60 S. Main, a now boarded up Romanesque style structure. At the turn of the century Memphis was the largest drygoods market in the South, and the Lemmon-Gale Co. was one of the city's largest drygoods companies.

FARNSWORTH BUILDING, 69 S. Main, stands 12 stories high and is a fine example of the Art Deco style. The Three Sisters Shop is on the ground floor.

CAST IRON TWINS, 87-91 S. 2nd, circa 1891, are the only remaining structures in Memphis whose facades are made entirely of cast iron. Structurally they are identical. The building at 87 2nd was for a time the home of the Memphis Daily Commercial and the Evening Democrat, the forerunners of the Memphis Commercial Appeal. Today the buildings house wholesale clothing stores.

The **PEABODY HOTEL* (NRHP),** 80 S. 2nd, the corner of Union and 2nd, was first located at the northwest corner of Monroe and Main. The original structure, built in 1869, was demolished in 1923, and the hotel rebuilt by R. C. Brinkley in 1925 on its present site.

In the '20s, '30s and '40s the Peabody was the social center of Memphis. The Skyway, its top floor nightclub, was slightly racy and very chic. Alonzo Locke, the black headwaiter, was famous for knowing everybody who was anybody. D. L. Cohn in his 1935 *God Shakes Creation* and Tennessee Williams in "Summer and Smoke" decreed that the Mississippi Delta began at the Peabody and ended at Catfish Row in Vicksburg. Socially and culturally it did. As Cohn said, the Peabody was to this area as the Ritz to Paris, Shepheard's to Cairo, and the Savoy to London.

The Peabody closed in 1975 but its present owners, the Belz-Hanover family, have since renovated the grand old building as a 456-room luxury hotel. It re-opened in fall 1981—hurrah!

Eloise would enjoy watching the ducks in the lobby's fountain, and so will your children.

Some commercial buildings along Main, between Union and Gayoso, built around 1905, are interesting architecturally:

NATIONAL EXCHANGE SALOON, 95 S. Main, now houses Hardy Shoes.

GOLDSMITH'S DEPARTMENT STORE, 123 S. Main, was started in 1870 by Isaac and Jacob Goldsmith as a drygoods store. It was first located on Beale Str. between Front and Main. In 1881 the store moved to Main at Union, in 1896 to a five-story building at Main and Gayoso, and in 1901 to its present location. Goldsmith's grew and in 1962 expanded into the neighboring **GAYOSO HOTEL,** 139-141 S. Main. The original hotel structure, built in 1842 by Robertson Topp, was the early town's most imposing structure. It burned in 1899 and was rebuilt in 1902. The luxury hotel was the city's leading hostelry until 1925. Goldsmith's bought the hotel in 1948 and closed it in 1962 when they expanded into the space.

MAJESTIC THEATRE, 145-149 S. Main, circa 1913, is visually exciting with its extravagant use of polychromed terra cotta ornamentation. The Blue Light Studio is on the ground floor.

BEALE STREET/SOUTH MEMPHIS

MATA: Showboat Bus or #50 running from 2nd east on Linden.

Everyone who loves the blues has heard of Beale Str. where black

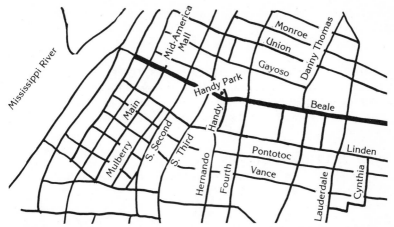

musicians wove the sorrows of sharecroppers and day laborers into one of the world's great art forms. Today it is several sad blocks of mostly boarded up buildings, and only memories linger of the days when the sounds of guitars, harmonicas, and horns drifted among the saloons and dance halls.

In the first half of the 19thc. Beale was the main road in South Memphis, a separate river town with its own busy docks. Near the river landing were warehouses, rooming houses, and saloons. There were retail stores between Main and 3rd, and farther east, churches and beautiful houses. From the 1830s through the 1850s many first families farmed plantations to the south and lived in the area bounded by Beale on the north, Vance on the south, Lauderdale on the east, and Wellington (now Danny Thomas Blvd.) on the west. The area remained fashionable through the 1890s.

In 1849 South Memphis was annexed by Memphis. The two met where Union Ave. runs.

By the 1880s increasing numbers of freed blacks were living in Memphis. Until after World War I when blacks began to enjoy greater mobility, Beale Str. was their "main" street. By day it was respectable; by night there was music, gambling, prostitution, drugs, and voodoo. Between 2nd and 3rd Strs. were the pawn shops, most owned by members of Memphis' Jewish and Italian communities. Here gamblers raised money for the crap games in the parlors and night spots between 3rd and Turley Strs. This was the infamous legendary Beale Str. that W. C. Handy* immortalized in his "Beale Street" blues.

In the early 1900s prohibition was little enforced on Beale, but by 1920 nightlife was forced underground, and the organized underworld gained more control. After World War I, blacks began to gain greater mobility, and Jim Crow laws slowly began to be thrown out. Beale Str. fell on hard times. From 1910-1955 Beale was officially designated Beale Ave. In the

1960s the area was practically urban renewaled into oblivion. Today rehabilitation is underway.

To see the area, walk up Beale from the river eastward. You'll pass:

LINDEN STATION and the **REICHMAN-CROSBY WAREHOUSE, (NRHP)** 245, 281, & 291 Wagner (near corner of Beale & Wagner), are being rehabilitated. Stop for lunch, dinner, drinks, or entertainment in #1 Beale (See American restaurants) or Captain Bilbo's (See Nightspots with Music).

ORPHEUM THEATRE (NRHP)

197 S. Main, southwester corner of Main & Beale. 523-6188 (ticket information), 523-6049 (tour information).

Tours: *Regularly scheduled tours 10:30am-1:30pm M. Bring your own lunch along; soft drinks for sale. Special group tours by appointment.*
Cost: *50¢/person. $10 minimum for special group tours.*
MATA: *Downtown buses.*
E&H: *First and second floors, wheelchair accessible.*

The land where the Orpheum now stands, the corner of Main and Beale Strs., was first a homesite for John Manning. Manning moved here from a house on Adams which he sold to Eugene Magevney*. Later the land became a coal yard. Then in 1888 the site was purchased for a lavish new theatre, Hopkins' Grand Opera House, built in 1889. In 1907 the theatre became part of a chain of vaudeville theatres. It was during this phase that such stars as Harry Houdini and Sarah Bernhardt appeared on the stage. In 1923 the original building was destroyed by fire, ironically while a burlesque dancer billed as "The Hottest Girl in Town" was playing.

The present Orpheum, built for vaudeville and movies, opened in 1928. The theatre's large Wurlitzer organ named Louise and the great chandeliers were only part of the lavishness expended on the new theatre. Then in 1933 the vaudeville circuit went bankrupt; the Memphis Orpheum ran as an independent theatre. In 1937 the Bluff City Amusement Co. took over the Orpheum for live musical events, and such greats as Louis Armstrong, Duke Ellington, the Mills Brothers, and Cab Calloway appeared on the state.

In 1940 M. A. Lightman bought the Orpheum, changed its name to the Malco, and showed motion pictures. In the late '60s and early '70s difficult times hit downtown Memphis and the theatre.

In December, 1976 the Memphis Development Foundation bought the building and changed its name back to the Orpheum. Today it offers live theatre, music, and special films.

ELVIS PRESLEY* PLAZA, southeast corner of Main and Beale, commemorates the "King of Rock 'N Roll". A 9½ foot bronze statue of Elvis by Eric Parks of Unionville, Pa. was unveiled in 1980 and dominates the plaza.

LANSKY, 126 Beale, is a men's clothing store. Story has it that Elvis bought on credit his first suit of clothes here for his high school graduation. Even as a star Elvis shopped here, sometimes buying $3000 worth of clothes at a time.

BEALE STREET HISTORIC DISTRICT (NRHP)
Between 2nd and 4th on Beale, designated a National Historic Landmark in 1966.

The buildings in this area were clothing stores, pawn shops, grocery stores, hotels, and saloons. Today most are just shells, the result of urban renewal attempts. Novick's, Hutkins, and Schwab's are exceptions; they're open for business.

NATHAN NOVICK'S LOAN OFFICE. 142 Beale. This pawn shop specializes in musical instruments. Elvis Presley* bought one of his first guitars here.

146-152 BEALE, circa 1895 and 1900. Boarded up, the store is architecturally typical of many on Beale.

HUTKINS HARDWARE. 149 Beale. Open for business, this store has changed little since the '50s.

SONNY'S LOAN OFFICE/EPSTEIN'S. 162-164 Beale, circa 1894. Now boarded up, the building is architecturally significant for its eclectic style which mixes a cast iron store front, stone arched window head, carved stone parapet, and ornate Victorian ironwork.

A. SCHWAB'S. 163-165 Beale. The general store is open for business and definitely worth a visit. Founded in 1876, it is run by the founder's grandchildren, Abram Schwab and Eleanor Schwab Braslow, who sell everything from 24¢ ties to love potions, suspenders, and kitchen utensils. A collection of local memorabilia is on the mezzanine, and visitors are given a free souvenir packet.

GALLINA BUILDING. 177-181 Beale, circa 1891. Built in the Richardsonian Romanesque style, this building was a combination hotel, restaurant, saloon, and office. Theatre and sports celebrities often stayed here in the "gay '90s".

HANDY PARK, between 3rd and Hernando, was created in 1930 on the site of South Market, one of the city's market places from 1859-1872.

The statue of W. C. Handy* was erected in 1960, two years after Handy's death.

SOLVENT SAVINGS BANK AND TRUST CO. 197 Beale. This site was a second home of the bank founded in 1906 by Robert R. Church Sr. Church is said to have been the South's first black millionaire.

He was born in 1839 in Holly Springs, Miss. and came to Memphis in 1851. Church's first career, working on steamboats, ended with the capture of Memphis by Federal forces. He then opened a hotel/saloon at 2nd and Gayoso serving the city's black population. Eventually Church branched out into real estate and banking.

In 1899 he built a 2,000-seat auditorium and a six-acre park for blacks near Beale Street Baptist Church*, 379 Beale.

Church's son, Robert R. Church Jr., became involved in politics and in 1916 helped found and finance the Lincoln League, a Republican organization that encouraged blacks to register and vote. He was a delegate to eight Republican national conventions.

HARRY'S DISCOUNT DEPARTMENT STORE. 205 Beale, circa 1884. This Victorian building housed Oakie's Saloon from 1884-1915.

BATTIER'S PHARMACY. 207-211 Beale, circa 1895. This meeting place for Beale Str. regulars was known after 1929 as Abe Plough's Pantaze Drug Store. The second and third floors of this building were known as Club Handy in the 1930s and later as the Old Mitchell Hotel. The building is notable for its cast iron window heads and elegant masonry details. This is the first structure being renovated in the city's Beale Str. Historic Preservation Project.

Blues musicians congregated on Beale between Hernando and 4th, a block also known as the headquarters for the Memphis underworld. Today most of the block's buildings have been torn down. Those standing are boarded up:

PEEWEE'S PLACE, 317 Beale, was torn down for road construction. Legend has it that W. C. Handy* wrote "Memphis Blues" there in 1900. Virgilio Maffei, known as Peewee, was an Italian immigrant who came to Memphis in the 1880s with ten cents. He made enough money shooting dice on Beale to open his first saloon at Beale and Hernando. His saloon offered gambling and a phone musicians could use to book engagements.

OLD DAISY THEATRE, 329-331 Beale, circa 1920, was originally a movie theatre. The ornate building with its Moorish arched facade is boarded up, but still standing.

MONARCH CLUB, 340 Beale, was once a saloon/dance hall/gambling hang-out with a mirrored entrance. It opened about 1910 and is said to have been known in the underworld as the Castle of Missing Men.

PANAMA CLUB was on the ground floor of a building which stood at the southwest corner of Beale and 4th. The owners of this club were known as the bosses of Beale. Mary Wonder, a voodoo queen, occupied the second floor.

HAMMITT ASHFORD'S SALOON, known as one of the hottest spots in town, was located at the southeast corner of Beale and 4th.

The historic district ends at 4th, but four buildings to the east are of note:

BEALE STREET BAPTIST CHURCH* (NRHP). 379 Beale.

The new **BEALE STREET CINEMA.** 380 Beale. The building may be rented for parties or theatre performances.

The boarded up **TRI-STATE BANK** building **(NRHP),** 386-390 Beale, is reported to have been the site of Handy's publishing house.

Of the 1830s-90s fashionable Beale Street residential area, little is left. Of the ante-bellum mansions only the **HUNT-PHELAN HOUSE* (NRHP),** 533 Beale, remains.

For legal buffs - the William Randolph home, circa 1865, stood at 546 Beale. In the 1890s Randolph, a prominent white lawyer, defended a black man's right to a seat on the railroad. Randolph and his client, Homer Adolph Plessy, lost the case. In its decision of *Plessy v. Ferguson,* 163 U.S. 537 (1896), the U.S. Supreme Court recognized a separate but equal doctrine that remained the law of the land until 1954 when the Court held in *Brown v. Board of Education* that separate facilities were inherently unequal. Randolph's Italian Rennaissance house, later owned by the Memphis Urban League, was in the National Register of Historic Places until it burned in 1976.

The streets crossing Beale, Hernando, Mulberry, DeSoto, and 4th also were well known for their saloons, night spots, and houses of ill-repute. Johnny Mills', which stood at 150 S. 4th, was the late night spot to go for barbecued ribs. Legend has it that one night a band in New York began to reminisce about the Peabody and Johnny's ribs and phoned for some to be flown to Manhattan.

To note in the area are:

LORRAINE MOTEL/MARTIN LUTHER KING* ROOM
406 Mulberry Str., Mulberry & Vance. 525-6834.

Hours: 9am-8pm daily.

Cost: $1/person to visit Martin Luther King Room. Groups may make a donation instead of paying the standard fee.

Lunch: Motel dining room open 7am-6pm.

MATA: Catch any bus going south on 2nd or Main at the mall's end. #39,13,16,44,4,12 and 45 are some of these. Get off at Vance and walk east one block to Mulberry.

E&H: The Martin Luther King Room is not accessible to wheelchairs.

The Lorraine Motel is a working motel, but it is known primarily as a memorial to Dr. Martin Luther King Jr. who died here. Dr. King stayed at the motel in 1968 when he was in Memphis organizing demonstrations in support of better benefits for local sanitation workers. As he stood on the balcony outside his room on Thursday, Apr. 4, 1968, King was shot and killed by James Earl Ray. A bullet fired from a rifle entered his jaw and neck at 6:01pm; he died in the emergency room at St. Joseph's Hospital at 7:05pm. Nationwide riots and mourning followed the assassination.

His room has been turned into a memorial. Photos, editorials, and memorial plaques now hang on the walls.

The headquarters for the nation's third largest black insurance company, **UNIVERSAL LIFE,** is in this area at 480 Linden. The company was organized in 1923 by Dr. J. E. Walker shortly after he moved to Memphis from Indianola, Miss. "Jet" and "Our World" magazines called him one of the ten most powerful blacks in America. He died in 1958. His son, A. Maceo Walker, Sr., is now in charge of the company which has over 800 employees and more than 500,000 policy holders. The Company operates in ten states and the District of Columbia. The Walkers have been active in the civil rights movement and helped found the Shelby County Democratic Club in 1936, the first black Democratic organization in the South.

Victorian homes in disrepair still stand in the **VANCE-PONTOTOC DISTRICT,** roughly along Vance and Pontotoc, between Danny Thomas and Orleans. The area contains Queen Anne and Victorian frame houses and a large outstanding collection of Italianate townhouses. Most of the homes were built from 1858-1918. The Robert S. Bowles House (544-548 Vance) and the Patrick S. Hayley House (604 Vance) are both in the National Register of Historic Places. Other homes in this area include the Davis House* (440 Vance), Busby House (678 Vance), Gale House (306 Cynthia), Collier House (587 Pontotoc) and Woodson House (666 Pontotoc).

HISTORIC HOMES

Unless hours are given these homes are *not* open to the public. Many remain private residences—please respect the owners' right to privacy.

PRE-1850

The earliest houses were built of roughhewn logs; sawmills began making finished boards in the 1830s. In the 1840s bricks sometimes replaced lumber in the homes of the wealthy.

Among the pre-1850 homes still standing:

DAVIES MANOR (NRHP) · circa 1807
9336 Davies Plantation Rd. (go about 16 miles northeast of Memphis on I-40 to Hwy. 64, then east about a mile to Davies Plantation Rd., then two miles to the manor).

Hours: *1-4pm, Tu only, May-Oct.*
Tours: *Docents guide you through.*
Cost: *Adults/$1, children 12 and under/50¢.*
E&H: *Not equipped for wheelchairs.*

A two-story log Colonial house surrounded by a 30-acre grove of trees. Legend has it that the two original rooms, west parlor and upstairs bedroom, were built by an Indian chief about 1807. An Indian trail and mound in the east front yard lend credence. You can see the original native boulders used as foundation pillars. A few years later the duplicate east side was built and linked to the older wing by an open hall. The "dog trot" was enclosed in 1931 and other rooms added to the rear.

Joel W. Royster, a Virginian, is the earliest recorded owner. In 1850 he sold the house and land to Logan E. Davies. The Davies family turned it over to the Davies Manor Asso. Inc. in 1976. Today it is the headquarters for Zachariah Davies chapter of the Daughters of the American Revolution, Shelby Chapter of the Sons of the American Revolution, and Old Stage Road Society of the Children of the American Revolution.

Warning: The house has not been restored to any one period. Be prepared for incongruities like storm windows set in the hand-hewn white oak log walls and Victorian wardrobes alongside early American plantation desks.

HUNT-PHELAN HOUSE (NRHP) - circa 1834
533 Beale. Built with slave labor in the Federal style for George H. Whyett, the house took on a Greek Revival look in the 1850s when additions were made to the back and the large Greek Revival portico was

added to the facade.

The house has quite a history. Five presidents are believed to have slept here and Federal generals to have planned the Battle of Vicksburg in the front parlor. General Grant made his headquarters here early in the Civil War. Later during the war, the house was a home for disabled Federal soldiers. After the war, it housed school teachers sent by the Freedman's Bureau to educate freed blacks. President Andrew Johnson returned the house to Col. William Hunt, its rightful owner. Legend has it that the ghost of a Negro slave, Uncle Nathan, haunts the house.

Today the grounds are surrounded by a barbed wire fence, and the house is awaiting restoration. It belongs to the Memphis Housing Authority and Stephen Phelan.

MAGEVNEY HOUSE (NRHP) - circa 1835
198 Adams 38103, Adams Ave. Historic District*. 526-4464.

Hours:	*10am-4pm, Tu - Sat.*
Tours:	*Wander alone or with a guide. Reservations requested for groups of 10 +. Costumed tours for school classes may be arranged through the house office.*
Cost:	*Free.*
MATA:	*#53 (ex Sun).*
Other:	*1) Special Christmas, Easter, and Valentine displays and school programs. 2) Bathroom facilities are limited; there is no running water in the house.*
E&H:	*Wheelchair accessible.*

Magevney house is the oldest surviving story and loft building in Tennessee. Restoration altered the exterior of the pioneer frame house. The four downstairs rooms are open for viewing and are furnished with pieces from the 1850 period. The upstairs is office space. A carriage house, stable, and herb garden are located behind the house.

The house was bought in 1837 by Eugene Magevney, Memphis' first schoolmaster. Magevney, an Irishman, came to Memphis from Pennsylvania in 1833 when he was 35. It was in his home in 1839 that the first Catholic mass was said in Memphis. Magevney's first school was a log cabin in Court Square. Tuition was sometimes paid in land. After his marriage in 1840, the first Catholic wedding in the city, Magevney gave up teaching for real estate. He died in the 1873 yellow fever epidemic.

The house, given to the city and restored in 1940, is run by the Park Commission and Pink Palace.

WILKES BROOKS HOUSE - circa 1835
2000 Old Oak Drive. Wilkes Brooks came to Memphis in 1834 from North Carolina and constructed this Greek Revival style house on his plantation, 13 miles east of Memphis. The house remains in his family.

HILDEBRAND HOUSE - circa 1838
4571 Airways. This Greek Revival residence was once part of a large plantation.

OLD COWARD PLACE - circa 1843
919 Coward (East & Coward, one block south of Crump Blvd.) This pre-Civil War house was built by H. W. Grosvenor who farmed several thousand acres fronting on Lamar, then called Pigeon Roost Road, the main stage coach route to north Mississippi. The house was modeled after New Orleans' French colonial homes. Handmade bricks are of clay removed while digging the basement.

After an 1862 Civil War skirmish on the grounds, the house was bought by Major William Coward. The major's son and daughter-in-law moved here from Court Street to live after the yellow fever epidemic of 1879.

Justine and Dayton Smith now own the house and have operated it as Justine's, a French restaurant*, since 1958.

The house has been altered during renovations.

MASSEY (CLEO BARTHOLOMEW) HOUSE (NRHP) - circa 1846
664 Adams, Victorian Village*. Built for Benjamin A. Massey, an early Memphis lawyer, this one-story Neo-classical cottage is clapboard with Doric columns. Its center hallway was used for parties and receptions by Sophie Harsson and her husband James C. Maydwell who lived here in the second half of the 19thc. Among guests entertained were Jefferson Davis, President of the Confederacy, and Mrs. Davis.

JACOB BURKLE HOUSE - circa 1849
826 N. 2nd. This house was built in the Greek Revival style.

WRIGHT CARRIAGE HOUSE (NRHP) - circa 1850
688 Jefferson, Victorian Village*. Built of handmade brick and hand-hewn timbers, this house was originally a simple farm house. In 1868 a new and larger house was built just to its south and the present structure converted to a carriage house. The later larger home has been demolished.

The present owner, Eldridge Wright, is the fourth generation of his family to live on this property. His great-grandfather, Luke Edward Wright, purchased the site with its two structures in 1902 and lived there until his death in 1922. Wright, a Confederate officer, became Attorney General of Shelby County and was active in relief work during the 1878 yellow fever epidemic. In 1900 he was Governor-General of Cuba. In 1904 he was appointed Governor-General of the Philippines and subsequently in 1906 became America's first Ambassador to Japan. In 1908 he was appointed Secretary of War by President Theodore Roosevelt.

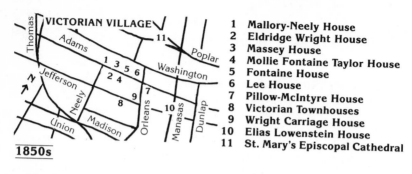

1 Mallory-Neely House
2 Eldridge Wright House
3 Massey House
4 Mollie Fontaine Taylor House
5 Fontaine House
6 Lee House
7 Pillow-McIntyre House
8 Victorian Townhouses
9 Wright Carriage House
10 Elias Lowenstein House
11 St. Mary's Episcopal Cathedral

1850s

The 1840s and '50s saw life in Memphis develop from a simple life into that of a complex city society. From 1850 to 1860 it was the fastest growing city in the nation, with Brooklyn in second place and Chicago in third, and by 1860 it had a population of 22,623. Native American immigrants from the Tidewater, many of whom were propertied and educated, and European immigrants, mainly Irish and German, were lured west by the cotton and lumber land and by the growth of railroads and steamboats. Memphis was expanding as a market center; in the 1850s it began to rival New Orleans.

During these boom years, fashionable city houses stood in the South Memphis/Beale Street* area and in the Washington/Court/Jefferson/Adams area. Part of the latter area has been preserved in the Victorian Village Historic District (NRHP) which stretches on Adams from Neely to Orleans. Large houses also were built on the rich farms surrounding the city and in Memphis' first suburb, the Greenlaw Addition*.

Among the houses remaining from this period are:

FOWLKES-BOYLE HOUSE (NRHP) - circa 1850
208 Adams, Adams Ave. Historic District*. A two-story, Victorian Italianate townhouse, built by Sterling Fowlkes in the 1850s, the house later belonged to the Boyle family. Now a law office.

MOSBY-BENNETT HOUSE (HUNTER LANE HOUSE) - circa 1852
6256 Poplar. Built of heavy timber as a Greek Revival style plantation home. Victorian ornamentation was added later. Now a real estate office.

PILLOW-MCINTYRE HOUSE (NRHP) - circa 1852
707 Adams, Victorian Village*. This two-story brick and stucco home has Corinthian columns. In 1873 Confederate General Gideon Johnson Pillow acquired it. In 1880 Peter McIntyre, a Memphis merchant, bought it. McIntyre was married to Ella Goyer, the daughter of Charles Wesley Goyer who owned the Lee* house during the second half of the 19thc. In 1942 it became the home of the Memphis Art Association's free art school, operated by Miss Florence McIntyre. The school closed in 1963

and in 1969 the house was purchased by Larry van Landingham, Inc. Today Margie van Landingham has an interior decorating shop here. Phone 527-5479 for an appointment.

MALLORY-NEELY HOUSE (NRHP) · circa 1852, 1883
652 Adams 38105, Victorian Village*. 523-1484.

Hours: 10am-4pm daily, May · Sept, 1-4pm daily Oct · Apr. Closed holidays.

Tours: Guided tours for groups and individuals. For groups of 10+, make arrangements in advance.

Cost: Adults/$2; students, military, & children 6+/$1; children under 6/free.

Lunch: The Lee-Fontaine Carriage House, also in Victorian Village, has been converted to a restaurant serving lunch and dinner (See American restaurants).

MATA: #53 (ex Sun).

Other: 1) Mallory-Neely House's carriage house may be rented, 4 hours/$15. It has bathroom and kitchen facilities. 2) Mallory-Neely house itself may be rented, morning or evening/$150. 3) Special exhibits, art displays, music programs, and antique seminars are announced in the local papers.

E&H: 1) First floor is wheelchair accessible. 2) Senior citizens can arrange reduced rate group tours, 75¢ per person.

Built by Isaac B. Kirtland, a banker from New York in the Victorian Italianate style. The second owner, Benjamin Babb, was a cotton factor. Around 1883 the house was purchased by James Columbus Neely and restyled to its present 25 room, towered size. The brick and stucco walls are 18″ thick.

In 1900 James Neely's daughter, Daisy Neely, married Barton Lee Mallory, hence the house's name. She raised three children here and died in 1969 at the age of 98. The Mallory heirs donated the house and family antiques in 1972 to the Daughters, Sons, and Children of the American Revolution Chapters in West Tennessee to be preserved as an historic attraction.

CLANLO · circa 1853
1616 Central. Built by William Richard Harris, brother of Isham Harris who served as governor of Tennessee during the Civil War. It has been owned by several different families, the Hennings, Morrows, Parters, and Schwamms, and has been architecturally altered.

ELAM LOG HOUSE · circa 1854
1428 Fox (½ mile north of Lamar & Prescott). This house of undisguised roughhewn logs was the home of Edward Simpson Elam who settled in this area, today known as Cherokee, in 1849. Only two of the present 14 rooms were part of the original house. The house was later the home of Russell Gardener, owner of the Memphis Chicks* baseball team, and the man for whom Russwood Park was named. The Elder family bought the

house in 1943 and later subdivided the land.

The surrounding Cherokee subdivision was developed at the end of World War II by Wallace Johnson, co-founder of Holiday Inn. In the 1960s, Cherokee's golf course was subdivided by Boyle Investment Co. The neighborhood is known as Cherokee Heights.

ANNESDALE (NRHP) - circa 1855

1325 Lamar. Annesdale was originally the home of Dr. Samuel Mansfield, a wholesale druggist. During the Civil War, the house served as a hospital. Many of those wounded at Shiloh* were brought by wagon the 100 miles to Annesdale to be treated and to recuperate. Robert C. Brinkley, a prominent railroad man, purchased the home in 1869 as a wedding present for his daughter, Annie Overton Brinkley, the granddaughter of the original Memphis proprietor, John Overton, when she married Robert Bogardus Snowden. Their descendants continue to live in the private residence today.

The house was built in the Italian Renaissance style and the gardens designed by an Italian landscape architect. During the 1800s the house was surrounded by a 200 acre estate. Present day Lamar Ave. was then known as Pigeon Roost Road, the stage coach route to Holly Springs and Oxford, Miss. Even earlier this route was the main path used by Chickasaw Indians* traveling between their homes in northern Mississippi and the Mississippi River.

RAYNER HOUSE (NRHP) - circa 1856

1020 Rayner (south of Lamar, east of Elvis Presley Blvd.). About 1853, Eli Rayner bought this land from Solomon Rozelle, a speculator who had acquired 1600 acres from the state of North Carolina. Rayner, a cotton farmer, built his two-story, Greek Revival style house facing the Memphis & Charleston Railroad at what was then Gill's Station. The house was surrounded by a grove of trees which, during the Civil War, served as a campground for Federal troops and, during the yellow fever epidemics, as a camp for fleeing Memphians. Rayner cut roads through his property and subdivided and sold some land. He died in 1892.

Most development in this area, known as the Rozelle-Annesdale Neighborhood, occurred after the city annexed the land in 1898. Today the house is being renovated as a private home.

CHASE-WALSH HOUSE - circa 1856

686 N. 7th, Greenlaw*. Only a portion of the Chase-Walsh home remains from the Greenlaw Addition.

William Chase came to Memphis from Washington, Penn. around 1840. He was a feed merchant, an agent for Portland Cement, and a real estate developer.

In 1901 the Chases sold the house to the Walsh family. The two Walsh brothers, John and Anthony, grew wealthy in the retail grocery business. What at first glance appear to be gargoyles on the building at 330 N. Main, once their store, are actually busts of the brothers. They were influential political leaders and started the North Memphis Savings Bank* in 1904; it merged with Union Planters in 1923.

In 1964 the house was sold to the Girl's Club.

COSTEN-WILLEY HOUSE - circa 1856

274 Mill, Greenlaw*. A raised cottage ante-bellum house, built by Stephen B. Costen in the original Greenlaw subdivision, the house has been little altered. Costen owned the Costen Brickyard and built the home with bricks he produced.

The house has changed hands many times. During the Civil War, it was the home of Thomas Gailor, the future Episcopal Bishop of the Diocese of Tennessee.

1860s and '70s

During the Civil War*, Memphis escaped destruction and actually prospered; it was a center for contraband trade between the North and South. Business activity remained near the pre-war level.

In the war's aftermath, however, Memphis faltered and lost her position as a cosmopolitan city. The rail lines were broken. By the war's end, the surrounding Tennessee-Mississippi-Arkansas trading area had been devastated. Ten thousand untrained jobless freedmen moved to the city. In 1866 race riots left 44 blacks killed and churches and schools burned.

Unlike most Confederate states, Tennessee was not subject to federal reconstruction acts. The state had freed its own slaves and ratified the 13th, 14th and 15th amendments that proscribed slavery and extended civil rights to blacks. Friction, however, between the sections of Tennessee resulted in the election of Governor "Parson" William G. Brownlow of east Tennessee. Bitter toward the pro-Confederacy middle and western sections of the state, he issued his "damnasty oath" denying voting rights forever, in actuality until 1870, to all who had in any way supported the Confederacy. The city's pre-war leaders were disenfranchised. Many feel that Memphis suffered more severely under Brownlow than she would have under federal reconstruction legislation.

Memphis was severely stricken by a yellow fever epidemic in 1873. Twenty-five thousand refugees fled the city. Five thousand of the remaining 15,000 contracted the fever; 2,000 died. Then in 1878 an even worse epidemic of yellow fever struck. Five thousand one hundred fifty of the 17,600 stricken died. The city's population declined from 40,000 to 33,000. Many of those who fled the city refused to return.

The municipal government had long been corrupt and inefficient and in 1878-79, Memphis defaulted on interest payments on bonds. The

Memphis city charter was repealed, and Memphis became a taxing district of the state.

The city's social, economic, and political instability discouraged large capital investments from the North so necessary for the city's recovery.

Among the house additions and new construction in the '60s and '70s were:

RAMSEY-RUTLAND HOUSE - circa 1860, 1870

487 Goodwyn, Buntyn. This red brick house was started before the Civil War but not completed until after the war. It is a mixture of several styles and probably most closely resembles Italianate Victorian. The brick walls are 18" thick, and the floors are of hand-hewn pine. The home was built by G. O. Buntyn for his daughter Euzelia and her husband, George W. Rutland. The house is still a private residence.

Ramsey-Rutland House is in Buntyn Station, an area which developed as a stop along the Memphis & Charleston Railroad (Southern). Trains stopped here from the 1850s until 1960s. The station was named for Geraldus Buntyn, a prominent citizen and a director of the Farmers and Merchants Bank.

Before his death in 1865, Buntyn lived in a house at the corner of Goodwyn and Southern on the property that is now the Memphis Country Club. Jefferson Davis Jr., son of Jefferson Davis*, President of the Confederacy, died of yellow fever in Buntyn's house in 1878 while the house was rented to Davis' older sister and her husband, Margaret Davis and Addison Hayes. The house was sold to the Memphis Country Club for their clubhouse in 1905, but burned in 1910.

The Buntyn Station area was annexed by the city in 1929. Many imposing 50-75 year old homes are in the neighborhood. Among the noteworthy houses is Boyce-Gregg House (NRHP) at 317 S. Highland. Built in 1920 in an Italian Mediterranean style, it now houses the Day Foundation.

BRADFORD-MAYDWELL HOUSE (NRHP) - circa 1859, 1868

648 Poplar. James Maydwell, a stone cutter, purchased the federal style townhouse and in 1868 added the Italianate facade. At writing, work is almost complete to renovate the home as a French restaurant, The Bradford House, 523-1915. To be open 5:30-10:30 W-Sun, to have a full bar, and to accept AE,MC, Visa. Sounds marvelous—we can't wait to try it.

MAXWELTON (SNEED HOUSE) - circa 1868

3105 Southern, Buntyn. This Victorian cottage was built near the Memphis & Charleston Railroad's Buntyn Station. The 5-room cottage has 12' ceilings, planked pine floors, and several outbuildings.

The home was built by Judge John Louis Taylor Sneed who came to Memphis from North Carolina in 1843. He served as Brigadier-General in the Civil War, Attorney General of Tennessee, member of the Tennessee Supreme Court, President of the Memphis Law School, and Chancellor of Chancery Court. He died in 1901. His descendants maintain the house as a private home.

1st JAMES LEE HOUSE (NRHP) - circa 1868

239 Adams, Adams Ave. Historic District*. Captain James Lee*, who lived in this Victorian Italianate house, later moved east to the Lee House*, 690 Adams. The house is now boarded up, but plans are underway to restore it as a law office.

LEE HOUSE (NRHP) - circa 1848, 1865, 1871

690 Adams, Victorian Village*. Being restored by the Memphis Chapter of the Assn. for the Preservation of Tennessee Antiquities, the house is not yet open to the public. The present rear section of Lee House was built by former Baltimore lumberman William Harsson around 1848 as a two-story farmhouse outside the city limits. In 1865 the present center section was added for his son-in-law, Charles Wesley Goyer. Then in 1871, Goyer built the present three-story front section and ornate tower. This addition was designed by Memphis architects E. C. Jones and M. H. Baldwin. The Goyer family lived in the house for 42 years. Story goes that Goyer, a sugar and molasses importer, grew so rich that he helped form Union Planters Bank in order to have a place to keep his money.

Captain James Lee Jr. moved to the house in 1890 from his earlier home at 239 Adams. His father had begun steamboating* in the early 1800s and in 1866 had formed the Lee Line of river packets and steamers based in Memphis. Captain Lee joined his father's river empire in 1877. His daughter, Miss Rosa Lee, gave the home and the Fontaine House (next door) to the city in 1930 as a memorial to him.

The house is in the Historical American Buildings Survey, and its plans are recorded in the Library of Congress.

FONTAINE HOUSE (NRHP) - circa 1871

680 Adams, Victorian Village*. 526-1469.

Hours: 10am-4pm M-Sat, 1-4pm Sun. Apr-Dec.; 1-4pm daily Jan-Mar.

Tours: Guided tours for individuals and groups. Make advance arrangements for 10+. Special Sat morning tours and slide show possible for Scout troops and school groups.

Cost: Adults/$2, senior citizens (60+)/$1.75, students, military, & children 6+/$1, children under 6/free.

Lunch: Lee-Fontaine Carriage House serves lunch and dinner (see American restaurants).

MATA: #53 (ex Sun).

Other: 1) Gift shop. 2) Public, clubroom facilities for 125 people in the basement. 3) Fashion show from the collection of 19thc. clothing and accessories

> *may be arranged with the social secretary, fee about $25. 4) Carriage house restaurant will cater dinner parties.* 5) *Occasional accessory displays and walking tours of the district announced in the newspapers.*

E&H: *First floor accessible to wheelchairs through back porch entrance. Carriage House also wheelchair accessible.*

A French-inspired Second Empire style home, designed by two Memphis architects, Edward Culliatt Jones and Mathias Harvey Baldwin, for Amos Woodruff, a builder. The mansion has three floors, a mansard slate roof, tower, and full basement. It is constructed of handmade brick.

In 1883 Woodruff sold his home to Noland Fontaine, a partner in Hill, Fontaine & Co. which grew to be the world's third largest cotton and supply company. During the next 46 years when the Fontaines lived here, the home was a center of Memphis society. Socially and politically important people, from exiled princes to governors and Vice-presidents, were entertained at the home. On one occasion John Phillip Sousa was the guest conductor at a lawn party for 2,000. Noland Fontaine came to Memphis from Kentucky in the 1860s. In addition to his cotton business, he served on several bank and insurance company boards.

Also on the grounds are the Lee-Fontaine Carriage House and a small, 19thc. doll house with antique doll furniture. The circa 1890 Handwerker "Gingerbread Playhouse" was originally on Thomas Street in North Memphis.

The house is maintained by the Memphis Chapter of the Assn. for the Preservation of Tennessee Antiquities.

DAVIS HOUSE · circa 1870
440 Vance, Vance/Pontotoc*. This imposing house was built by Frank S. Davis to replace his earlier home at this location. At the end of the Civil War, Davis who had come from Cincinnati to Memphis, organized the First National Bank. In 1882 he moved to New York and sold the home to W. B. Mallory. The house is now the Southern Funeral Home.

The Davis house is in the once fashionable area of the city now loosely referred to as the Vance-Pontotoc* area. Ante-bellum mansions with large farms were first in this area of Beale/South Memphis*. Later, from the 1850s-1890s, large imposing houses were built in the fashionable neighborhood. Many of these have been destroyed. Others are in bad states of repair.

H. H. METTE HOUSE (NRHP) · circa 1872
253 Adams, Adams Ave. Historic District*. This Victorian townhouse built for Herman Henry Mette was renovated in 1968 and is now a law office. (See Hein House.)

STEPHENS-COCHRAN HOUSE - circa 1874
784 Poplar. William H. Stephens, a lawyer, built this Victorian Italianate house in 1874-75 and sold it in 1876 to Marcus E. Cochran, a lumberman. Today the house is boarded up, for lease, and awaiting restoration.

JOHN S. TOOF HOUSE - circa 1875
246 Adams, Adams Ave. Historic District*. This Victorian Italianate townhouse was the home of John S. Toof, a well-known international financier who did business in London, New York, and Paris. The house is being completely renovated as a residence.

TOWNHOUSE APARTMENTS (NRHP) - circa 1875
669 and 671 Jefferson, Victorian Village*. Two Victorian townhouses, now apartments.

1880-1980

Optimism returned to the city, and building boomed in the 1880s and '90s. New levees turned swamps into rich, profitable farm land, and fortunes were made in lumber as the land was cleared. New railroads were built. A rich trading area again flourished and expanded. Memphis revived—good days were here again.

Home rule was restored to the city in 1893, and in 1899 the municipality enlarged from 4½ to 16 square miles. By 1900 Memphis was the third largest city in the South with a population for the first time of more than 100,000. These were the days of horse racing and private railroad cars, Beale Street was nurturing the blues*, its music that would spread world-wide. Memphis was a rough city; from 1900 to 1916, it was the murder capital of the U.S.

Tennessee's prohibition of horse racing in 1905 and of alcohol in 1909 were locally unpopular, but city government reform was a rallying cry. Most of the 68,000 newcomers to Memphis in the '80s and '90s were blacks and whites from farms in Mississippi and Tennessee. As the city's population became dominated by rural-born native Southerners, the city became more homogenous, and politically, economically, and socially more conservative. In 1909 the city adopted a commission form of government, and in 1910 elected a reform minded mayor, "Boss" Crump*. The commission form of government was in effect until the city voted in a referendum in 1967 to switch to its present Mayor-Council form of government. Today executive duties are vested in the Mayor. Legislative power is assigned to the thirteen member council, seven from districts and six at-large. Subject to council approval, the mayor appoints the directors of the 12 city government divisions and the members of various commissions. The county is governed by a county mayor and county court. Some government functions are shared, others di-

vided between the two. Jurisdiction occasionally overlaps.
Through 31 annexations, the city has absorbed a third of Shelby County. In the early 1900s the state legislature authorized the purchase of Overton* and Riverside* Parks, and a scenic drive was designed to connect them. In 1909 the city extended its boundaries to this parkway. Discouraged by the Wolf River and Nonconnah River floodplains to the north and south, the city grew primarily toward the east. The depression and World Wars I and II temporarily slowed down growth, but by 1949, developers built the city's first shopping center, Poplar Plaza*.

During the 1950s and '60s new was good and old was bad. Much was lost. Better control of flood levels and more sophisticated highways and bridges eliminated earlier natural boundaries, and the city grew rapidly in all directions. Today the city is continuing to spread, but there is also a new appreciation of the old and a desire to preserve and invigorate our heritage.

Homes built during the turn of the century and afterward illustrate the city's pattern of growth. Many were built in older, established neighborhoods. Then, as the city expanded, houses were built first along train and trolley lines and later along fashionable avenues.

MILL HOUSE - circa 1885
297 Mill, Greenlaw*. Victorian home built by G. T. O'Haver, a police captain. The home was purchased and renovated by Memphis Heritage Inc., a non-profit preservation organization. Today it is a private home.

PATTON-BEJACH HOUSE (NRHP) - circa 1885
1085 Poplar. A home built here in 1877 for Thomas N. Patton burned and the present structure was built in 1885. This Italianate residence has been the Four Flames Restaurant since 1958.

MOLLIE FONTAINE TAYLOR HOUSE (NRHP) - circa 1886
679 Adams, Victorian Village*. 523-7514.

Tours: By appointment 11am-3pm M-Sat.
Cost: Adults/$2, children/$1. Group discounts possible.
MATA: #53 (ex Sun).
E&H: Not equipped for wheelchairs.

The house is architecturally High Victorian with Queen Anne elements. Noland Fontaine, who lived across the street, gave it to his daughter Mollie as a wedding present when she married Dr. William Wood Taylor. Today it is a private house, and tours are given by appointment.

ELDRIDGE WRIGHT HOUSE (NRHP) - circa 1892
657 Adams, Victorian Village*. Late Victorian, the house's exterior has

been altered extensively. The interior remains almost in original form with high ceilings, windows to the floor, interior shutters and fine wood-work.

The rear section of the house is Jimmy Graham's interior design shop. Phone 527-0633 for an appointment.

LOVE HOUSE (NRHP) - circa 1890
619 N. 7th, Greenlaw*. George Love was one of a number of northerners who moved to Memphis in the 1870s and '80s and settled in the Greenlaw Addition. Born in 1845 in Indiana, Love moved to Memphis as a young man in 1862 and prospered in the wood stave business and in real estate. Around 1890, he built this home combining several Victorian styles popular at the turn of the century.

A member of the city commission, Love was credited with the con-struction of the Bayou Gayoso Pumping Station in 1912. He was mayor from Nov. 1915 to Feb. 1916, after E. H. Crump* was ousted from the of-fice.

Love House and the surrounding block was given to the city by the Love family in 1979. It will be used as office space by the Memphis Land-marks Commission.

ELIAS LOWENSTEIN HOUSE (NRHP) - circa 1891
756 Jefferson, Victorian Village*. 525-1960.

Tours: *By appointment 9:30am-2:30pm M-F.*
Cost: *Free.*
Lunch: *You are invited to the 40¢ noon lunch, but you most make reservations in advance.*
MATA: *#3 (ex Sat & Sun), 53 (ex Sun).*
E&H: *First floor and lunchroom are accessible to wheelchairs.*

Four Lowenstein brothers emigrated from Germany to Memphis in the mid 1800s. The first brother, Benedict, sold sundries door-to-door and in 1855 opened a store at 242 Main Street. In 1869 he sent for his brothers, Elias, Abraham, and Bernard. Elias built this Late Victorian home where he and his family lived from 1891 until his death in 1919. Elias was presi-dent of B'Nai Israel from 1870-1874 and from 1883-1893. His daughter, Mrs. Celia Samelson, gave the house to the Nineteenth Century Club which administered it as a boarding home for young women. In the 1920s an annex was built to the original three-storied structure.

Today Lowenstein House is a private charitable organization that helps people returning to the community from psychiatric hospitals. It offers a day program, transitional employment help, and an apartment program.

HARRIS HOUSE (NRHP) - circa 1897
2106 Young (west of Cooper, south of Central). Built in the Queen Anne

Style, the house originally faced Cooper. Real estate developer Frank Trimble built it and sold it to Captain Harris of Ripley, Miss. in 1900.

A feud between the Harris and Faulkner families was a basic theme in William Faulkner's *Requiem for a Nun* and *The Unvanquished*. The feud grew from a business dispute over the construction of the railroad through Ripley. Col. Sartoris is modeled on Col. Falkner, William Faulkner's grandfather, and Ben Redmond on R. J. Thurmond, Captain Harris' son-in-law.

ASHLAR HALL - circa 1900
1397 Central. Annie and Col. Robert Bogardus Snowden, who lived next door in Annesdale*, had five children. One of their sons, Robert Brinkley Snowden attended architecture school and designed this castle next door to his parents' home. The Gothic Revival house was built as a wedding present for him and his bride, Sara Day.

The residence is now a steak restaurant, Conestoga's Ashlar Hall. (See American restaurants.)

Ashlar Hall adjoins Annesdale Snowden Historic District (NRHP), an area developed in architectural styles popular from 1906-1929.

Nearby is Annesdale Park Historic District (NRHP), a four block area bounded by Goodbar, Rosenstein, Peabody, and Cleveland. It was developed by Col. Snowden's two sons, Robert Brinkley Snowden and John Bayard Snowden, as a 125-house subdivision around 1903. The first housing subdivision in the U.S., it set precedents for modern planning. The houses reflect a transition from Victorian styles to Bungalow.

SAMBUCETTI HOUSE - circa 1905
700 N. 7th, Greenlaw*. Prosperous Italian families moved into Greenlaw in the late 1870s. Louis Sambucetti, who built this home, was successful in the real estate and liquor businesses and was active in politics. He served on the Board of Education and City Council.

The home now is the Convent of the Holy Names, home for Sister Elizabeth Bonia and three other Marist missionary sisters. The former carriage house is their office and the workshop for CoDeNorth, a community group that is active in the restoration and rehabilitation of the area. They make wooden lace, sidings, spindles and cutouts for use in the restoration of houses. They will teach those interested in learning these skills. For information contact Sister Elizabeth at 523-7713.

BEVERLY HALL (GREENWOOD) (NRHP) - circa 1905
1560 Central. The Colonial Revival style home was built by Hunter Raine, president of the Mercantile Bank, now called Union Planters. It was designed by the architects Marshall and Fox of Chicago, and the grounds were landscaped by architects from Louisville and Kansas City.

In 1914 the home was purchased by Mrs. Leila Robinson Boyd. She gave the house its name, Beverly Hall, after her paternal grandfather, an early explorer of Kentucky. Returning from a trip to China, Mrs. Boyd planted the first gingko tree in Memphis on the grounds.

In 1950 the house was sold to the Southern College of Optometry to be used as the president's house. Since then the house has changed hands several times and is currently a private residence.

The section of the city around this house is broadly known as the Central Gardens Area of Midtown. Many of the homes were built about 1900, but the majority of the sturdy houses here were built from 1920 to 30. To get a feel, wander across Willett and Belvedere, and up and down Peabody, Carr, Vinton, Harbert, and Central. Of particular beauty and note are Stark/Gautier house at 665 S. Willett, Reese/Smithwick House at 653 S. Willett, Kent-Carrier House at 642 S. Willett, E. H. Crump* House (NRHP) at 1962 Peabody, Cary House at 1649 Central and Grant/Thompson House at 1785 Harbert. The Grant/Thompson House built by Peter Grant in the early 1900s is a copy of the exterior of John Hancock's home in Boston.

GALLOWAY HOUSE (PAISLEY HALL) - circa 1905
1822 Overton Park Ave. This residence, named Paisley Hall after an ancestral town in Scotland, was built by Col. Robert Galloway. Galloway was president of the Galloway Coal Co. and served as chairman of the Memphis Park Commission. Galloway Park was named in his honor. Galloway died in 1918 and his widow, the former May Edmonds, in 1942. In 1943 Galloway House was sold by the Galloway heirs to Southwestern for use as its music department. The building is now again a private residence.

Stone columns frame the entrance to the Colonial Revival style home built of solid masonry construction with steel reinforced floors. Pressed tin trim decorates the exterior, and much of the interior woodwork is from Europe. The entire third floor was designed as a ballroom.

DARNELL HOUSE/19th CENTURY CLUB (NRHP) - circa 1907
1433 Union. Built by Rowland Jones Darnell, the house was once one of many fine homes that lined Union Ave. In 1922 the street was widened, and in the 1950s most of the fashionable homes were replaced by car dealerships.

Darnell, who moved here from Indianapolis, was one of the first to realize Memphis' potential as a lumber market. The north had depleted its forests and new timber was needed for the country's expansion and building. By the end of the 19thc. Memphis was the second largest lumber market in the world and the largest hardwood lumber market in the world.

The home was purchased in 1918 by Leslie M. Stratton. In 1926 it was purchased by the 19th Century Club for their headquarters. The 19th

Century Club was founded in 1890 by 30 women as a cultural, literary, and social organization. Many interesting public speakers have appeared here. Check the visitors register.

CRAWFORD HOUSE - circa 1910

1 E. Parkway N. Inspired by the early 20thc. city beautiful movement, Memphis leaders built an elegant new parkway* system edging the city limits and connecting Overton Park with Riverside Park. West J. Crawford, founder and president of the Commercial Publishing Company and the Memphis Cotton Exchange, had planned to build this mansion on Beale. At the last minute he changed plans and built his house on the new parkway, then a dirt road. It was the first of many mansions to line the parkway.

Designed by George M. Shaw, the Greek Revival style house is rich in detail. Symmetrically designed, it has five porches, 11 rooms, upper and lower halls, and a cantilevered spiral staircase. Marble urns that formerly marked the street entrance are now in the garden of Brooks Memorial Art Gallery*.

Other lovely houses along the parkway from this period include the Newburger Home, southeast corner of Union and Parkway, now the Memphis Theological Seminary, and the William Goodman House, circa 1912, at 159 E. Parkway N., southwest corner of Parkway and Poplar.

PINK PALACE*, ORIGINAL BUILDING - circa 1922

3050 Central Ave. 38111. 454-5600.

Tours: Guided tours of original building 1:30-5pm, third Sun each month.
Cost: Tour cost included in general entrance fee to the museum: Adults/$1.50, ages 6-18 and senior citizens (62 +)/75¢, children under 6/free.
MATA: #50 (ex Sun).
E&H: First floor and lobby can be reached by wheelchair with help.

Clarence Saunders, the supermarket pioneer, meant his mansion of pink Georgia marble to be the finest money could buy. It was built at a cost of approximately $1-million in 1922-23 on an 155-acre tract. Saunders named the home Cla-Le-Clare for his children, Clay, Lee, and Amy Clare. Saunders lost his first fortune in 1923 when the house was still unfinished. Developers gave it to the city, and it has been used as a museum since 1930.

Clarence Saunders' life was a classic rags-to-riches story. He was born in Virginia in 1881 and came to Memphis as a grocery salesman in 1904. Twelve years later, in 1916, he opened his first revolutionary Piggly Wiggly grocery store at 79 Jefferson. By 1922 there were 1,241 stores in 388 towns in 41 states; sales in 1923 were reported at almost $200 million. Instead of waiting at the front counter, customers went through the store and served themselves. They paid cash and took the groceries home with them. In 1923 Saunders went broke playing the stock market and lost Piggly Wiggly. Kroger now owns the remaining Piggly Wiggly franchised stores.

Saunders started a second chain of grocery stores under the name of Clarence Saunders, Sole Owner of My Name Stores, Inc. The chain folded in 1933, a result of the depression.

Saunders sought a third fortune with the Keedoozle. In these revolutionary stores the customer viewed the object, pushed a key into a slot below it, and the article moved on a conveyor belt to the rear of the store. Here the customer again inserted the key and the selected goods arrived, bagged and accompanied by a totaled bill. The first Keedoozle opened in 1937 at 1628 Union. The timing was bad; automation was not perfected, and World War II was coming. Keedoozle closed in 1941.

Saunders has been highly honored as an inventor and entrepreneurial pioneer. In 1949 he was made an honorary member of the Swedish Inventors' Assn., in 1969 the "Sunday Times Magazine of London" named him one of the 1,000 makers of the 20thc., and during the 1976 Bicentennial, the Smithsonian Institution cited him as one of the 200 shapers of American history.

The original Pink Palace is an educational facility for the natural history museum. The mansion never served as a home, and there is little in the interior of historical note.

The Pink Palace Museum* next door has a scale replica of the first Piggly Wiggly.

HEIN HOUSE · circa 1927
2250 N. Parkway. This private residence was the home of the family of W. A. Hein, founder of Memphis Steam Laundry. In 1927 the Heins, Mettes (see Mette House), and Gerbers laid out the streets between N. Parkway, Trezevant, Jackson, and Charles Place, and developed this area known as Hein Park.

JOHNSON/FISHER/LEDBETTER HOUSE
337 S. Goodlett at Central. This house better than any portrays the city's eastward growth. Built on the southeast corner of Bellevue and Madison, it was moved east to its present location around 1925. W. C. Johnson, a civic and industrial leader, lived in the house at its first location. John T. Fisher moved the house to its present location and added the columns. The two-story white brick house is now the private home of the E. R. Ledbetters.

Today such old communities as Germantown, Raleigh, West Memphis, and Whitehaven, while in some cases still separate corporate bodies, illustrate the city's sprawling growth.

GERMANTOWN

Germantown, incorporated in 1841, is a town of about 23,000 people, located three miles east of Memphis. Today it is one of the county's fastest growing and wealthiest areas. The town offers excellent shopping and a preserved small town atmosphere.

Germantown is famous as the site of Nashoba, a utopian plantation colony founded in 1825 by Frances Wright and her sister Camilla. Wright, a wealthy Scottish woman, believed blacks must be educated to support themselves and live in freedom. The colony covered about 2,000 acres running from what is now Old Poplar Pike to Wolf River. In 1829 the experiment ended because of public criticism and mismanagement. About 30 blacks there at the time were recolonized in Haiti.

By 1852 a railroad provided an all-weather connection from Memphis to Germantown and points east. If you drive along Old Poplar Pike from Riverdale Rd. to Forrest Hill Rd., you can see about 20 homes built along the railroad tracks in the second half of the 1800s. You might want to stop at Cloyes Nursery, 7831 Old Poplar Pike, to see the circa 1854 house; let your children ride Cloyes' train, and see the beautiful azaleas. You'll pick up early Germantown anecdotes and see some relics.

Historic churches remain in Germantown. Germantown Baptist Church (NRHP), 2216 S. Germantown Rd., was founded in 1838. The present chapel was built in 1870. Germantown Presbyterian Church, 2363 S. Germantown Rd., was organized in 1838, and the present structure completed in 1851.

Germantown Village Square Mall and numerous small stores along Germantown Rd., between Poplar Ave. and Old Poplar Pike, offer excellent shopping. Two popular stores in converted old homes are Town & Country Antiques and Babcock Galleries (See Specialty Shopping).

The Germantown Chamber of Commerce has published a "Guide For Newcomers to Germantown", available from local merchants or from the Germantown Chamber of Commerce, P.O. Box 38441, Germantown, Tn. 38138, 755-1200.

RALEIGH

Raleigh, located north of Memphis on Wolf River, provided a good harbor for flatboats and, in the early 1800s, competed with Memphis for river traffic. In 1827 the county seat of Shelby County was moved from Memphis to Raleigh, where it remained until 1870. Popular warm mineral springs were located near present day Jackson Ave. bridge over Wolf River. Raleigh Springs Hotel, built by tobacco millionaire B. I. Duke and destroyed by fire in 1912, was quite fashionable and could accommodate about 50 families. The town of Raleigh, described as cosmopolitan during this period, boasted an open air dance pavilion, rail and streetcar service to Memphis, and river excursion boats on then clear Wolf River.

The J. M. Coleman house, now a dentist's office at 4225 Stage Rd., and Raleigh Cemetery, just off Stage Rd. near its intersection with Jackson, are remnants of old Raleigh. The wooded cemetery on Sanderlin's bluff was used as early as 1831. Isaac Rawlings*, Memphis' second mayor, was buried here in 1839.

Goodwinslow (NRHP), the home of M. Winslow Chapman, is located on six acres at 4066 James Rd. Begun in 1875 and completed in 1900, it has three sections: the northern section circa 1875 modeled after a Medieval English castle, the middle one-story section circa 1880 with a steep gable roof, and a final southern section inspired by an Italian villa circa 1890. The house has been visited by such literary notables as Robert Penn Warren, Vachel Lindsay, Allen Tate, and John Crowe Ransom. Mrs. Chapman is the author of a history of Raleigh, *I Remember Raleigh.*

Today Raleigh is a neighborhood within the city limits of Memphis. This whole northern area of the city and its neighbors, Frayser, Bartlett, and Millington*, are growing rapidly.

WEST MEMPHIS

West Memphis, Ark., incorporated 1929, is Memphis' western neighbor. The Frisco (1892), Harahan (1916), Memphis & Arkansas (1949) and Hernando DeSoto/I-40 (1973) Bridges have increasingly spanned the gap between East and West and have brought interaction between Memphis and its neighbor.

The land immediately on the river is in the river's floodplain and is used for farming. Five miles farther west is the town of West Memphis with its Southland Greyhound Race Track*, Spott's Drugstore (see Ice Cream restaurants), Bill's (see American restaurants), and cheap liquor. West Memphis Senior High School is home of the Blue Devils, voted the #2 U.S. high school basketball team by UPI in 1980 and 1981.

WHITEHAVEN

Best known today as the site of Elvis Presley's Graceland Mansion*, Whitehaven began as a railroad stop south of Memphis. Most early landowners were speculators; permanent settlers did not arrive until the 1840s. The railroad was laid through farmland here in the 1850s, and a stop named White's Station Haven, later White's Haven, was named for the White family of Como, Miss.

Whitehaven is bound by Nonconnah Creek on the north, Airways on the east, State Line Rd. on the south, and Old Lake Rd. on the west. The area used to be somewhat isolated from Memphis. Nonconnah Creek often flooded the only road to town. The trip by road took a full day and part of the night. For years the railroad was the area's primary means of transportation.

In 1926 the J. B. Holmes land was bought for Memphis' municipal airport, a major factor in the modern development of the area. Around

1937 land began to be subdivided for housing. In 1948 Anna Leigh Mc-Corkle, author of *Tales of Old Whitehaven*, led a fight to have the zoning along Hwy. 51 changed. The town needed a doctor, and Dr. John J. Sohm was ready to come but needed office space. The decision to permit business along the road has been an important one for Whitehaven. From the mid-1960s on, large shopping centers like Southland Mall have been developed along the highway.

Among the few non-commercial sites on Hwy. 51 today are Hale House, Graceland*, and Hoyt Wooten House, circa 1937, whose civil defense bomb shelter is said to be the largest in the U.S. George Hale's house is one of the few remaining historic houses in Whitehaven. Located on Hwy. 51 between Holmes and Winfield, the circa 1885 house can only be glimpsed from the highway. Will Hale, a relative, was a Crump* man and local political boss in the first half of the 1900s.

Old Whitehaven may best be found in Edmiston Cemetery on State Line Road between Millbranch and I-55, and even here it is difficult. The cemetery has been cleaned, relatively new trees planted, and a new brick wall built, but the tombstones mark the past. The cemetery, actually located in Mississippi, was next to a circa 1845 Presbyterian church. Many of Whitehaven's early families are buried here.

DOWNTOWN CHURCHES

Memphis, located in the heart of the "Bible belt", is reputed to have more churches than filling stations. Many faiths are represented. Specialized religious programs serve every segment of society and deal with every facet of life. For specifics phone LINC* or individual churches. They are listed in the yellow pages of the phone book both by location and by denomination.

Memphis was a rough river port and formalized community religious services did not begin until the late 1820s. Early Baptists, Methodists, and Presbyterians all worshipped in a log house in Court Square*. The Methodists organized the first church in 1826 and in 1832 were the first to erect their own building. By the 1840s the Presbyterians also had built a church building, and most Christian denominations were represented in the town. More churches went up as the community prospered.

Of the original ante-bellum church structures only three remain: St. Peter's Catholic Church, Calvary Episcopal Church, and Third Presbyterian Church. Of these only St. Peter's was designed by a trained architect.

No Jewish congregation is included in this listing because none is active today in downtown Memphis. The only standing synagogue downtown, Anshei Mishne Synagogue at 112 Jackson, was built in 1927 and is now a nightclub. The first Jewish settler came to Memphis about 1838 and by 1854 the B'Nai Israel Congregation, the original name for Temple Israel, had grown out of the Hebrew Benevolent Society. This congregation, the oldest in Memphis, worshipped in a rented hall until they converted the Farmer and Mechanic's Bank at Main and Exchange into what was their home from 1858 to 1884. This building no longer stands, and Temple Israel Synagogue is now at 1376 E. Massey Rd. (761-3130). The Baron Hirsch Congregation, the largest Orthodox congregation in the U.S., was also organized in North Memphis*. It met on the second floor of Isaac's Bookstore, N. Main near Poplar, from 1890 to 1914. Its synagogue now is at 1740 Vollintine Ave. (274-3525) and its religious school at 5631 Shady Grove Rd. (683-4767) in a house that until 1977 belonged to recording star Isaac Hayes. For more information on Memphis' Jewish community see *Jewish Memphis*, a tour book written by Alan Singer for the Memphis Jewish Federation in 1980.

BELLEVUE BAPTIST CHURCH
70 N. Bellevue Blvd. 725-9777.

Hours: *Services, 8am, 10:45am, & 7pm Sun, 6:30pm W. TV & radio broadcasts, 10:45am Sun on Channel 13 & AM 60, 9:30pm Sun on Channel 24. Office hours, 8:30am-4:30pm M-F.*
Tours: *By arrangement.*
Lunch: *Th noon lunch for businessmen and W night supper before the services.*
MATA: *#5, 55 (ex Sun).*
Other: *1) Large singles ministry. 2) Family enrichment and counseling service. 3) Seminars open to the public. 4) Large sports facility and program.*
E&H: *1) Signer during services. 2) Fellowship and Bible study for blind. 3) Special programs for the divorced and widowed.*

Early Baptists in Memphis organized in 1839 and worshipped in the log house in Court Square*. In 1849 the denomination built their first Memphis church on land now occupied by the Shelby County Court House*.

Bellevue Baptist Church, today the largest Baptist church east of the Mississippi River, was started in 1898 as a suburban branch of Central Baptist Church which stood at 146 S. 2nd Str. A small stone church was dedicated in 1903, and by 1924 the congregation needed more space and built Lee Auditorium. The present 3,000-seat sanctuary was built in 1952. The church today has about nine buildings and covers more than a block. Dr. Adrian Rogers, the church's senior minister since 1972, was president of the Southern Baptist Convention in 1980.

CALVARY EPISCOPAL CHURCH (NRHP)
102 N. 2nd Str. 525-6602.

Hours: *Services, 7:30, 9:15, & 11:15 am Sun. Office hours, 9am-4pm M-F.*
Tours: *By appointment.*

Lunch: 1) During lent (except holy week) after the noon services. 2) On W after the art programs.
MATA: Downtown buses.
Other: 1) Occasional music programs. 2) Free 20-minute art programs, 12:05pm W: 1st W/theatre, 2nd W/classical music, 3rd W/gospel, jazz, blues, or rock, 4th W/organ music.
E&H: No wheelchair ramp; five steps at entrance.

The first local Episcopal services were held on a boat, the Tobacco Plant, by Rev. Thomas Wright. In 1832 Wright and ten parishioners formed Calvary, the first Episcopal church in Shelby County. The Gothic nave of handmade brick was begun about 1840 and is the oldest surviving public building in Memphis. The tower was added in 1848, and the building renovated and chancel added in 1881.

CHRISTIAN METHODIST EPISCOPAL CHURCH (CME)
International headquarters, 531 S. Parkway E. at Lauderdale. 947-4188.

Hours: Office, 8am-5pm M-F, 9am-1pm Sat. Service, 10:45 Sun.
Tours: By appointment, 8:30am-4:30pm Th.
Lunch: You may arrange to eat in the employee's cafeteria.
MATA: #16, 13 (ex Sun).
Other: 1) Girl and Boy Scout programs. 2) Community outreach programs.
E&H: 1) Not equipped for wheelchairs. 2) Special senior citizen programs.

The Christian Methodist Episcopal denomination grew out of the Methodist Church South and was founded in 1870 in Jackson, Tn. Today there are more than 3,000 CME churches internationally and more than 32 in the greater Memphis area.

The CME international headquarters and publishing house are in Memphis. CME Temple, purchased from Boulevard Baptist Church in 1966, is part of the headquarters and holds Sun. services and religious programs. Other CME churches are listed in the yellow pages of the phone book.

CHURCH OF GOD IN CHRIST
International headquarters - 272 S. Main. 527-1422.

Hours: The information officer is usually here 10am-4pm M-F. Visitors are welcome, but you should phone ahead. No Sun. services at headquarters. See phone directory for church locations.
MATA: Downtown buses.
E&H: Wheelchair accessible.

The Church of God in Christ, a predominantly black Pentecostal-Holiness sect, has its international headquarters here. The church was planned at a camp meeting in Jackson, Miss. by Charles Harrison Mason of Shelby County who organized the first congregation in Lexington, Miss. in 1897. By Nov. 1907 there were seven congregations in the Mid-South. At Mason's death in 1961, the church had about 5,000 congregations around the world. The current bishop, Rev. J. O. Patterson of Memphis, took office in 1968. Today there are more than 15,000 congregations.

The international headquarters building, formerly the Chisca Plaza Hotel, was given to the church in 1971 by the Snowden-Todd family. Plans are underway for an adjoining eight square block multi-building church center.

Bishop Patterson's church, Pentecostal Temple Church of God in Christ at 229 S. Danny Thomas (527-9202), is the sect's mother church. Services are at 11am and 8pm Sun and 8pm W & F. The first tabernacle built in Memphis, Temple Church of God in Christ, is at 672 S. Lauderdale.

Mason Temple at 938 Mason, south off Crump Blvd. just east of 4th, is now a headquarters building for the church. Dr. Martin Luther King Jr.*, in Memphis in support of a strike by the city's sanitation workers, delivered his famous prophetic "I've Been to the Mountaintop" address to a crowd of about 13,000 here on Apr. 3, 1968.

> *I've been to the mountaintop. And I don't mind. Like anybody, I would like to live a long life. Longevity has its place. But I'm not concerned about that now. I just want to do God's will. And He's allowed me to go up to the mountain. And I've looked over. And I've seen the promised land. I may not get there with you. But I want you to know tonight, that we, as a people will get to the promised land.*
>
> Copyright © 1968 by Estate of Martin Luther King, Jr.
> Used by permission of Joan Daves.

Dr. King was assassinated the next day, Apr. 4, 1968, on the balcony of the Lorraine Motel*.

CHURCH OF THE RIVER
292 Virginia Ave. 526-8631.

Hours: Service, 11am Sun. Open, 9:30am-2:30pm M-F.
MATA: Take the Showboat bus to Holiday Inn-Rivermont. The church is a five minute walk across the parking lot.
E&H: Wheelchairs can enter the building, but, because of the church's design, movement inside the building is difficult.

Designed in the 1960s, this Unitarian church offers a spectacular view of the river.

CLAYBORN TEMPLE/FORMERLY SECOND PRESBYTERIAN CHURCH (NRHP)
280 Hernando at Pontotoc.

MATA: *#50 (ex Sun) or 36 (ex Sun) to Linden and Hernando. Walk one block south to Pontotoc.*

This church is not in use and has fallen into disrepair. Second Presbyterian Church, organized in South Memphis in 1844, built this structure in 1891. It was designed by Jones, Hain, and Kirby in the Richardsonian Romanesque style. The plain gray stone exterior has been little altered. The massive auditorium seating 2000 was unique for 19thc. Memphis.

The original congregation moved to a new church at the intersection of Central, Poplar, and Goodlett in 1949, and the building was purchased by the African Methodist Episcopal Church to be used as a convention center. It was renamed the Clayborn Temple AME Church. The building was a center for civil rights demonstrations in the 1960s.

FIRST BAPTIST CHURCH BEALE STREET (NRHP)
379 Beale. 527-4832.

Hours: *Services, 11am & 6:30pm Sun and 7:30pm W. Open 9am-3pm M-F while its day care program is in operation.*
MATA: *#6 (ex Sun).*

The Baptists in South Memphis first worshipped in the Randolph Building at Main and Beale. Blacks went to church with their masters and sat in the gallery. Legend has it that the congregation decided the blacks were overly emotional and disruptive so it set up separate services for blacks either in the basement or private homes.

First Baptist Church Beale Street was organized in 1854 in meetings at Reverend Scott Keys' home on Beale near Turley. Completed in 1885, the present building is believed to be the first brick church built for and by an all black congregation. It is considered the "mother church" of all black Baptist churches in Mississippi, Arkansas, and Tennessee. It is here that President Grant spoke in 1870 when he came to Memphis.

The church was designed in the Romanesque Revival style by E. C. Jones, and before alterations, was High Victorian in spirit. Tall towers, one topped by a sculpture of John the Baptist pointing to heaven, were part of the two-story building's elaborately ornamented facade.

FIRST PRESBYTERIAN CHURCH
166 Poplar at 3rd. 525-5619.

Hours: *Service, 11am Sun. Open, 8:30am-4pm M-F.*
Tours: *Phone to arrange. Brochures available for visitors.*

Lunch: A $2.10 lunch is served 11:30am-1:15pm M-F.
MATA: #5, 55 (ex Sun), or other downtown buses to 2nd & Poplar.
Other: The church is urban oriented and sponsors neighborhood youth and criminal justice programs.
E&H: No ramps, but an elevator serves the second-floor sanctuary.

First Presbyterian Church, organized in 1828 by five men and women, was the second congregation in the city. Early members worshipped in the log house in Court Square*.

Originally there was a cemetery on the church's present site. John Overton gave this land to the city with the stipulation that it no longer be used as a cemetery. The cemetery was moved, and the city deeded the land to the church in 1834. The first building, of wood, was replaced in 1854 by a brick building which was destroyed by fire in 1883. The present two-story Romanesque Revival style building was built in 1884.

FIRST UNITED METHODIST CHURCH (NRHP)
204 North 2nd at Poplar. 527-8362.

Hours: Service, 10:50am Sun. Open, 9am-4:30pm M-F.
Tours: Phone to arrange.
Lunch: A lunch and speaker program, First Forum, is held each Friday. Lunch is $1.00; various civic leaders speak. Phone the office to make reservations.
Other: Dinner and a fellowship service, 6pm W; make reservations in advance for dinner.
MATA: Downtown buses.
E&H: 1) Sunday school building is accessible to wheelchairs, but help is needed to reach the sanctuary. 2) Hearing aids are provided. 3) Senior citizen activities, 4th floor 9am-3:30pm daily.

Memphis' first Methodist church was organized in 1826. Early members worshipped in the log house in Court Square*. They built the first church building in Memphis in 1832. Wesley Chapel was built in 1845. The present church structure was completed on the same site about 1890. It is built of stone, unusual in Memphis. The exterior remains basically the same today, but the interior has been totally altered. The pulpit Bible is a gift from Ben Abernathy, a former slave and for forty years the sexton of the original church. The hand-needlepointed cushions depict the history of Memphis.

NEW FIRST BAPTIST CHURCH/FORMERLY THIRD PRESBYTERIAN CHURCH/CHELSEA AVENUE PRESBYTERIAN CHURCH
299 Chelsea at 7th Str. 523-7734.

MATA: #8, 11 (ex Sat & Sun).

Third Presbyterian Church was founded in 1856 by 34 residents of

Greenlaw*. The two level brick church was dedicated in 1860. During the Civil War, the church's minister left to be a chaplain in the Confederate army. Grant's soldiers stabled horses on the first floor of the church building and used the upper floor as a hospital.

In 1899 the exterior and interior were altered, and in 1910 the exterior was stuccoed. The steeple was removed from the building, and the church's name changed to Chelsea Avenue Presbyterian Church in 1916. In 1973 the building was sold to New First Baptist Church.

ST. MARY'S CATHOLIC CHURCH (NRHP)
155 Market at 3rd. 522-9420.

Hours: Mass, 5:30pm Sat, 5:30am, 8am, 10:30am (broadcast on radio WMQM 1480), and 5:30pm (guitar music) Sun. Open, 9am-4pm M-F. To enter, ring bell at Market Str. side door.
Tours: Phone to arrange.
MATA: #11 (ex Sat & Sun) or any downtown bus and walk two short blocks.
E&H: No ramp and about three steps at entrance on Market, so help would be necessary for those in a wheelchair.

St. Mary's, the second oldest Catholic church in Memphis, was founded in 1862 by German Catholics who wanted a German ministry. The cornerstone was laid in 1864 with a salute by Federal soldiers. The building was finished in 1870. A Franciscan monastery was added in 1871 and closed in 1976. The interior is highlighted by Franciscan handwork and stained glass.

ST. MARY'S EPISCOPAL CATHEDRAL, CHAPEL, and DIOCESAN HOUSE (NRHP)
692 Poplar. 527-3361.

Hours: Services, 7:30 & 11am Sun. Open, 8:30am-4:30pm M-F.
Tours: Phone to arrange.
MATA: #5, 55 (ex Sun).
E&H: 1) Accessible to wheelchairs through east entrance. 2) Ecumenical service for deaf in chapel 9:30am Sun.

St. Mary's Parish was founded in 1857 by the women of Calvary Episcopal Church on a plot of land donated by the Brinkley family. A board and batten Gothic structure was built in 1871 and presented to the bishop as his cathedral church. This was one of the first Episcopal cathedrals in the U.S.

In 1873, at the bishop's request, the Order of St. Mary sent sisters from New York to establish a school for girls at the cathedral. In 1887 a red brick chapel with leaded windows and cherry columns was built for the sisters in High Victorian Gothic style. It was later faced with Sewanee stone to match the present cathedral building.

Plans for the present Late Gothic Revival cathedral were designed in 1895 by W. Halsey Wood of New York. The cornerstone was laid in 1898 and the building finished in 1926. The 41 stained glass windows were designed by Len Howard between 1926 and 1955. The Diocesan House, built about 1902 as a dwelling for the Bishop of Tennessee, and the Parish Hall and Church School Building, completed in 1952, are also on the property.

The cathedral's treasured possessions include a silver communion service presented by Jefferson Davis to the Episcopal Church of Arlington, Tn., a stone in the western transcept which was part of the balustrade surrounding the pool of Bethesda, and a stone in the eastern transcept which was part of a column in the Abbey of Glastonbury, the legendary resting place of Arthur and Guinevere.

ST. PATRICK'S CHURCH
277 S. 4th Str. 527-2542.

Hours: *Services, 9am, 11am, & 5:10pm Sun. The church is locked except during services. There is a bell on the priest's house to ring for admittance.*
MATA: *#50 (ex Sun).*
E&H: *Wheelchair accessible.*

St. Patrick's is the third oldest Catholic church in Memphis and was built around 1904. At the time, it served a thriving Irish parish. The building is a replica of a 16thc. Italian Renaissance church.

ST. PETER'S CATHOLIC CHURCH (NRHP)
190 Adams at 3rd Str. 526-6882.

Hours: *Services, 8:30 & 11:30am Sun, 12:10pm daily. Open, 8am-6pm daily.*
Tours: *Phone to arrange.*
Lunch: *Lenten lunches, 11:30am-2pm W.*
MATA: *#53 (ex Sun) or any downtown bus to 2nd & Adams, then walk east one block.*
E&H: *Ramp at church's garden entrance. The garden is open for Sun. services. Phone the office to use this entrance at other times.*

St. Peter's is the oldest Catholic church in Memphis and originally served a predominantly Irish congregation. The parish was founded in 1840 and the first church built in 1842. The present building was built between 1852 and 1857 around the earlier brick building. When the new church was completed, the old eave structure, which was only 70 feet long by 30 feet wide, was dismantled and carried out through the new doors.

The present Victorian Gothic church looks much like a medieval fortress. Its brick walls are stuccoed and modeled to resemble stone. The stained glass windows were imported from Germany in the early 1900s. Except for the altars and some minor decoration, the church is much the same as when built. Three of the church's former priests, who served during the yellow fever epidemics of the 1870s, are buried beneath the building.

TRINITY LUTHERAN CHURCH
210 Washington (encircled by the Criminal Justice Center). 525-1056.

Hours: 8am-4:30pm M-F. To enter ring bell by education building's front door.
Tours: Phone to arrange.
MATA: Downtown buses.
Other: Lunch with noon reviews of current popular books, 11:45am-1pm for eight W after Easter and eight W before Thanksgiving.
E&H: 1) Accessible to the handicapped by an elevator at the rear door. 2) In the 1960s, the church's deaf congregation branched off, establishing their own church, Eternal Mercy Lutheran Church for the Deaf, at E. Parkway and Monroe.

Seventy-four German families in Memphis organized this church in 1855. The downstairs level of the church building was completed in 1874 and the second floor sanctuary in 1888. The Gothic style structure is noted for its Belz glass windows from Germany. The interior retains much of its original appearance. The brick veneered exterior was covered with a Permastone finish in 1950.

Trinity Lutheran Church grew to serve 600 German families in the early 1870s. The Germans were struck hard by the yellow fever epidemics of the '70s; many survivors left Memphis for St. Louis and Cincinnati, and only 200 families remained in the church.

CEMETERIES

Ironically the history of a city often comes alive in its old cemeteries. In the city, cemeteries were usually owned and run by private corporations; in the country, they were usually family plots on farms or church graveyards. The public library's Memphis Room (528-2961) has two volumes of information on local cemeteries, "Gravestone Inscriptions from Shelby County, Tn. Volumes 1 & 2" copied and compiled by Charlotte Edmondson Elam, Margaret Inabinet Ericksen, and Ruth Wyckoff Hunt.

CALVARY CEMETERY
1663 Elvis Presley Blvd. 948-1529.

Hours: Gates, 7am-7pm daily; office, 9am-4:30pm daily.

Tours: A map in the office diagrams the cemetery. Phone to arrange a tour of highlights.

MATA: #43 (ex Sun).

Calvary was established by the Roman Catholic Diocese of Nashville in 1865. In 1897, 1,300 bodies, earlier buried in St. Peter's Catholic Cemetery on Madison Ave., were moved here. Such moves were not unusual as the city expanded. In this case progress meant the new city hospital. In 1970 the cemetery became the property of the Roman Catholic Diocese of Memphis.

The rolling site of the cemetery is well maintained, and tombstones run the gamut from simple to ornate. The life of Joseph F. McMullen, a truck driver who died in 1962, is commemorated by the truck carved on his tombstone. The 1873 yellow fever deaths of Fathers Daley, Carey, O'Brien, Sheehy, and Leo and the seven sisters of St. Dominic and St. Francis are commemorated in a monument erected in 1876. The 18-foot high altar and Gothic cross flanked by kneeling angels was made in Carrara, Italy.

EDMISTON CEMETERY*.

ELMWOOD CEMETERY
824 S. Dudley (just south of Crump Blvd., near I-240). 774-3212.

Hours: Gates open 8am-5pm daily summer, 8am-4pm daily winter. Office open 8am-3pm M-Sat.

Tours: Visitors may wander through the cemetery on their own and make rubbings from the gravestones. A free guide-brochure is available in the office.

Lunch: School groups—with proper supervision—may bring lunch, but they must not litter.

MATA: #7 (ex Sat & Sun) and then walk about two blocks.

E&H: There are several steps into the office and no ramp is available. The cemetery itself is accessible to wheelchairs.

Kit Dalton, an outlaw in the James Gang, and Annie Cook, the proprietor of the Mansion, a house of prostitution, are both buried here—but they are not typical. Elmwood, established in 1852 by 50 businessmen, is primarily the cemetery of Memphis' early elite. The graves of 22 mayors of Memphis and South Memphis, two governors, four U.S. senators, 17 Confederate generals, one Yankee general, 12 veterans of the War of 1812, one soldier of the American Revolution, and the city's first black millionaire, Robert Church, are all here. But the cemetery is not only for the elite. More than 1,000 Confederate veterans and many victims of the yellow fever epidemics are buried here.

Of special note are the 1880s office (NRHP), the city's only remaining example of Carpenter Gothic architecture, and the 1903 north bridge entrance (NRHP).

HOLLYWOOD CEMETERY*.

RALEIGH CEMETERY*.

SOURCES OF INFORMATION

Historic Sites is a compilation of information gathered from in-depth **historical studies.** I have drawn particularly from:
Gerald Caper's *The Biography of a Rivertown,*
Paul R. Coppock's *Memphis Sketches* and newspaper articles,
Charles Crawford's *Yesterday's Memphis,*
Alan Karchmer's *Time and Place, a Review of Memphis Architecture,*
Les Passes, Inc.'s 1967 tour book, *Reflections of a Rivertown,*
Memphis Landmark Commission's 1980 "Survey and Preservation Plan",
Metropolitan Inter-Faith Association's "Neighborhood Series", by Betty Tilly and Peggy B. Jemison,
Kitty Plunkett's *Memphis A Pictorial History,*
Bennie Hugh Priddy, Jr.'s "Nineteenth Century Architecture in Memphis: Ten Surviving Structures",
William D. Miller's *Memphis During the Progressive Era 1900-1917,*
Robert A. Sigafoos' *Cotton Row to Beale Street, A Business History of Memphis,*
many "Memphis Magazine", "Commercial Appeal" and "Memphis Press-Scimitar" articles, especially those by David Bowman, Paul Coppock, and Kenneth Neill.
"The Souvenir Edition of the Memphis Appeal, Memphis, Tn., Dec. 1890", "Souvenir Edition of the Memphis Evening Scimitar, Oct. 1891", "Art Work of the City of Memphis, W. H. Parish Publishing Co. 1895", "Art Supplement to the Greater Memphis Edition of the Evening Scimitar, Apr. 1899", and the "Art Work of Memphis, Tn., Gravure Illustration Co. 1900" were extremely interesting and helpful.
Mary Winslow Chapman's *I Remember Raleigh* and Anna Leigh McCorkle's *Tales of Old Whitehaven* provided information on these areas of the city.
Two architectural history books are currently in the works, one by the Junior League of Memphis and the other by Mary Wallace Crocker, author of "Historic Architecture in Mississippi". Also to come: "Central Gardens Handbook", a guide to the neighborhood and tips on restoration by James Williamson and Carl Awsumb, and an updated walking tour booklet of downtown historic districts, "Walking Through Old Memphis", by Memphis Heritage Inc.

Memphis Room—Memphis and Shelby County Public Library and Information Center, Main Branch, Peabody at McLean. 528-2961. Most of the formerly mentioned sources for this chapter plus a bibliography of in-print Memphis history books, additional books, newspaper articles, photographs, studies on Memphis history, and Memphis City Directories are available here. A thank you to the staff!

The library staff will present a slide show, talks, and displays on Memphis history, the ante-bellum South and women's history free of charge on two weeks' notice.

Memphis Landmarks Commission—Falls Building, 22 N. Front, Suite 901. 528-2834. A division of the Housing and Community Development Administration, they have listed and mapped candidates for landmark and district designation. The public may look at their files and pick up a free copy of their excellent 1980 Survey and Preservation Plan.

Historical Hiking Trails—P.O. Box 17507, 38117. 683-3505. Maps, instruction, and historical information available on historic Mid-South hiking trails.

Metropolitan Inter-Faith Assn. (MIFA)—166-A Poplar (2nd floor of First Presbyterian Church). 527-0208. MIFA has originally researched and compiled studies on eight Memphis neighborhoods: Greenlaw, Cooper-Young, Rozelle-Annesdale, Cherokee, Douglass, Buntyn, Vollintine-Evergreen, and Overton Park. Studies are on file in the Memphis Room of the library and at MIFA headquarters. Brief free historical tour pamphlets of Greenlaw and Buntyn also are available in the office.

The following **organizations** will provide programs on Memphis history and architecture:

American Institute of Architects, Memphis Chapter—P.O. Box 4941, 38111. 525-6663. Speakers on architecture, history, current trends and local design. One week's notice required. No fee.

Assn. for the Study of Afro-American Life and History—2460 Arlington 38114. 743-8723. Speakers, films, and slide shows on Black history, culture and civilization. Arrange for speaker two weeks ahead and for film, one month in advance. Free.

B'Nai B'Rith Women Simcha Chapter, #1509—4887 Dee Road 38117. 767-5671. Speakers on Jewish history. Arrange one week in advance. Free.

Center for Southern Folklore—1216 Peabody 38104. 726-4205. Produces, rents, and sells films, photographs, recordings, books, and slide shows which research and document folklore (folktales, crafts, music...) of rural Arkansas, Mississippi, and Tennessee. Arrange for the Center's materials and/or an hour long speaker's program a month in advance. Fees vary based on the material used. The Center's materials also are available at the Memphis and Shelby County Public Library and Information Center, Main branch, Peabody at McLean.

Future Memphis— 100 N. Main Bldg., Suite 2909, 38103. 525-5395. Speakers on Memphis' future, growth, and development. Free. Arrange one month ahead.

Memphis Heritage Inc.—P.O. Box 3143, 38103. 327-3086. Citizens' support group to the Memphis Landmark Commission. Walking and driving tour brochure of historic areas in Memphis. For $25 they will provide groups with speakers and a film on preservation and adaptive uses of old buildings and historic sites in Memphis. Arrange two weeks in advance. Various members might be persuaded to give historical guided tours of the city.

Speakers on various facets of Memphis history are listed in the Memphis and Shelby County Public Library and Information Center's annual "Program Resources and Techniques". The booklet is for sale for $1 at the library's main branch on Peabody at McLean. Included are:

James Robert Chumney, Jr.
Mitchell Hall, Rm 111, Memphis State University 38152. 454-2518. Topic: Old/New South. Fees vary. Arrange one month in advance.

Charles W. Crawford
Administration Bldg., Rm. 324, Memphis State University 38152. Topic: Tennessee Politics; Memphis Becoming a City. Free. Arrange three weeks in advance.

David Bowman
524 Reese 38111. 452-4277. Topic: Restoration and preservation of old buildings and historical Memphis sites. Free.

Mrs. G. W. Huckaba
215 Kimbrough 38104. 324-7395. Topic: Historic sites in Tennessee, with slides. Free. Arrange six weeks in advance.

Mrs. Eleanor Hughes
4140 Chanwill Ave. 38117. Topic: Victorian Village Historic District, with slides. No charge, but honorarium accepted. Arrange two weeks in advance.

Gerald Patrick Smith
Administration Bldg., Rm. 324, Memphis State University 38152. 454-2606. Topic: Chucalissa. Free. Arrange three weeks in advance.

Music/ The Memphis Sound

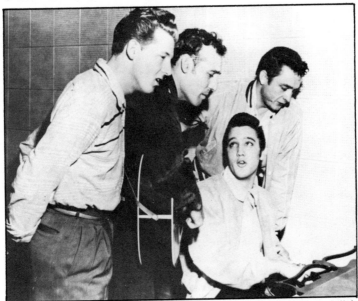

Knox Phillips

Jerry Lee Lewis, Carl Perkins, Elvis Presley, and Johnny Cash, rockabilly's million dollar quartet, recording at Sun Studio 1955.

HISTORY

In 1838 Memphis received a Norwegian violinist coldly, but black fiddle and hoe-down music could always bring out the crowds. It was a rough and simple society, and most importantly, a place where whites and blacks listened to one another's music. This seems the key to the development of the Memphis sound.

The music created in Memphis is an amalgam of the region's styles and cultures. Poor whites and blacks have come to the city and played and sung their hearts out. They have created a rich and powerful musical idiom. Although Memphis' recording industry never rivaled the "big three"—New York, Los Angeles, and Nashville—the jazz, blues, rock, and soul recorded here have influenced music around the world.

19th CENTURY

In 1846 music publisher P. Flavio opened the city's first music store. In 1850 German settlers organized the city's first brass band. During the 1850s many touring musical and dramatic shows came to Memphis, and in 1851 thousands turned out for Jenny Lind's performance. Tickets were being auctioned for as much as $30, a tremendous sum in those days. The showboats, "floating palaces", brought everything from musical comedy companies to minstrels, opera singers, and circuses.

Festivals, dances, and band concerts were an important part of the city's social and cultural life. In February of 1872 Memphis celebrated its first Mardi Gras pageant and that same month honored Grand Duke Alexis of Russia at a ball. In 1875 John Phillip Sousa directed an orchestra for the first time here. He returned to Memphis many times.

As the city revived from the yellow fever epidemics of the 1870s, there was a surge of musical activity. By 1880 there were 13 music schools. During the '80s choral and instrumental clubs and societies proliferated. An opera house opened in 1889, a school of fine arts was built in 1894, and a music conservatory was founded in 1895.

Bands were the rage in the 1890s. West Dukes, Jim Turner, and Charlie Bynum had popular bands, the forerunners of William Christopher Handy's band in the early 1900s.

HANDY ERA

Brass bands, vaudeville, classical music clubs and societies, a small orchestra, black rural music, and white country music were all a part of Memphis' musical milieu when William Christopher Handy came to the city in 1903. A trained musician and band leader, Handy took the sounds created by black laborers and sharecroppers and wove them into formal compositions. Handy is often call the "father of the blues"; more accurately, he was the stenographer of the blues.

Born in Florence, Ala. in 1873, Handy was the son of people who had been born in slavery. His father and grandfather were both Methodist ministers. (His childhood home is a museum.) Handy had been tutored in formal music, but when at 13, he bought his first cornet for $1.75, his family disapproved of what they considered his frivolous interest in secular popular music. He mastered the cornet and left home to make a career of music. He hooked up with traveling bands and eventually with minstrel shows, touring the country with Mahara's Colored Minstrels.

Handy conducted his own orchestra in the Memphis-Clarksdale area from 1903 to 1921, playing mostly for private parties at places like the Memphis Country Club and the Alaskan Roof Garden atop the Falls Building. One night Handy's band was playing for a dance in Cleveland*, Miss; someone requested "native" music. Handy didn't understand until he heard a local band fill in during intermission. After that he began writing down the blues sounds he heard in the countryside, and his band began playing the blues.

For a while Handy settled at 659 Jennette Str. in Memphis and had an office at 390 Beale. His band played for funerals and political rallies as well as for dances. Handy wrote "Mr. Crump Don't 'Low", later retitled the "Memphis Blues", as a campaign song for E. H. Crump*. First played at a rally on the corner of Main and Madison, the song was immediately popular. In 1912 Handy published the piece. It was the first written song to have a jazz break in it.

In 1914 Handy composed "St. Louis Blues" at the cigar stand in Peewee's Place*. It is said that every piece of polyphonic ragtime is a descendant of "St. Louis Blues", the song that spread the Beale Street* sound worldwide. Handy also wrote many spirituals.

In 1913 Handy formed a music company and in 1917 moved to New York. The company, Handy Brothers Music Co., is run by one of his sons today. In 1931 Handy visited Memphis for the dedication of Handy Park*, but he continued to live in N.Y.C. until his death in 1958. The Reverend Adam Clayton Powell, Jr., then a U.S. Congressman, spoke at his funeral service in Abyssinian Baptist Church in Harlem, and crowds lined the street to mourn his death. In 1980 one block of 52nd Street, between Avenue of the Americas and 7th Street, in N.Y.C. was renamed 52nd Street—W. C. Handy's Place.

Handy took the music of southern blacks and made it an art form. The rest of the country learned about the blues at the tent show performances of vaudeville singers like Gertrude "Ma" Rainey and through the recordings, after 1926, of authentic rural bluesmen. Three outstanding local musicians who played with Handy continued the blues tradition—drummer Alex Dukes, trumpeter Sun Smith, and violinist Thomas Pinkston. Out of Beale Street came noted blues singer and guitarist Memphis Minnie Lawler and Booker T. "Bukka" White. Another blues great, Walter "Furry" Lewis came to Memphis from Greenwood, Miss. in 1900, and

Handy bought him a "good" guitar. Furry played the blues from Peewee's Place on Beale to Madison Square Garden in N.Y.C. Clarinetist Buster Bailey was a star in Louis Armstrong's band of All-Stars, and Lil Hardin, who married Armstrong, composed several jazz masterpieces and played piano in Armstrong's "Hot 5" and "Hot 7" bands. These bands recorded the finest in traditional jazz.

ROCK 'N ROLL BREWS

In the 1920s the rise of the recording industry had an homogenizing effect on music. Black musicians melded western country swing into the blues and borrowed horns and drums from jazz. The bluesmen, playing in city honky-tonks, picked up heavier and faster rhythms. Texan T-Bone Walker developed a modern blues technique using the volume of electric amplifiers to create vibrato. B. B. King made the technique famous. Walker also developed the fast rhythmic guitar chording that Chuck Berry adopted as his trademark.

During the '20s and '30s there were no local record companies, only national ones. Radio grew rapidly from 1922 to 1925 and began to cut into the record companies' sales. Looking for new markets, the companies realized that few radio stations played blues, gospel, or country & western. These types of music and the South became an increasing market for records, and until 1940 the large companies sent representatives south to make field recordings of the region's music.

Non-commercial hillbilly music and the blues were popular here in the '30s. Sophisticated jazz was the uptown rage. Memphis jazzmen adopted stronger bass rhythms from the blues. The result was a raw throbbing boogie. The Manassas High School band was a big hit playing the Memphis-born boogie at Harlem's famous Cotton Club. In the '40s and '50s such jazz greats as Phineas Newborn, George Coleman, Booker Little, Hank Crawford, Herman Green, and Harold Mabern were all playing in Memphis at Club Handy in the old Mitchell Hotel. Blues stars like Bobby Blue Bland, Johnny Ace, Junior Parker, B. B. King, and Rufus Thomas were playing local gigs.

After the war, radio stations reached out for black listeners. Black performers had short live shows. In 1948 WDIA put on a half hour rhythm and blues show; within a year, the station's whole programing was R&B. In 1950 Howlin' Wolf and Sonny Boy Williamson were broadcasting R&B from West Memphis. B. B. King and Rufus Thomas played on Memphis' WDIA*, the first black-operated radio outlet in the South.

Sam Phillips founded Memphis' first record company in 1950. His Memphis Recording Service and Sun Records* recorded such greats as B. B. King, Bobby Blue Bland, Howlin' Wolf, Junior Parker, Little Milton, Elvis, Jerry Lee Lewis, and Johnny Cash in the '50s and '60s.

Phillips leased these cuts to independent record companies like Chess in Chicago. His first hit in 1951 was "Rocket 88" played by Ike Turner's band with Jackie Brenston singing. It combined western swing and urban boogie blues, an early form of rock and roll.

ELVIS PRESLEY—THE KING

In 1952, Phillips started Sun Records with Jim Bullet of Nashville. The first 15 releases on the now famous yellow label with sunburst and crowing rooster were by black musicians. Phillips sensed that white teenagers were bored by sugary ballads and would take to earthier R&B rhythms. Because of the racism of the time, however, white stations would not play black music. Phillips was looking for a white who could synthesize the styles and cultures.

Then Phillips discovered Elvis Presley. In 1953 Presley paid $3.98 to cut a disc as a present for his mother on Phillips' custom recording service. In January 1954 he came back and cut another song. Phillips heard the sound he had been looking for. In "Sam Phillips: The Sun King, A Revised History of the Roots of Rock and Roll" Robert Palmer wrote, "It was the sound of a white man with a look, a style, and a genuine feeling for the vitality that America's minority musics—white country and black rhythm and blues—had in common. It was rock and roll."

Phillips asked Elvis to make a ballad "demo". On July 5, 1954 Elvis recorded his first hit, "That's All Right", a traditional blues number written by Arthur "Big Boy" Crudup. "Blue Moon of Kentucky", a country song, was on the flip side. Dewey Phillips, no kin to Sam, played Elvis' record on his "Red Hot and Blue" WHBQ radio show and instantly began receiving calls and requests. Dewey, one of the first radio disc jockeys to ad lib shows, was probably the first person who played black music for whites and blacks. Some say without him there would have been no boogie woogie. Elvis' record sold 300,000 copies and was briefly #1 on the Memphis country and western charts. What had been "race" music was breaking through to white audiences. Elvis' dazzling music career would revolutionize the musical and cultural scene.

Elvis Aron Presley was born Jan. 8, 1935 in Tupelo, Miss., the only child of Gladys and Vernon Presley. (Elvis' twin brother, Jesse Garon, died at birth.) Vernon shifted from carpentry to sharecropping, truck driving, and painting jobs, and the family had little money. Elvis' first contact with music was in church; the family often sang at dinners in Tupelo's Pentecostal 1st Assembly of God Church. The blues he learned listening to the radio and to blacks in the area. At age 11, Elvis got his first guitar. When he was 13, the family packed all their belongings into a 1939 Plymouth and moved to Memphis.

The family lived in a city housing project in Memphis, and Elvis attended Humes High School. He was rejected and lonely. In 1953 he graduated and got a job as a driver for Crown Electric Co.

After making "That's All Right" in 1954, Presley played gigs around Memphis. He sat in with the Starlight Wranglers at Bel Air and Airport

Inn, played briefly with the Blue Moon Boys at the Eagle's Nest, and did a country show at the Overton Park Shell*. Then he went on the road, opening shopping centers throughout Texas and Mississippi. Elvis' style didn't fit a slot; he was too much a hillbilly for the black R&B stations and too bluesy for the white country and western stations.

In 1955 Elvis cut "Baby, Let's Play House" which made the national C&W charts. Colonel Tom Parker, a booking agent from central Tennessee, heard and began booking Elvis. In 1955 Parker signed Presley with RCA and paid Sun $35,000 plus $5,000 in back royalties for his contract. RCA wanted to move into the country field, and its competitors had the Nashville country and western stars all signed up.

In January 1956 in RCA's Nashville studio, Elvis recorded "Heartbreak Hotel" with the Jordanaires. The hit brought him an invitation to the Ed Sullivan Show. He swiveled his hips, sneered at square reality, and was an instant celebrity. He had 14 consecutive million-sellers; at one point his records held all five top spots on the best seller charts.

In 1956 Elvis went to Hollywood to make movies, but his career was sidetracked when he was drafted in 1958 and stationed in Germany. He returned to the U.S. and civilian life in 1960 to find his music eclipsed by Bob Dylan, the Beatles, and the Rolling Stones. In 1967 Elvis married Priscilla Beaulieu, and nine months later their daughter, Lisa Marie, was born. Elvis and Priscilla were divorced in 1973.

In 1968-69 Presley's music began to re-emerge. Elvis was a hit on a NBC-TV special and, for the first time in almost 14 years, again recorded in Memphis. In these sessions at American Studios* under Chips Moman, he cut six gold singles and two gold albums, among them "In the Ghetto", "Kentucky Rain", and the album "Elvis Back in Memphis". Elvis also went back on the road and performed for sell-out crowds in Las Vegas.

The "King of Rock and Roll" had sold more than 45 million records when he died Aug. 16, 1977. He is buried on the grounds at Graceland*.

THE '50S

B. B. King, a star of the traveling rhythm and blues reviews of the 1950s, is credited with introducing the blues to white America almost single-handedly. Riley B. King, born near Itta Bena, Miss. in 1925, was brought up in the country blues tradition. His cousin Bukka White helped him get a 15-minute radio show on KWAM in Memphis. Playing his wailing guitar, he picked up the nickname "Beale Street Blues Boy", eventually shortened to B. B. King. His radio show, broadcast from 1948 to 1952 on WDIA, was very popular, but in the '60s his popularity among black audiences waned. He often shared the stage with Bobby Blue Bland, an urban style R&B artist, and in 1966 King's lyric guitar work was discovered by white rock fans. He inspired a generation of blues-rock guitarists, among them Eric Clapton and Jimi Hendrix.

In the mid-'50s Memphis and Sun Records produced a hybrid of blues, rock and roll, and country and western—rockabilly. Among its star performers were Carl Perkins, Jerry Lee Lewis, Johnny Cash, Charlie Rich, Roy Orbison, and, of course, Presley.

Carl Perkins recorded rockabilly's anthem, "Blue Suede Shoes", on the Sun label. Presley cut the song for RCA, and it made the national charts.

Jerry Lee Lewis, one of rockabilly's biggest stars, forsook his father's egg business to record with Sun. His first hit, "Whole Lot of Shakin'" showed the diverse appeal of rockabilly—it was big on the rhythm and blues, country and western, and pop charts. Jerry Lee Lewis plays in an unrehearsed style what he calls the "devil's music". The scandal when he married his 13 year old cousin, Myra Brown, in 1958, decimated his popular appeal. Today he primarily records country and western music. In 1980 Lewis was the first entry in the new Memphis Music Hall of Fame.

Another first generation Sun star, Roy Orbison, had a big rock hit, "Ooby Dooby". Orbison, however, was not comfortable with the black blues influence and shifted to Nashville and pop country songs.

Other early Sun artists, Johnny Cash and Charlie Rich, also made the shift from Memphis' blues oriented rock to Nashville's country and western. One of Johnny Cash's first big performances was in 1955, as an extra on the bill with Elvis at the Overton Park Shell. Cash went to Nashville and became a superstar of country music. Charlie Rich, a noted jazz pianist, still lives in Memphis, but records country and western music in Nashville.

SOUL—THE '60S

Soul music was born of rhythm and blues and gospel in the 1960s. One of the first nationally known soul singers was Rufus Thomas, an ex-minstrel show hoofer and Memphis disc jockey. Thomas and his daughter Carla cut a record in 1960 for Satellite, a fledgling Memphis recording company. In 1961, Satellite became Stax, and Atlantic records began distributing and promoting its recordings of Thomas, Booker T & the MGs, Sam and Dave, and other local artists. Stax became one of the hottest soul labels in the country. A new lazy-beat sound was coming out of the haphazard recording sessions here, at Hi, and at Chip Moman's American Recording Studios.

One of Stax's bigget stars literally walked in off the street. In 1962 a young man from Macon, Ga. named Otis Redding drove a friend, Johnny Jenkins, to Memphis to record for Stax. The session ended early, and Redding asked to use the left-over time to make a recording. He cut "These Arms of Mine" which soared to the top of the national pop charts. Redding's sensational career was cut short; in 1967 he and members of his band, the Bar-Kays, were killed in an airplane crash.

In 1965 Atlantic's Jerry Wexler brought R&B singer Wilson Pickett to the Stax studios to learn the hard-edged soul sound. Pickett and guitarist Steve Cropper sat down and wrote "In the Midnight Hour", one of the biggest soul hits of all times.

Two great albums cut during this period are Stax-Volt's 1966 "The Otis Redding Dictionary of Soul" and Carla and Rufus Thomas' "King and Queen". A Stax-Volt review toured Europe to tumultuous acclaim, but nationally soul was relegated primarily to the South and the black circuit. In 1967 Aretha Franklin put soul on the pop charts.

UNREST IN THE '70S

The Stax-Atlantic alliance was brief. After a disagreement, Stax barred Atlantic artists from recording at its studio. This was good news for Fame Studio in Muscle Shoals, Ala. where Atlantic artists began recording. Atlantic stopped distributing Stax nationally. Redding and the Bar-Kays died. Sam and Dave split. Isaac Hayes, former songwriter and keyboard player at Stax, had become known as the "black Moses". He added strings to rock in "Hot Buttered Soul", a harbinger of the '70s. The Memphis soul sound gave way to psychedelic rock emanating from California and New York.

Al Green, soul's heir apparent, was the decade's most successful local recording star. Working with producer Willie Mitchell at Cream-Hi Records (office at 1320 S. Lauderdale), he had gold singles and albums. Green combined the cool Detroit with the hotter Memphis sound on hits like "Tired of Being Alone", "Call Me", and "Take Me to the River". He retired from the music scene for two years, and then in 1980 returned with his first all-gospel album, "The Lord Will Make a Way".

In 1980 Willie Mitchell brought his trumpet out of retirement and with Michael Toles cut his first album in ten years at Bearsville Records.

Ardent Recording Inc. (studio at 2000 Madison) is probably the busiest independent studio in town today. They have the city's largest facility and only 48 track studio. The Bar-Kays, Larry Raspberry, Keith Sykes, Mud Boy and the Neutrons, ZZ Top, Shaun Cassidy, Ann Peebles, and Dorothy Moore have all worked here.

Sam Phillips Recording Service Inc. (studio at 630 Madison) is directed by Knox Phillips, Sam's son. John Prine and the Amazing Rhythm Aces record here.

Estelle Axton and Jim Stewart, founders of Satellite/Stax, are both still active. Axton's label, Fretone (production company at 3114 Radford Rd.) had a 4-million worldwide hit with "Disco Duck", a novelty record by ex-Memphis disc jockey Rick Dees. Two other Stax Veterans, Homer Banks and Chuck Brooks, have moved their production company back to Memphis from the West Coast.

Charly McClain, Shiloh, and Ricky Nelson have recorded at Lyn-Lou Music Inc. (1518 Chelsea). American Sound Studios of Memphis* (827

Thomas) is another active independent. Others are listed under Recording Service - Sound & Video in the yellow pages of the phone book.

Memphis State University's High Water Recording Co. has cut four releases designed to preserve regional music. They are funded by a grant from the National Endowment for the Arts.

Many well known musicians hail from Memphis. Duck Dunn and Steve Cropper are members of the Blues Brothers Band. Alberta Hunter carries on the blues/jazz tradition in New York nightclubs. Such blues artists as Booker T. Laury, Jessie Mae Hemphill, and R. L. Burnside tour internationally.

Peter Chatman, internationally known as Memphis Slim, was born in Memphis in 1915. He grew up in Memphis, but moved to Chicago and in 1956 to Paris. In 1959 he performed in N.Y.C.'s Carnegie Hall and in the Newport Folk Festival. Today a super star, he lives in Paris and performs around the world. In 1977 the U.S. Congress passed a resolution giving him the honorary title U.S. Ambassador-at-Large of Good Will.

No description of Memphis musicians and their impact would be complete without the Blackwood Brothers. This traditional male gospel group has recorded 118 albums and sung in 35 countries. Their headquarters is at 3935 Summer Ave.

W. B. Tanner Co. Inc. (2714 Union Ave. Extended and 711 Poplar) is the world's largest producer of radio jingles. Rita Coolidge, now a progressive-country star, used to sing jingles here.

CURRENT INFORMATION AND SOURCES

For current information on the local music scene see Joe Mulherin's monthly articles in "Memphis Magazine", Walter Dawson's articles in the "Commercial Appeal", and the "Memphis Concert Calendar" put out by radio Rock 103 and available free at all Ticket Hub locations (725-HUBB).

The Center for Southern Folklore produces valuable information on Southern folk traditions. This non-profit organization is at 1216 Peabody Ave., P.O. Box 4081-E, 38014 (726-4205). Their award-winning films, records, and books are available for sale or rent. The Memphis/Shelby County Public Library and Information Center* has a collection of their work; rental fees here are cheaper.

One way to enjoy Memphis' musical heritage is to listen to "Beale Street Saturday Night", produced by Jim Dickinson for the Memphis Development Foundation. The blues album is on sale for $7.50 at the Orpheum* or can be borrowed from the main branch library's music department.

Another excellent record is "Tennessee: The Folk Heritage, Volume 1: The Delta" produced by Harry E. Godwin for the Tn. Folklore Society and the Tn. Arts Commission. Godwin (685-0722) also will arrange traditional jazz and blues programs.

At Memphis State University, regular classes on Memphis and regional music are offered by Professors David Evans, John Bakke, and Jackson Baker. In addition, a day-long free open to the public Elvis/Memphis music seminar is offered each Aug. 16th on the campus.

The museum on Mud Island* promises Memphis music exhibits.

For more information about Memphis music read:

Kay Myracle's 1975 thesis at MSU, "Music in Memphis 1880-1900",

W. C. Handy's autobiography, *Father of the Blues,*

George Lee's *Beale Street, Where the Blues Began,*

Bert Olsson's *Memphis Blues,*

the *Rolling Stone Illustrated History of Rock and Roll,*

Collin Escott and Martin Hawkins' *Catalyst: A Sun Record History,*

Jerry Hopkins' *Elvis: A Biography,*

and in "Memphis Magazine": Jackson Baker's "Elvis: End of an Era", Robert Palmer's "Sam Phillips: The Sun King", and Joe Mulherin's "Ear to the Ground".

SITES

AMERICAN SOUND STUDIOS
827 Thomas at Chelsea. 525-0540.

Tours: *10am-4pm daily, May-Sept; rest of year, by appointment.*
Cost: *$2/person. Prearranged group discounts possible.*
MATA: *#11 (ex Sat & Sun).*
Other: *Souvenirs and records for sale.*
E&H: *Wheelchair accessible.*

A currently active studio as well as an historic treat, American is where Elvis made his return to the U.S. recording industry. In 1969 he cut six gold singles, among them "Kentucky Rain" and "The Bear is Moving On", and two albums, "Elvis in Memphis" and "Elvis Back in Memphis", here. During the '60s and early '70s Chips Moman owned the studio and recorded such other stars as Neil Diamond, Petula Clark, B. J. Thomas, Paul Revere and the Raiders, Aretha Franklin, and Dionne Warwick. He produced hits like "You've Lost that Lovin' Feeling", "I Just Can't Help Believin'", "Son of a Preacher Man", "Hey Jude", and in one year had 150 records on the charts.

In 1972 Moman sold the studio and moved his rhythm section first to Atlanta, then later to Nashville and present success. In 1977 Bill Glore reopened the independent studio and today records such local artists as Hatchie River Band and Charlie Feathers.

DELTA BLUES MUSEUM*.

ELVIS PRESLEY MUSEUM
3350 Elvis Presley Blvd. 396-6200.

Hours: *9am-9pm daily.*
Tours: *Just wander on your own.*
Cost: *Adults/$3, children/$1.*
MATA: *#43 (ex Sun).*
E&H: *Wheelchair accessible.*

Lots of Elvis memorabilia—jewelry, cars, guns, clothing. furniture....

GRACELAND
3764 Elvis Presley Blvd. (Previously Bellevue, the street was renamed for Elvis in 1971.) For information phone 345-0551.

Hours: *9am-4pm Tu-Sun, weather permitting. Closed M.*
Tours: *None.*
Cost: *Free.*
MATA: *#43 (ex Sun), from downtown, catch it going south on 2nd Str.*
Other: *1) House is not open to the public—only the Presley gravesite. 2) Many souvenir shops in the area.*
E&H: *Wheelchair accessible.*

People from all over the world flock to Graceland to pay their respects to Memphis' most famous musical son, Elvis Presley*.

Graceland was built about 1940. The land, once owned by S. N. Ford and W. F. Taylor, was sold to the Toof family in the mid-1800s. Graceland was named for Grace Toof, whose family built a cottage-home here. Mrs. Toof's husband's niece, Grace Moore, built the present 20-room house. Elvis Presley bought the home in 1957.

The Presley gravesite, Meditation Gardens, has monuments to Gladys Smith Presley, Elvis' mother (1912-1958), to Vernon Elvis Presley, Elvis' father (1916-1979), and to Elvis (1935-1977).

ELVIS PRESLEY BIRTHPLACE*.

SUN RECORDING STUDIO
706 Union. 345-8687.

Hours: *9am-5pm daily, May-Sept. Groups by appointment other months.*
Tours: *Gray Line Tour Co. leases the building and gives brief tours of the ex-studio.*
Cost: *$2 ($1.50 as part of a Gray Line bus tour).*
Lunch: *Try Ronnie Grisanti & Sons Restaurant next door at 710 Union. Many Sun business deals were made over a cup of coffee here when it was Taylor's Restaurant. See Italian restaurants.*
MATA: *#34 (ex Sat & Sun), 56.*

Other: *Records, tapes, and T-shirts sold here.*
E&H: *Wheelchair accessible.*

Copies of some of Sun's early records hang on the walls—notably Carl Perkins' "Blue Suede Shoes" and Jerry Lee Lewis' "Save the Last Dance for Me", "Whole Lot of Shakin' Going On", and "Sweet Little 16".

WDIA

2265 Central (earlier located at 2074 Union where the First Tennessee Bank Building now stands). 278-4550.

Tours: *By appointment. 9am M-W preferred. All ages but probably best for those 10+.*
Cost: *Free.*
MATA: *#50 (ex Sun).*
Other: *Station personnel will come to the classroom and give lectures on radio broadcasting.*
E&H: *Not equipped for wheelchairs.*

In the early days tapes by such great bluesmen as Bobby Blue Bland were cut here. Started in 1947 by two Memphis businessmen, John Pepper and Bert Ferguson, the station began broadcasting predominantly for black audiences Oct. 1948. It was the first black-operated radio station in the South.

DRIVE-BYS

Beale Street*.

Handy Park - on Beale, between 3rd and Hernando. Dedicated 1931 to W. C. Handy*, "father of the blues".

Handy's Home - 659 Jennette.

Handy's Publishing Office - 390 Beale.

Peewee's Place* - 317 Beale. Some claim W. C. Handy wrote "St. Louis Blues" here.

Hollywood Cemetery - 2012 Hernando Rd. Blues guitarist Furry Lewis was buried here in 1981. His performance in N.Y.C.'s Madison Square Gardens in the 1950s is credited with stimulating the revival of the blues. Lewis was the second black man honorarily named a Tennessee Colonel. (Lieutenant George W. Lee, the first Negro to be commissioned in the U.S. Army and author of *Beale Street, Where the Blues Began*, was the first.) Sun Smith, trumpeter for the Beale Street Originals, is also buried

here. During the 1920s and '30s he was a regular in Henry's Pool Room on Beale Str. Also buried in the cemetery is Tom Lee for whom Tom Lee Park* is named.

New Park Cemetery - 4536 Horn Lake Rd. Thomas L. Pinkston, Memphis blues musician, was buried here in 1980. His Thomas Pinkston Trio played for years at the old Tennessee Club*. Pinkston narrated the album "Beale Street Saturday Night".

Elvis' Memphis Homes (Prior to Graceland*):
Lauderdale Court Housing Project - 32 Exchange, just east of 3rd. The window to the right of the door is in what was the Presley's apartment. The family moved when Elvis' mother got a job as a nurse's aid at nearby St. Joseph's Hospital.
371 Carroll - boarding house, east off Danny Thomas.
1034 Audubon - Elvis lived here in 1957. Fans blocked the street trying to catch a glimpse; after 18 months, Elvis moved to Graceland in search of privacy.

L. C. Humes High School - fronts on Manassas just south of Jackson. Elvis attended high school here.

Crown Electric - 353 Poplar, now B&H Hardware. Elvis worked here as a truck driver.

Memphian - 51 S. Cooper. Elvis rented this theatre for private late-night movie showings.

Baptist Hospital - 899 Madison. One of the largest private hospitals in the U.S. Elvis was pronounced dead on arrival at the emergency entrance.

Lansky Men's Shop - 126 Beale. The story goes that Elvis bought on credit his first suit of clothes here for his high school graduation. Even as a star Elvis shopped here, sometimes buying $3000 worth of clothes at a time.

Elvis Memorial - Elvis Presley Blvd. across from Graceland. $2 entry fee. An eternal flame honoring Elvis was moved here from Elvis' Circle G Ranch on Goodman Rd. in Mississippi (just south of Memphis and north of Walls). Developers sold shares of a one acre plot on the ranch to Elvis fans for $10 apiece. The flame was ignited Aug. 16, 1979 but extinguished three months later. It was relighted at the current site summer 1981.

Elvis Statue - Elvis Presley Plaza, Beale between Main and 2nd. The 9½ foot bronze statue by Eric Parks was dedicated Aug. 1980. It was commissioned by the Memphis Development Foundation.

Stax Studios - College and McLemore Strs., just west of Bellevue; now boarded up.

Full Gospel Tabernacle - 787 Hale Rd., in the Whitehaven area. Soul/gospel singer Al Green* started this church in 1976 and preaches here.

First Assembly of God Church - 255 N. Highland. The Blackwood Brothers* worship here when they're in town.

Record Stores*..

Musical Equipment - See Strings and Things under miscellaneous shops*.

NIGHTSPOTS

The Tennessee legislature imposed prohibition in 1909, but Memphians protested and looked the other way. In 1916, Mayor Crump* was ostensibly forced to resign his office for not enforcing the law. Things tightened up periodically as public sentiment demanded, but, even in the severest days, President's Island* was a haven for bootleggers. There were always things to attract country boys to the city.

Prohibition's repeal in 1923 brought a proliferation of private clubs and brown bagging. The Plantation Inn in West Memphis and the Sharecropper in Memphis were the places to go for fantastic live music in the '40s, '50s and '60s.

Memphis approved a liquor-by-the-drink statute in 1969. The law required that bars serving whiskey be a certain size and operate full kitchens. As a result, many of today's best spots are also good restaurants.

WITH LIVE MUSIC

Music festivals and special-occasion performances are the best places to hear most regional and Memphis musicians. Two outstanding events are the annual Beale Street Music Festival every May and the Memphis Music Heritage Festival sponsored each Labor Day by Schlitz Brewing Co. Each summer, June-Aug, the Blues Foundation sponsors free blues in Handy Park 11am-2pm M-F, 2-6pm Sat & Sun.

Big name concerts are usually booked into the Orpheum Theatre at 197 S. Main (523-6188), the Cook Convention Center Auditorium at 255 N. Main (523-7645), the Coliseum in the Fairgrounds off Central and E. Parkway (274-7400), and the Peabody Hotel's Skyway at 149 Union (529-4000).

This section lists some of the city's best nightspots, but things change quickly. It's probably best to phone before you go, or check the listing in the Friday "Commercial Appeal" and "Memphis Press-Scimitar". Many of the hotels/motels in the area have live entertainment ranging from piano bars to big show bands. "Key Magazine" has a full listing of these. See also The Arts/Summertime Treats.

Antenna Club
1588 Madison. 725-9812. Everyone is doing the pogo here—it's Memphis' new wave bar. Go on fashion show night. Open: 9pm-2:30am W-Sat. Live new wave or rockabilly 10pm-2am W-Sat. Cover: W about $1/person, Th-Sat about $2/person. Beer or BYOB. No cards.

Bad Bob's Lounge
3126 Sandbrook (behind the Quality Inn on Brooks Rd. at I-55). 332-9559. It's hard to find the corrugated tin warehouse that houses this country bar/dance hall. Follow the signs and look for rows of pick-ups parked out front. Open 4pm-2am Sun-Th, 4pm-3am F&Sat. Live top 40 and country: 9pm-1:30am Sun-Th, 9pm-2:30am F&Sat. Cover after 7:30pm: F&Sat $3/person or $5/couple, Sun-Th ladies/free, men/$2. Happy hour: 4-7:30pm. Full bar. Burgers, chili, ribs. AE, DC, MC, Visa.

Blue's Alley
60 S. Front. 523-7144. Authentic Memphis blues plus ribs. An album, "Beale Street Blues — Alive and Well at Blues Alley, Memphis, Tennessee", was cut here and is on sale from the cashier. Open: 11am-1am M-Th, 11am-2am F&Sat, 6pm-2am Sun. Live blues: 6pm-closing nightly. $5 minimum after 6pm F&Sat. Happy hour: 11am-6pm M-Sat. Full bar. Barbecue sandwiches and ribs. AE, MC, Visa. Reservations until 8pm; recommended on F&Sat.

Bombay Bicycle Club. See American restaurants - jazz.

Brittenum's Corner
1300 Airways Blvd. 452-9118. Small neighborhood blues club. Hear the real thing live 8pm-midnight Sun. Cover, $2/person. Beer or BYOB. No cards.

Captain Bilbo's
263 Wagner. 526-1966. Big popular bar/restaurant. Super river view.

Open: 4:30pm-1am Sun-Th, 4:30pm-2am F&Sat. Live music: jazz 6-9pm M-Sat, rock 'n roll and '50s show groups 9pm-1am M-Sat, big band jazz 6-10pm Sun. No cover. Happy hour: 4:30-6pm M-F. Full bar. Seafood and steaks. AE, MC, Visa.

Classing Room

60 S. Front (above Blues Alley). 523-7144. A blues showcase bar owned by Blues Alley. Varied schedule. Open most summer weekends and for private parties. $5 minimum; occasional cover charge. Full bar. Barbecue. AE, MC, Visa. Reservations.

Club Paradise

645 E. Georgia. 774-4871. Memphis' answer to N.Y.'s Apollo and Detroit's Rooster Tail. Space for 3000 and lots of dancing. Nearly every big rhythm and blues performer has appeared here. You'll pass through a metal detector as you enter. "Sunbeam" Mitchell, who ran Club Handy in the old Mitchell Hotel on Beale Str, runs Club Paradise. Open: 10pm-4am W, F, & Sat. Live music: some nights; call for schedule. Cover: $1/W&F, $3/Sat. Special show admission, around $8. Food. Reservations for big shows.

Doebler's Dock

110 Wagner Place. 521-1300. Go hear Mary Jane Collins play the piano, everything from college pep songs to Broadway show tunes. Sing along if you like. (Starts 8:30pm Tu & W, 9:30pm F&Sat.) There are also waiter and waitress cabarets at 9&11pm F&Sat. Open 11am-1am M-F, noon-1am Sat. Closed Sun. Kitchen closes 8:30pm M-Th, 11pm F&Sat. No cover. Happy hour: 4-7pm M-F. Full bar. Catfish. AE, MC, Visa. Reservations recommended F&Sat.

Fantasia

1718 Madison. 725-6748. A place for conversation or listening to classical music. Open 11:30-2am Tu-Sat, 4pm-2am Sun. Live music: classical 8:30-10pm Tu-Sat, jazz 8-11:30pm Sun. No cover. Happy hour: 11:30am-7pm Tu-F. Full bar. Full dinner, sandwiches, or Vietnamese spring rolls. AE, DC, MC, Visa. No reservations.

The Goddaddy & Cat's Lounge

1285 Thomas. 525-5495. Odetta went to this club to hear "Memphis jazz" when she was in town. Open: 7am-4am daily. Honeymoon Garner and Fred Ford play live: 8:30am-midnight Sun. Beer or BYOB. No cards.

Huey's and Louie's. See Beer & Burger restaurants. - Jazz on Sundays.

J&J Lounge

1037 Mississippi Blvd. 775-9216. A neighborhood spot with live blues 10pm-3am F. Cover, $2. Beer or BYOB. No cards.

Jefferson Square Restaurant

79 Jefferson. 523-1897. The music makes this neighborhood beer and burger* spot a special place. On F & Sat one of Memphis' favorite blues guitar players, Syd Selvidge, is here. Open: 11am-3am M-Sat, 2pm-3am Sun. Live music: 9:30pm-1am Th-Sat. Cover: after 9:30pm Th-Sat, $1/person. Happy hour: 4:30-7pm & midnight-3am. Full bar. AE, DC, MC, Visa. Reservations taken for large parties.

The London Transport. See Beer & Burger restaurants - Keith Sykes plays rock 'n roll here.

The Music Hall

4069 Lamar. 794-9111. A showcase music hall. Open only when they have something scheduled which is most F&Sat nights and some weeknights. There are no standard hours; you'll have to call to find out what's going on and when. Cover charges range $2-$13.50. Beer or BYOB. No food. No cards. Tickets may be purchased through Ticket Hubs or at the door. Private parties possible.

No. 1 Beale. See American restaurants - mellow jazz.

Peabody Hotel Lobby

149 Union. 529-4000. Watch the ducks splash to classical and easy listening harp, harpsichord, or piano music in the lobby. 11am-11pm daily. Full bar. AE, DC, MC, Visa.

Plantation Roof. See Good Happy Hours.

Skyway

Peabody Hotel, 149 Union. 529-4000. Dress up and have a fling. The Art Deco Skyway first opened in 1939, and big bands like Paul Whiteman, Jan Garber, Les Brown, and Ted Weems played here. Their music was broadcast live by WREC/CBS from the Skyway. Only two other places in the U.S. broadcast big band music nationwide: the Roosevelt Hotel in New Orleans and Frank Dailey's Meadowbrook in N.J. Today well-recognized national and regional dance bands, musicians, and/or singers perform live on weekends in the rejuvenated Skyway. Schedules and rates vary. Full bar. Dinner. AE,DC,MC,Visa. Reservations. Private parties possible.

Solomon Alfred's

2144 Madison. 725-0684. Locals and out-of-towners, some big names, perform in the back room. Rock 'n roll M-Sat, jazz Sun. The front room, called the Filling Station, serves D. Open 3pm-midnight M-Th, 3pm-1am F&Sat, 3-10pm Sun. Live music: 10pm-midnight M-Th, 10pm-1am

F&Sat, 6-10pm Sun. Cover after 7pm: F&Sat $3-$5 range. Happy hour: 3-7pm daily. Full bar. Quiche, salad, specials. AE, MC, Visa. Reservations except F&Sat.

Vapors
1743 E. Brooks. 345-1761. They must be doing something right. This supper club has been here for years with the same band playing a little bit of everything and a steady bunch of regulars. Open: 2pm-1am M-Th, 2pm-2am F&Sat, closed Sun. Live music: 3:30-7:30pm & 8pm-1am M-Sat. Cover after 7pm M-Sat (and they collect from those who entered earlier): $2.50/person, $5/couple, single women/free. Happy hour: 2-7pm M-Sat. Full bar. Full menu. AE, CB, DC, MC, Visa. Reservations recommended for dinner time.

Varsity Inn. See Beer & Burger restaurants.

Western Steakhouse and Lounge. See American restaurants - good country bands.

NON-COMMERCIAL COUNTRY MUSIC SPOTS
There are several non-commercial inexpensive family spots where you can hear country music on the weekends. Alcoholic beverages prohibited. The musicians make the circuit, and shows usually run from 8pm to between 10:30pm and 1am.

Arkansas Jubilee—Marion Shopping Center in Marion, Ark. 8pm Sat. Bluegrass. Adults/$2, children 6-12/50¢, under 6/free.

Bluegrass Shack— 4325 Pleasant Ridge Rd. in Lucy. 8pm F. Closed during summer. Bluegrass. Donations.

Country Music Showcase—Strand Theatre, 7979 Wilkinsville in Millington* Gospel 8pm F; country 8pm Sat.

Lucy Opry—Kiwanis Building, just off old Raleigh-Millington Rd. in Raleigh. 8pm F. Bluegrass. Donations.

Mid-South Jubilee—Kiwanis Building, just off old Raleigh-Millington Rd. in Raleigh. 8pm Sat. Country. Admission/$2.

Quito Community Center—Center, five miles northwest of Millington on Quito-Drummonds Rd. 8-11pm Sat. Country. Adults/$1.50, children under 12/free.

Saturday Night Country—Auditorium, Auburndale School, 2100 Germantown Rd. 8-11pm Sat. Country. Adults/$2, children under 12/free.

Saturday Night Jamboree—Jaycee's Civic Center, 1583 Brookhaven in Southaven, Miss. 8-11:30pm Sat. Country. Adults/$1.50, children/50¢.

WITHOUT LIVE MUSIC

Some of our favorites.

Alex's Tavern
1445 Jackson. 278-9086. An unpretentious neighborhood bar. Open: 8am-3am daily. Beer only. Hamburgers and sandwiches. No cards.

Bennigan's Tavern. See Beer & Burger restaurants.

Circle Cafe. See Beer & Burger restaurants.

Cockeyed Camel. See Beer & Burger restaurants.

Dooley's
5100 Poplar in Clark Tower (west side). 761-0771. Nostalgia is "in". Popular singles spot to listen to "oldies". M night there are free hot dogs and football games, Tu/50¢ beer, and W/50¢ drinks for women. Open: 5pm-2am M-Sat, 8pm-2am Sun. Cover: $1 F&Sat. Happy hour: 5-8pm M-Sat. Full bar. Sandwiches. AE, DC, MC, Visa. No reservations.

élan
5100 Poplar in Clark Tower (west side). 761-0990. Branches in Atlanta, Dallas, Houston, Philadelphia, and Washington, D.C., but in Memphis élan is *not* a private club. It's a sophisticated singles bar. Open: 11:30am-2am M-F, 7pm-2:30am Sat. Closed Sun. Taped disco. Cover for non-cardholders: $2 F&Sat. Happy hour: 5-8pm M-F, complimentary hors d'oeuvres. L 11:30am-2pm M-F, D 7-11pm M-Sat. Cafe menu 'til midnight M-Th, 'til 1 am F&Sat. Full bar. AE, DC, MC, Visa.

T.G.I. Friday's. See Beer & Burger restaurants.

The Half Shell. See Beer & Burger restaurants.

Murphy's Oyster Bar
1589 Madison. 725-4946. A neighborhood pinball/juke joint. Open: 3pm-2am M-F, noon-2am Sat & Sun. Happy hour: 4-5:30pm M-F, noon-5pm Sat & Sun. Beer only. Burgers, oysters ($3.25/doz.) No cards.

The Outlaw
4730 Poplar. 761-2880. Urban-western at its best. By 9:30 or 10pm people are lined up waiting to get in. If you don't come with a hat and want to get in the spirit, you can buy one at the door. Prices seem a bit steep; they're probably paying off their good interior designer. Open: 4pm-3am M-F, 7pm-3am Sat & Sun. A dj plays progressive country and disco. Cover: 7pm-2am F&Sat/$2. Happy hour: 4-7pm M-F; free snacks. Full bar. Buffalo stew, chili, tamales, and barbecue plus an early morning breakfast. AE, MC, Visa. No reservations.

P&H Cafe
1528 Madison. 274-5522. It's a neighborhood watering hole known affectionately as a home for the city's "poor & hungry" artists. Open: 11am-3am M-F, 4pm-3am Sat. Closed Sun. Beer or BYOB. Daily plate lunches, chili, barbecue, burgers. (Kitchen 'til 1am). No cards.

Poor Red's
851 Loeb (just off Park, near Getwell). 323-2175. A friendly neighborhood bar. Baseball and softball teams often come here for a drink after the game, so it can be noisy. Open: 11am-3am M-Sat, noon-3am Sun. Happy hour: 5-6:30pm M-F. Full bar. Burgers, sandwiches, spaghetti, chili. MC, Visa.

Rendezvous. See Barbecue restaurants.

2001
1331 Union (on top of Mid-City Building). 276-2001. You might see successful Memphis politicos at this disco. Open: 7pm-2:30am Sat-Th, 5pm-2:30am F. Tapes only. Cover: Sun-Th/$2, F&Sat/$4. Happy hour: 5-8pm F. Full bar. Short order, breakfast. MC, Visa. Reservations for 10+.

Zinnie's. See Beer & Burger restaurants.

GOOD HAPPY HOURS

Bennigan's—5336 Poplar. 685-2088. 11am-7pm M-F. 2 for 1. Popular spot among young professionals and singles.

Bombay Bicycle Club—Overton Square. 726-6055. 4-6:30pm M-F. $1 off drinks. An on-the-way home spot.

Captain Bilbo's—263 Wagner, 526-1966. 4-6:30pm M-F. 2 for 1. Super river view.

èlan—5100 Poplar. 761-0990. 5-8pm M-F. ½ price drinks. Shrimp and oyster buffet.

Juleps—Holiday Inn-Rivermont lobby. 525-0121. 4-7pm M-F. Live mellow guitar. Try a strawberry or mint julep.

The Loft—2514 Mt. Moriah. 794-1480. 4-7pm M-F. 2 for 1. Free snacks, oysters 6/$1. Live mellow jazz Tu-Sat.

No. 1 Beale—1 Beale. 525-1116. 4-6:30pm M-F. 3 for 1.

The Pier—100 Wagner Pl. 526-7381. 4-6pm M-F. 2 for 1. Sit out front and watch the river flow by—fabulous sunsets.

Plantation Roof—Peabody Hotel, 149 Union. 529-4000. 5:30-7pm daily *warm weather only*. Live jazz outdoors on top. Marvelous sunsets. $1 cover.

Vapors—1743 E. Brooks. 345-1761. 2-7pm M-Sat. 2 for 1. Live dance music 3:30-7:30pm.

Colleges & Universities

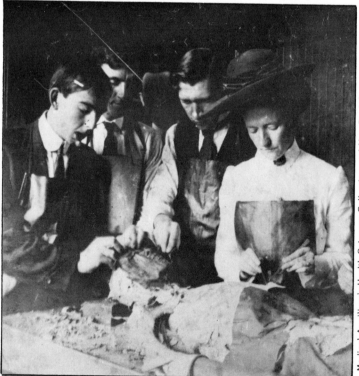

Anatomy class, University of Tennessee, College of Medicine. The lady in the hat is Sara Conyers York Murray, M.D., the school's first female graduate. She was in the class of 1913.

The arts*, sports*, and continuing education programs at the city's colleges and universities contribute to the mix that makes city life appealing.

In addition to general higher academic schools there are six religious colleges, a school for the deaf, occupational adult training schools, and business schools. For a complete listing look in the yellow pages under Schools—Universities & Colleges (Academic).

CHRISTIAN BROTHERS COLLEGE
650 E. Parkway S. 278-0100.

Hours: Day and night classes daily.
Lunch: Cafeteria, B 7:30-8:30am, L 11:30am-1pm, D 5:30-6:30pm. Also snack bar.
MATA: Showboat Bus or #50 (ex Sun) to corner Parkway & Central, walk north about one block to main section of campus.

A private undergraduate college offering four year degree programs in business, engineering, liberal arts, and science, the school has about 1,000 students, one third of whom are women.

CBC was established in 1871 at 612 Adams. In 1939 it moved to its present location. The college is run by the Christian Brothers, a Catholic male religious community founded to educate the poor.

LE-MOYNE - OWEN COLLEGE
807 Walker Ave. 38126. 774-9090.

Hours: 9am-4pm daily.
Lunch: Dining hall in the Student Center.
MATA: #4.

LeMoyne-Owen, formed by the 1968 merger of LeMoyne College and Owen College, is a predominantly black co-educational private college offering BA and BS degrees.

LeMoyne College was started at Camp Shiloh in 1862 by the American Missionary Assn. as an elementary school for blacks. The school moved to Memphis in 1863 and became known as Lincoln School in 1866. During the race riots of 1866, after federal troops left Memphis, Lincoln Chapel was burned. It was rebuilt and in 1867 reopened with about 150 students. In 1871 the school's name was changed to LeMoyne Normal and Commercial School in honor of a benefactor, Dr. Francis Julius Le-Moyne. It began educating black teachers. In 1901 the curriculum was broadened to include high school. The school moved to its present site in 1914, became a junior college in 1924, and in 1934 became a four year school known as LeMoyne College.

Owen College began in 1946 as a junior college founded by the Tennessee Baptist Missionary and Educational Convention. The first class was graduated in 1956, and the school became accredited in 1958.

LeMoyne-Owen is primarily a commuter college. There are no dormitories on the 15-acre campus. The campus' oldest structure, Steele Hall (NRHP) at 807 Walker, was built in 1914 and from then until 1923 served as the city's only black high school.

MEMPHIS ACADEMY OF ARTS
Overton Park. 726-4085.

Hours:	*Gallery open 9am-5pm M-F, 9am-noon Sat. Free.*
Lunch:	*Snackbar.*
MATA:	*Showboat Bus or #5, 55 (ex Sun), 3 (ex Sat & Sun), then walk about three blocks through the park.*
Other:	*1) Student, faculty, and visiting artist shows throughout the year. 2) Annual Christmas bazaar and summer sale. 3) Day and night adult community education classes. 4) Sat. and summer classes for children.*
E&H:	*Wheelchair accessible, enter through ground floor, east entrance (under main steps).*

A private, non-profit institution, the academy offers a four year course leading to a Bachelor of Fine Arts degree. Major areas of study include painting, sculpture, design, crafts, advertising, printmaking, and photography.

The academy was established in 1936 and was first located on Adams in the Fontaine* and Lee-Mallory* homes. It moved to its present location in 1964. Original plans were for the construction of a cultural center to include the art school and facilities for the visual and performing arts. In 1955 Roy Harrover's architectural firm won the design competition, and the first stage of the art academy was begun. The second stage was completed in 1967. Additional plans for a cultural center in the park have been abandoned.

MEMPHIS STATE UNIVERSITY (MSU)
Information Office at Central & Patterson, 38152. 454-2040 or 454-2041; recorded calendar of events & announcements, 24 hours daily/454-2079.

Hours:	*Day and night classes daily year-round.*
Lunch:	*Three cafeterias on campus.*
MATA:	*#50 (ex Sun).*
Other:	*1) Continuing education courses for Memphians who are neither full nor part-time students at the university. These include special courses like diaper gymnastics and water babies for children. For information phone 454-2381. 2) The athletic department and the performing and visual arts departments offer many events and programs to the community. 3) Occasional lectures, open to the public. 4) For William Blake scholars—a col-*

lection of the poet/artist's works, books by his contemporaries, and
criticism in The Center for the Study of William Blake, Rm. 335, Patterson
Hall; open 9am-noon M, W, F, 1-3pm Tu & Th. Check with Kay or Roger
Easson at 454-2651 for more information. 5) Guest rooms, meals, and
meeting space available in Richardson Towers for conferences,
workshops, or seminars. Contact 454-2021 for information and help in
designing your program.

E&H: 1) Most of the campus is wheelchair accessible. Pick up a free brochure on
campus wheelchair routes at the Information Center. 2) Anyone over 60
can take any non-credit course free of charge on a space available basis.

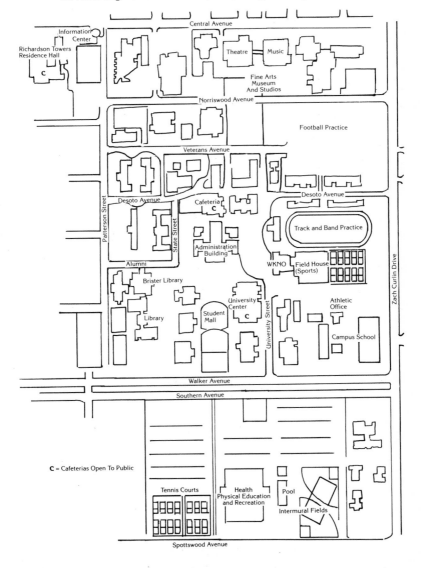

First known as West Tennessee Normal School, Memphis State University has grown rapidly. Its first building went up in 1912. The school became a university in 1957 and now occupies 1000 acres and over 100 buildings at three sites. About 20,000 students attend MSU.

The university is composed of six undergraduate colleges: the College of Arts and Sciences, the College of Business Administration, the College of Communication and Fine Arts, the College of Education, the Herff College of Engineering, and the University College. MSU offers advanced degrees through its Graduate School and its School of Law.

SHELBY STATE COMMUNITY COLLEGE
P.O. Box 4568, 38104. 528-6700, 528-6888 recorded calendar of events.

Hours: Day and night classes M-F.
Lunch: Cafeterias on campuses.
MATA: Call 523-2521 for information on how to reach the various campuses.

Shelby State Community College, opened in 1972, has an enrollment of abut 5,000. The college is part of the State University and Community College System of Tennessee and offers academic courses leading to certificates and associate degrees. The open admission policy of this urban oriented college encourages part time and continuing education students.

The coeducational college offers classes at more than 50 sites including shopping malls. For information on what's offered near you phone 382-0500. Major campuses are:

Mid-Town Campus	737 Union	528-6700
Gragg Campus	3772 Jackson	382-0500
Allied Health Annex	889 Linden	528-6825
Frayser Heights Center	2450 Frayser Blvd.	357-5520
Millington Center	Naval Air Station	872-8115
Neshoba-Germantown Center	7772 Old Poplar Pike	754-2528
Southeast Center	2969 South Mendenhall	363-3241
Whitehaven Center	4184 Graceland	332-8436

SOUTHERN COLLEGE OF OPTOMETRY
1245 Madison. 725-0180.

Hours: 9am-5pm M-F.
Tours: May be arranged. Phone the Dean of Students' office.
MATA: Showboat Bus.
Other: A community clinic, open 9:45am-4:30pm M-F, is on the first level of the building. Make appointments. Eye examination/$15. The dispensary for eyeglasses is across the street.
E&H: Wheelchair accessible.

Founded in 1932, the college moved to its present location in 1954 and into its present building in 1970. It is an independent coeducation four year professional school offering OD and BS degrees.

SOUTHWESTERN AT MEMPHIS
2000 N. Parkway. 274-1800.

Hours:	*9am-5pm, M-F.*
Lunch:	*Dining room and grill open to visitors.*
MATA:	*Showboat Bus or #53 (ex Sun).*
Other:	*1) Continuing education courses and seminars are offered throughout the year. 2) Lectures, music programs, plays, films, art shows, and sports events open to the public. The annual lecture series named "Dilemma" is held each March. Famous innovators and thinkers analyze a particular facet of our society.*

Southwestern is a four year private coeducational liberal arts college noted for academic excellence. The school has about 1,000 students, offers BA, BS, and BM degrees, and is affiliated with the Presbyterian Church.

Southwestern began in Clarksville, Tn. in 1848 as Montgomery Masonic College. In 1855 the name was changed to Stewart College and later to Southwestern Presbyterian University. In 1925 the college moved to Memphis.

Twelve of the campus' buildings, built since 1925 in the Collegiate Gothic style, are in the National Register of Historic Places. Of particular note is Halliburton Memorial Tower honoring Richard Halliburton, a 20thc., Memphian, adventurer, author, and world traveler. Halliburton crossed the Alps by elephant, swam the Hellespont, and circumnavigated the earth in a small biplane. He disappeared while trying to cross the Pacific on a Chinese junk in 1939.

STATE TECHNICAL INSTITUTE
5909 Shelby Oaks Drive. 388-4575.

Hours:	*Day and night classes. Office hours, 8am-4:30pm M-F.*
Lunch:	*Cafeteria.*
MATA:	*#54 (ex Sun).*
E&H:	*Wheelchair accessible.*

This coeducational state supported school offers a two year program leading to an associate degree in engineering, science, applied science, or computer technology for full and part-time students.

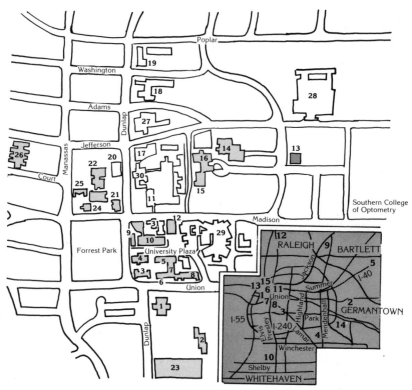

MEDICAL CENTER

(29) Baptist Memorial Hospital • (16) Bowld Hospital • (31) Campbell Clinic • (26) Child Development Center • (27) City of Memphis Hospital • (14) Coleman College of Medicine Building • (6) Crowe Pharmacy Building • (4) Dental Faculty Building • (15) Dobbs Medical Research Institute • (13) Doctors Office Building • (1) Dunn Dental Clinical Building • (9) Feurt Building • (30) Gailor Clinic • (25) Goodman House • (10) Humphreys General Education Building • (3) Hyman Administration Building • (18) Le Bonheur Children's Medical Center • (20) Les Passes Rehabilitation Center • (12) Library-Nursing Building (Proposed) • (19) Memphis Mental Health Institute • (7) Mooney Memorial Library • (8) Nash Chemistry-Physiology Building • (17) Newborn Center • (11) Pathology Building • (2) Physical Plant Purchasing Building • (22) Randolph Student-Alumni Center • (24) Randolph Student Dormitory • (23) UT Doctors Field • (13), (15), (16), (21) UT Medical Center • (21) Van Vleet Memorial Cancer Center • (28) Veterans Administration Medical Center • (5) Wittenborg Anatomy Building.

☐ = facilities which are primarily owned and operated by The University of Tennessee Center for the Health Sciences.

MEMPHIS AREA HOSPITALS

(1) Baptist Hospital • (2) Baptist Hospital East • (3) Crippled Children's Hospital • (4) Eastwood Hospital • (5) Lakeside Hospital • (6) Memphis Eye and Ear Hospital • (7) Memphis Medical Center (see medical center map) • (8) Methodist Hospital • (9) Methodist Hospital North • (10) Methodist Hospital South • (11) Mid-South Hospital • (12) Naval Regional Medical Center/ Millington • (13) St. Joseph Hospital • (14) St. Francis Hospital • (15) St. Jude Children's Research Hospital

UNIVERSITY OF TENNESSEE CENTER FOR HEALTH SCIENCES (UTCHS)
800 Madison. 528-5500.

Tours: May be arranged for high school students and those with a specialized interest in the health sciences. Phone 528-5544.

Lunch: Cafeteria in the Student Alumni Center, just north of Forrest Park, open to visitors.

MATA: Showboat or Hustle Bus (ex Sat & Sun).
Other: Special mini-courses offered to the public in subjects ranging from guitar,
         stained glass, disco, and scuba to philosophy and religion.

The University of Tennessee Center for the Health Sciences is one of
five major campuses of the University of Tennessee and is the state's
primary medical school. It has about 2,000 students enrolled in the colleges of Medicine, Dentistry, Pharmacy, Nursing, Basic Medical Sciences,
Community and Allied Health Professions, and the Graduate School of
Medical Sciences.

The first two medical schools in Tennessee, Memphis Medical College
and Botanico-Medical College, were both located in Memphis. They were
chartered by the state in 1846 and were based on different theories of
practice. Botanico-Medical College closed in 1861 at the beginning of
the Civil War; Memphis Medical College, the precursor of today's
UTCHS, had a more sporadic early period. It operated from 1846 to
1849, was reorganized and operated from 1852 until 1861. After the
Civil War, the college reopened in 1867. It closed in 1872, and until 1880
Memphis was without a medical school. Memphis Medical College's suc-
cessor, the Memphis Hospital Medical College, was organized in 1877
but, because of the yellow fever epidemics, it did not open until 1880. In
1906 another medical school, the College of Physicians and Surgeons,
opened. Then in 1911 the University of Tennessee College of Medicine
moved to Memphis and merged with the College of Physicians and
Surgeons. In 1913 Memphis Hospital Medical College joined the UT
facility, adding its property to the new institution. The final merger took
place in 1914 when the Medical Department of Lincoln Memorial University joined the UT College of Medicine.

The 45.2 acre UTCHS campus, located just east of downtown, is an in-
tegral part of Memphis' Medical Center, a six square block area of 14
hospitals and related buildings between Poplar and Union, Manassas and
Pauline.

Memphis Hospital, the city's first institution for the sick, was chartered
in 1829 by the Tennessee Legislature. Although there have been several
changes of name and location, the hospital operates today as City of
Memphis Hospital. From 1829 to 1836 the hospital provided care for
rivermen and sick travelers in a small wooden structure on Front Street.
By 1841 a larger brick building was completed on the ten acre tract that
is now Forrest Park. At the beginning of the Civil War, the State of Tennessee used this facility for military purposes. When Memphis was taken
over by federal forces, the hospital was enlarged and used as a smallpox-
contagious disease facility. A much needed new hospital, known as
Memphis General Hospital, was built in 1898 on Madison just east of
Dunlap. This building was torn down in 1936 and replaced by the John
Gaston Hospital, named in honor of a French immigrant whose widow's
bequest helped finance construction of the modern hospital. Gaston had

become famous and wealthy as proprietor of the Gaston Hotel and Restaurant, 33-35 Court Ave. By 1970 John Gaston Hospital had merged with the William Bowld, the E. H. Crump, the Frank Tobey, and the Gailor Psychiatric hospitals to form the City of Memphis Hospital. The city hospital has been under the control of the University of Tennessee since 1911 and has been managed by Methodist Hospital since 1981.

By the 1880s such private infirmaries and hospitals as Lucy Brinkley Hospital for Women were opening. One of the oldest private institutions, St. Joseph's Hospital, was founded in 1889 and staffed by the Poor Sisters of St. Francis. Two of Memphis' most prestigious and largest private hospitals, Baptist Memorial and Methodist, opened in 1912 and 1918 respectively. Campbell Clinic, an internationally recognized center for orthopedic surgery, opened in 1921. Its founder, Dr. Willis C. Campbell, also helped establish the Crippled Children's Hospital and the Hospital for Crippled Adults. Le Bonheur Children's Hospital*, founded by a women's philanthropic organization, Le Bonheur Club, opened in 1952 and has pioneered in pediatric hospital care. In 1962 entertainer Danny Thomas helped found the internationally recognized St. Jude Childrens Research Hospital* to conduct advanced clinical research on catastrophic childhood diseases.

Memphis can claim several medical firsts: The American Board of Ophthalmology, one of the early specialty groups, was organized here. Dr. Willis Campbell, who helped to establish the UT Department of Orthopedic Surgery, was the first elected president of the American Academy of Orthopedic Surgeons. Dr. L. W. Diggs, whose blood studies, especially in sickel cell anemia, are famous, started the South's first blood bank at John Gaston. UTCHS has pioneered methods of diagnosing and preventing glaucoma and was one of the first medical centers to use the Pap Smear in the detection of cervical cancer. The College of Dentistry is the Mid-South's oldest and one of the nation's largest dental schools.

For more information on the history of medicine in Memphis see "Early Medical History of Memphis 1819-1861", by Dr. S. R. Bruesch, *West Tennessee Historical Society Papers* (1948) and *History of Medicine in Memphis* edited by Drs. Marcus Stewart and William Black with Mildred Hicks. The Memphis/Shelby County Medical Society Auxiliary and the Health Sciences Museum Foundation are developing an exhibit on local medical history for the Memphis Pink Palace Museum*.

For a listing of hospitals, their phone numbers and addresses, see the yellow pages under Hospitals and the white pages under University of Tennessee Center for Health Sciences.

Science,
Nature,
& Amusement

The zoo's beginning—Natch the bear staked in Overton Park. Photograph taken about 1904.

SIGHTS

CARTWRIGHT NURSERY
Collierville. 853-2352.

Hours: *7:30am-4pm M-F summer and early fall.*
Tours: *Only for college and school groups with a special interest in horticulture. Tour involves both walking and riding; groups must provide own transportation. Call to arrange.*

Cartwright is one of the largest tree nurseries in the world. You'll see both their greenhouse and field operations.

CRAIGMONT PLANETARIUM
3333 Covington Pike 38128 (in Raleigh's Craigmont High School). 386-7820.

Hours: *Public shows, 1pm & 7:30pm Th, 1pm Tu, June-Aug; 7:30pm Th, 2:30pm Sun, Sept-May. Warning: late comers will not be seated. During the school year group programs may be arranged 7:30am-4:30pm M-F. Schedule well in advance.*
Cost: *Adults (18+)/$1, students (18 and under)/50¢. Pre-arranged group rates for 20+: 50¢/person, city & county school groups/free.*
Lunch: *The school's vocational food service program runs the Corner Tea Room—it's good. Reservations must be made in advance. Phone 388-1571.*
Other: *1) Advance study guides for kindergarten-6th grade levels. 2) Annual Christmas star program. 3) Vocational courses also operate a shop and FM radio station. Visit these too.*
E&H: *1) Wheelchair accessible. 2) Programs may be arranged for the visually limited and hearing impaired.*

Built in 1974 to supplement the city schools' science program, the planetarium can delight 130 star-gazers at a time. Changing 45-minute multi-media shows are informative and involve group participation.

DIXON GALLERY AND GARDENS*
4339 Park Ave. 38117. 761-5250.

Hours: *11am-5pm Tu-Sat, 1-5pm Sun.*
Tours: *Group tours may be arranged. You'll find a map of the grounds in the free pamphlet available in the museum foyer.*
Cost: *Adults/$1, children 3-11, senior citizens, & non-profit pre-arranged groups/50¢, pre-arranged school groups/free. Free to everyone on Tu.*
MATA: *#57, 52.*
Other: *1) Garden workshops, courses, and seminars at various times. 2) An internship program in horticulture.*
E&H: *Gardens are wheelchair accessible.*

The only sad thing about these beautiful 17 acres is that you can't picnic on them. Lovely in all seasons, the gardens include informal, formal, and cutting areas.

HORSESHOEING DEMONSTRATION BY JIM NOBLE
8450 Donelson Rd, Eads. 1-465-9712 (long distance) after 7pm.

Hours: Daylight M-Sat. Best months, Apr-Oct.
Cost: $40.
Other: Groups of 10 are best, and Noble will handle two different groups per demonstration.
E&H: This might be a good chance for seniors to reminisce.

Jim Noble will bring his horse and equipment to your school or backyard and demonstrate his craft, or, if you'd prefer, you can go to his house for the demonstration and take along a picnic. Something different for a child's birthday party, school group, or scout troop!

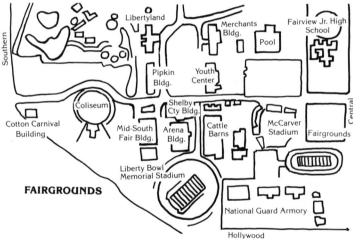

LIBERTYLAND/THEME PARK
Mid-South Fairgrounds (between E. Parkway, Central, Hollywood, and Southern). 940 Early Maxwell Blvd. 38104. 274-1776.

Hours: 11am-8pm Sat, noon-8pm Sun in Apr & May; 11am-10pm M-Sat, noon-10pm Sun in June, July & Aug; 11am-10pm Sat, noon-10pm Sun and as part of Mid-South Fair in Sept. Holidays have different, usually longer, hours. These change slightly each year, so phone ahead.
Cost: Adults/$6.95, children 3-10/$4.95, those under 3/free. Special rates for: 1) senior citizens M-F/$6.25, 2) groups of 20+ /$6.25 with 21st person free, 3) church groups before 5pm Sun/$6, 4) anyone after 5pm Sun-F/$5, 5) season pass, unlimited visits except during Cotton Carnival and the Mid-South Fair, adults/$29.95, children 3-10/$19.95.

Lunch: *Food available from stands and restaurants—a wide variety of usual fare plus corn on the cob, ham and biscuits, roast beef and turkey sandwiches, deli plates, sliced pies, pizza, milkshakes, and Pennsylvania funnel cake.*

MATA: *Showboat Bus or #9 (ex Sat & Sun), 20 (ex Sun), 50 (ex Sun), 32 (ex Sun).*

Other: *1) Gift shops. 2) Free strollers just inside the main entrance. 3) Free parking. 4) Special events, scheduled throughout the season, feature big name entertainers. The major one, Independence Day, also the park's birthday, features a birthday cake, special exhibits, and entertainment. 5) Libertyland is available for private parties. Companies or organizations may rent Libertyland for a minimum of three hours when the park would otherwise be closed. The rate is $3500 per hour. Organizations may also plan "mixins" where the company gets discount rates, use of the sundome, box lunches, and banners to announce their presence. Discounts vary according to size of the group, time of day, and time of year.*

E&H: *1) Park and all shows accessible to wheelchairs. 2) Personnel are glad to help you on and off rides. 3) Two wheelchairs available at front gate.*

Libertyland's theme is American history. It is divided into three "periods": colonial, frontier, and turn-of-the-century.

Near the main gate, in the colonial section, you'll see a large replica of Philadelphia's Liberty Bell, Independence Station where Casey's Cannonball train heads out for a tour of the park, and colonial style shops.

Next you'll wander into turn-of-the-century-land with its antique car ride, grand carousel, gay '90s games, and the "Zippin Pippin" ride. The "Jester Head" carousel, constructed in 1909 by Wm. H. Dentzel of Philadelphia, was installed at the Fairgrounds in 1923. It has 48 wooden horses, each made of 14 hand carved sections put together with wooden dowels.

Frontier-land features Tom Sawyer's island with rides and play equipment for young children, a war-canoe ride at Injun Joe's, a craft trading post, and such rides for the adventuresome as the Revolution and the log flume.

Shows of all kinds are presented in the park's theatres. The Delta Dolphins swim and perform to the crowds' delight. Broadway show tunes fill one musical show and progressive country, another. A "Memphis Music Show" at W. C. Handy Theatre offers a kaleidoscope of the city's musical history. Every song in the show, ranging from W. C. Handy's "Memphis Blues" to Rick Dee's "Disco Duck", was either written or recorded by a Memphian. Every hour at Bell Tavern there is an Elvis Presley tribute.

The grounds are well landscaped and well maintained.

MEDICAL SITES. See University of Tennessee Center for the Health Sciences, Le Bonheur Children's Medical Center, and St. Jude Children's Research Hospital.

MEMPHIS BELLE

Memphis Area Vocational Technical School, Aviation Complex (temporary home), 2752 Winchester. 345-1955.

Hours:	*7:30am-3:30pm M-F. Phone ahead to arrange a visit.*
Cost:	*Free.*
MATA:	*#20 (ex Sun).*
Other:	*An especially good outing for boys.*
E&H:	*There are no steps involved in viewing the plane.*

The Memphis Belle, one of three surviving B-17 Bombers used in the European theatre, was the first plane of its type to complete 25 missions over Europe during World War II and to return to the U.S. under its own power. The plane flew from Bassingborne, England in the 324th Squadron of the 91st Bomber Wing. Its crewmen shot down eight enemy fighters and among them earned 51 decorations. After their return to the U.S. in 1943, the crew and aircraft spearheaded a war bond drive and were used in flight training.

No member of the plane's crew was from Memphis, but the pilot's girlfriend, Miss Margaret Polk, was a Memphian. Captain Robert H. Morgan of Asheville, N.C. named the plane after her. Their engagement was later broken and each married another.

The plane is presently being refurbished. When work is completed, it will be moved to a temporary hangar on three acres next to 91st Bomb Group H Restaurant at 2156 Democrat (see American restaurants).

MEMPHIS BOTANICAL GARDEN AND GOLDSMITH CIVIC GARDEN CENTER

750 Cherry Rd, in Audubon Park 38117. 685-1566.

Hours:	*Gardens open sunrise to sunset daily. Center open winter: 9am-4:30pm M-F, 1-4:30pm Sat & Sun; summer: 9am-5pm M-F, 1-5pm Sat & Sun.*
Tours:	*Docent guided tours may be arranged for groups of 10+ at 10am and 1pm M-F. They last 15 minutes to 1½ hours depending on participants' age and interest. Arrange two weeks in advance. A free pamphlet available in the center includes a map of the groups.*
Cost:	*Free.*
Lunch:	*No facilities for eating or picnicking in the center or gardens; picnic grounds in nearby Audubon Park.*
MATA:	*#57 to W. Cherry; walk about 1/8 mile through Audubon Park to the center and garden entrance.*
Other:	*1) Occasional special lectures and programs. 2) Horticultural reference library. 3) Gift shop selling books, postcards, and occasionally plants. 4) You can get information on plant identification, disease symptoms, and care from the center's botanist in person or over the phone. 5) A monthly newsletter for members features horticultural tips. (Individual membership, $5).*
E&H:	*Wheelchair accessible.*

There is something for everyone in the 88-acre gardens—a conservatory of tropical and foliage plants, seasonal indoor-and-out exhibits, rose and iris gardens, magnolias, wild flowers, and a Japanese bridge.

MEMPHIS PINK PALACE MUSEUM
3050 Central Ave. 38111 (enter off Lafayette Str). 454-5600.

Hours: 9:30am-4pm Tu-F, 9am-4pm Sat, 1-5pm Sun.

Tours: For group tours phone the museum. Others, pick up a map at the reception desk. A 15-minute slide presentation explains the displays.

Cost: Adults/$2.00, children ages 5-18, college students with ID, & senior citizens (62+)/$1.50, children 4 and under/free. Free admission for all 9-10am Sat. Group rates for 20+ may be arranged. Free entry for museum members.

Lunch: Drinks and crackers available in machines. Bring your own lunch and picnic on the grounds.

MATA: #50 (ex Sun).

Other: Check with the museum's education department for information about the following: 1) Lecture/demonstrations for school groups. These often include films and puppet shows about nature. Programs are designed for k-6th grade students, are limited to 30, and must be reserved by teachers. They are free and are offered 9:30-11:30am & 12:30-2:30pm Tu-Th. Some are designed specifically for handicapped children. 2) Summer workshops in such areas as astronomy, archaeology, Memphis history, animals... for four year-olds through 12th graders, plus one adult education class. Fees vary. 3) Saturday workshops/demonstrations for pre-schoolers through 12th graders offered 9:30-11:30am. Fees vary. 4) Family programs, lectures, classes, and other activities 2-3pm Sat & Sun Oct-May. Free unless a puppet show is included. Special holidays and events are often themes: e.g. on Halloween weekend they feature pumpkin carving, a haunted house, and a costume contest. 5) Occasional field trips for adults and children. Fees vary. 6) Pink Palace staff identifies geological, natural history, and historical artifacts by appointment. 7) Reference library available by appointment. 8) Teachers can use the museum's laboratory and auditorium for 7th-12th grade anthropology, geology, and biology classes. 9) The public may tour the museum's education facilities, once the home of grocery tycoon Clarence Saunders*, on the third Sun of each month. 10) Gift shop. 11) Membership in support group (adults/$10, students & seniors/$5, family/$20) entitles you to free entry, discounts, and newsletter.

E&H: 1) Facility is accessible to physically handicapped. 2) Some school programs designed specifically for handicapped children.

Completed in 1977, the new Pink Palace is a regional science and history museum. The first floor is devoted to natural history exhibits with displays on birds, trees, and insects. Children love to push the multimedia buttons, climb in the tree house, and jump on the earthquake monitoring device. Live animals are shown 11am&2pm Sat, 2:30 & 4pm Sun.

Displays on the second floor illustrate the cultural history of the Mid-South. Slides tell the area's history, and log cabin and drugstore replicas show what life was like. A recreation of the first self-service supermarket, Clarence Saunders' Piggly Wiggly, even contains merchandise marked with 1916 prices. There are also a Memphis medical history exhibit, cotton bales, hats, a fire engine, and a stage coach. Clyde W. Parke's wooden miniature circus is on this floor. See it come alive from 11am-noon and 2-3pm Sat and 3:30-4:30pm Sun. The second floor also houses changing exhibits, about four different shows each year.

MEMPHIS PINK PALACE PLANETARIUM
3050 Central Ave. 38111 (enter museum off Lafayette Str; planetarium is to the right of the reception desk). 454-5600.

Hours: *Show times, 10am, 11:30am, 1:30pm, 3:30pm Sat, 1:30&3pm Sun. In summer and on school holidays, public shows, 11am & 3pm Tu-F.*

Cost: *Adults/$2, children (4-18), college students, pre-arranged school groups, & senior citizens (62+)/$1.50. Free to museum members.*

Lunch: *Drinks and crackers in machines, or phone ahead for permission to picnic on the grounds.*

MATA: *#50 (ex Sun).*

Other: *1) Children under four may become frightened by the darkness and special effects. They are welcome only at the 10am Sat family shows and at the weekday summer and holiday shows. 2) During the school year, group instructional shows, 9:30am, 10:45am, 12:15pm, & 1:30pm Tu-F. Teachers should contact the education department for information.*

A star-gazer's delight! Shows change periodically.

MEMPHIS ZOOLOGICAL GARDEN AND AQUARIUM
Overton Park 38112. 725-4768.

Hours: *Open seven days a week year round, 9am-6pm Apr-Sept, 9am-5pm Oct-March.*

Tours: *Free red pamphlet at the gate contains a good map. To arrange a guided tour by Zoo Action Program (ZAP), call the Education Department. Open 9am-noon M-F or write the Curator of Education.*

Cost: *Adults (12+)/$1.50, children (2-11) & senior citizens/50¢, children under 2/free. Free to all 9-10am Sat. Special school group rates for groups registering 14 days in advance with the zoo education department. The aquarium costs extra: adults (12+)/25¢, children 6-11 & senior citizens/10¢, children under 6/free.*

Lunch: *Three concessions sell popcorn, peanuts, and hot dogs, or pack a lunch and picnic in adjacent Overton Park. Zoo stands sell approved food for the animals.*

MATA: *Showboat Bus and #3 (ex Sat & Sun) go to zoo gate.*

Other: *1) Strollers for rent just inside the south entrance, 50¢ per day plus 50¢ deposit. 2) Besides the animals, there are train, carousel, ferris wheel,* boat, and airplane rides, 30¢ a ride or $5 for a discount book of 20 ride tickets. J. C. Levy, who operates the rides, also offers the city's children another treat—dial 278-2370 for a rhymed animal message.

E&H: The zoo is wheelchair accessible. Wheelchairs are for rent just inside the main gate, $1/day with a driver's license as deposit.

A treat for the young at heart, young and old alike! The Memphis Zoo, Tennessee's largest public zoo, covers 36 acres and houses more than 440 species of animals. It started when the Memphis baseball team gave its mascot, a black bear named Natch, to the Park Commission in 1901. At first the bear was tied to a tree in Overton Park. He acquired a following and his fans brought him company, a bobcat and a raccoon. In 1903 the city set aside money for animal houses and a zoo keeper. The 1909 Egyptian revival style elephant house is now the education building, but lions still live in the original lion house.

The Memphis Zoo, known as the Nile hippopotamus capital of the world, has bred more hippos than any other zoo in the world. It was home for the world's oldest hippo when he died at age 54 in 1965. The zoo was the first in the world to breed the West African dwarf crocodile, the Douc Langur monkey, Rothschild's Mynah starlings, and the bald crow. It has the largest population of Nilgiri Tahr goats outside of India and produced the first gorilla born through artificial insemination. Memphis Zoo is also famous as the home of M-G-M's roaring lion until his death in 1944 and as the home of Tarzanna, the lion who starred with Johnny Weissmuller in "Tarzan's Secret Treasure".

MUD ISLAND*.

TV APPEARANCE ON MAGICLAND
Channel 5 TV, 1960 Union. 726-0555 after 6pm any day of the week, adults only.

Hours: Program taped 7-8:30pm on alternate Th nights.
Other: 1) Adults may make a reservation for groups of up to five children; scout troops of up to 20. Shows are scheduled at three month intervals, so phone well in advance.

See how television works first hand. Children may make their TV debut at age 4, and ages often range up to 15.

PARKS

There are more than 150 parks and playgrounds in Memphis and Shelby County, ranging in size from tiny Carver Park (1552 Hanaur) to

13,000 acre Meeman-Shelby Forest State Park. Park statues commemorate such disparate figures as the Spanish-American War volunteers (Spanish Memorial Park, corner of the Central-East Parkway intersection) and Swayback Wilson, the black custodian of many Memphis homes during the yellow fever days and organizer of the black orphanage named in his honor (Douglass Park, 1616 Ash). For information on the park nearest you contact the Memphis Park Commission, 2599 Avery 38112, 454-5759.

Four large parks within the immediate vicinity of Memphis are: Overton Park, Meeman-Shelby Forest State Park, Plough Park in Shelby Farms, and T.O. Fuller State Park. Other parks are mentioned in the River, Sports, and Camping chapters of this book.

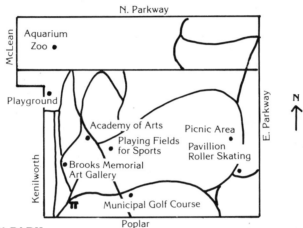

OVERTON PARK
Between Poplar, N. Parkway, Kenilworth and E. Parkway.

MATA: Showboat Bus and #3 (ex Sat & Sun), 5, 55 (ex Sun).

Overton Park, the Memphis equivalent of N.Y.C.'s Central Park, is 342.3 acres of center city parkland. It was designed by Olmsted Brothers, sons of the famous landscape architect Frederick Law Olmsted who designed Central Park.

In 1901 the Memphis Park Commission bought the land for Overton Park and Martin Luther King Riverside Park* and designed the 172 acre parkway road system to encircle the city and connect the two parks. The acreage now known as Overton Park, then on the extreme eastern edge of the city, was known as Lea's Woods. It was part of the original 5,000 acre tract of land owned by Judge John Overton, a city founder, and had been willed through one of his daughters, Mrs. John Lea, to her son Overton Lea of Nashville. When the city bought it, the land was undisturbed except for an electric streetcar line to Raleigh*. The park was briefly known as East Park until Park Chairman McFarland suggested naming it for John Overton, who had provided a system of parks and promenades when laying out the city. L.B. McFarland himself is memorialized in the park by a clock tower and 1918 drinking fountain, both located on the grounds around the art academy. A statue of "Boss" Crump* is near the park's main entrance on Poplar Ave. George Kessler who designed the streets for Kansas City and Dallas, laid out the roads, walkways, and bridges.

Today the park features nature trails and natural forest land, playground and picnic areas, volleyball* courts, softball* and soccer* fields, and a 9-hole golf* course. Also here are the Memphis Zoo*, Brooks Memorial Art Gallery*, Memphis Academy of Arts*, and the 1936 WPA open-air amphitheatre, scene of Memphis' summer arts-in-the-park* series.

The park has been the subject of 20 years of precedent-setting litigation between environmentalists and highway engineers fighting over the proposed routing of I-40 through the park (Citizens to Preserve Overton Park, Inc. v. Volpe, 401 U.S. 402 (1971)). The legal battle appears to have ended in 1981 and nature lovers and park goers to have had the last say.

MEEMAN-SHELBY FOREST STATE PARK
Millington 38053 (just off Hwy. 51, 12 miles north of Memphis). 876-5201. 876-5297 (swimming pool).

Other: *Trying to dream up an unusual party? —Phone 876-5756 to find out about scheduling a hayride and bonfire. The cost is $2/person with a $50 minimum.*

You can picnic, boat*, camp*, hike*, fish*, ride horses* and bicycles*, hunt*, or just observe nature on these 13,000 acres of preserved forest. Naturalists and recreation directors plan year-round programs and activities; special arts, crafts, and nature programs are presented in the late fall and winter at the museum and craft center. Bird watching is excellent, especially near the lake for water fowl.

Maps available at the park office, open 7am-5:30pm M-Th and 7:30am-10pm F&Sat. The park closes at 10pm daily.

SHELBY FARMS
Part of Shelby County Penal Farm property at Walnut Grove Rd. & Germantown Rd. 528-3279.

Other: *Organizations and companies may arrange to rent the Equestrian Center for picnics and events.*
E&H: *1) Garden plots for senior citizens. 2) Triumph Trail, a 1600 foot paved nature trail, and playground and picnic equipment specially designed for the blind and handicapped.*

A bird and wildlife watcher's delight! Shelby Farms, a 4,416 acre county run recreational area, includes an Equestrian Center on Germantown Rd, public soccer fields on Walnut Grove Rd, and Plough Park on Mullins Rd. Plough Park, free to the public, open 8am-sunset daily, has horse* stables ($4.50/hour to rent a horse and ride marked trails), a specially designed exercise trail, nature trails, picnic facilities, and playgrounds. The park has two fishing* ponds, one with a pier. (No license is necessary for residents of Shelby County. Live bait only. No boats.)

Plans are underway for an international Agri-Center to exhibit farming technology. Scheduled to open 1982-83 near the Equestrian Center.

T. O. FULLER STATE PARK
3269 Boxtown 38109 (in south Memphis, five miles west of Hwy. 61). 785-3950.

E&H: *¼ mile nature trail marked with pebbles and Braille signs for visually handicapped. Trail guidebook available in both bold type and braille.*

This 1,000-acre park was created in 1938 by the Civilian Conservation Corps (CCC) and named for T. O. Fuller, prominent clergyman, educator, and exponent of interracial cooperation. In 1940 excavation for a swimming pool unearthed the park's most significant feature, evidence of a prehistoric civilization. Now excavated and partially restored, the site is known as Chucalissa Indian Village*.

The park has camping* facilities, an 18-hole golf course*, and swimming*, picnicking, playground, and hiking* areas.

The park is open 8am-10pm in summer and 8am-sundown in winter.

🚲 ADDITIONAL SUGGESTIONS FOR CHILDREN

Children can learn about the world in their own backyard. Get on your knees, square off a foot of earth and see what surprises are there. Go walk along the same route at different times of day and in different weather. Notice what you smell, hear, touch, taste, and see.

How about a picnic in the park? Take along a leaf guide. Or at night, a weenie roast? Take a star guide.

Future zoologists might want to make a home for a stray dog or cat. The city animal shelter, 3456 N. Tchulahoma Rd, 362-5310, has puppies/$6, grown dogs/$15, kittens/$6, and cats/$12. They're open 9am-5pm M-F, 10am-3pm Sat. Or you might prefer to adopt from the Humane Society, 2238 Central, 272-1753. Befriend a homeless cat or dog for $25, 9am-4pm M-F, 10am-2pm Sat.

Memphis State University* Duration Children's Program, 3771 Poplar, 454-2120, offers a special summer nature study program for children ages 2-6.

Boy Scouts' (327-4193) and Girl Scouts' (767-1440) programs help children learn about their world.

Possible excursions for budding naturalists include a drive to Wapanocca* wildlife refuge to watch the waterfowl or to Reelfoot Lake* to see our national emblem. Each year about 175 bald eagles visit the lake on their migratory route. Free eagle tours are offered Dec-mid March by the Tennessee Department of Conservation. They're in great demand so reserve well in advance. For information and reservations phone 1-901-253-7756. Or plan a fall drive through Arkansas' Ozarks*. For leaf reports call toll free 1-800-643-8383. More weekend trip suggestions are in the chapter Worth the Drive.

Memphis At Work

Abe Frank classing cotton about 1900.

Tours of Memphis' businesses and government buildings are free unless otherwise noted. Most are by appointment only—so when it says call ahead, be sure to do so. School age children will enjoy most of these tours; some are equally fascinating for adults. If a place you want to tour is not listed, call the business' public relations office to find out if they give tours.

Other sources of information:

"Program Resources and Techniques" printed annually by Memphis/Shelby County Public Library and Information Center, $1.

"Places to Go, Hikes and Patches, Speakers and Demonstrations for Cub Scouts and Webelos" from the Boy Scouts of America, 171 S. Hollywood (327-4193).

"Eye-Opening Tours Given Free", article in the "The Commercial Appeal" by Ron Russell Jan. 18, 1980.

COTTON INDUSTRY

See Cotton Row, Shelby Cotton Co., and Cotton Exchange Building.

FARMS

CARTWRIGHT NURSERY*.

DAIRY FARM TOUR (arranged by Dairy Council Inc.)
3035 Directors Row. 726-1631.

Hours: Call the council between 9am and 4pm M-F to request a dairy tour.
Tours: Some dairy farmers give occasional tours. The Dairy Council will try to arrange one for your group. Remember: dairies usually do their milking very early in the morning. Age 8+. Groups of 5-25 (adult supervision needed).

LOFTIN DAIRY FARM
Red Banks, Miss. (12 miles from Collierville, off Hwy. 72). 851-7152.

Tours: By appointment 10am-noon M-Th. Groups of 1-30. Age 5+.
Lunch: You can picnic but be sure to clean up.
E&H: Wheelchair accessible.

See the cows being milked and fed. Visit baby calves. You may not go inside the bottling plant.

R-D CHICKEN FARMS
Tullahoma Rd, Collierville, 38107. 853-0931.

Tours: *By appointment 10am Tu-Th Apr & May only. Phone in Jan to set up Apr
         or May tour date. Groups of 20-50. All ages.*
Lunch: *Ask about arranging a picnic in the nearby two-room school house which
         has been converted to a clubhouse.*
E&H: *On one level, but the gravel may make access difficult for wheelchairs.*

Which came first, the chicken or the egg? You may not get the answer,
but you will see the farm, gather a few eggs in the hen house, and see the
eggs processed.

GOVERNMENT

MEMPHIS INTERNATIONAL AIRPORT*.

ALLEN STEAM PLANT
2574 Plant Rd. 785-7490.

Hours: *9am-5pm daily.*
Tours: *No reservations needed for small groups or individuals. By appointment for
         groups of 20+. Groups of 1-70.*
E&H: *There's a curb and one step outside, but once inside, wheelchairs can make
         the tour.*

Full tour lasts about 1½ hours, but can be narrowed. The equipment is
huge and fascinating, but the subject matter is highly technical. You'll
hear how coal is converted to steam to produce electricity.
The plant is part of the Tennessee Valley Authority (TVA) power
system. In a special election in the mid-1930s, Memphis voted to buy the
privately owned electrical system and to join TVA.

FEDERAL AVIATION ADMINISTRATION AIR TRAFFIC CONTROL
CENTER
3229 Democrat Rd. 365-0970.

Hours: *8am-4:30pm M-F (best 10am-3pm).*
Tours: *By appointment. Groups of 1-20. All ages, but children under 12 not
         allowed in the control room.*
Lunch: *Arrange in advance to eat in the cafeteria.*
MATA: *#30 (ex Sun).*
E&H: *Accessible to wheelchairs. Enter through ramp at back of building.*

The loosely structured tour begins with a 12-minute film tracing an airliner in flight from Los Angeles to Washington; there's dialogue between the pilot and traffic controllers. Then you see the control and computer rooms.

FEDERAL BUREAU OF INVESTIGATION (FBI)
8th Floor, Federal Bldg., 167 N. Main. 525-7373.

Hours: *10am-4:30pm M-F.*
Tours: *By appointment. Prefer groups of 15, but can take up to 20. Best for ages 8+. One hour.*
E&H: *Some spaces too small for wheelchairs.*

Check a criminal's name or a license number through the national crime information ticker. Look at the gun vault and learn how fingerprints are taken.

FEDERAL RESERVE BANK OF ST. LOUIS - MEMPHIS BRANCH
200 N. Main. 523-7171.

Tours: *By appointment 9am-1:30pm M-F. Groups of 5-20. Ages 16+. 1½ hours.*
MATA: *Downtown buses.*
E&H: *Wheelchair accessible.*

Sign in through a security check. You'll see a film on the Federal Reserve System and tour the check accounting/data processing, securities, and internal services departments.

MEMPHIS FIRE DEPARTMENT
Go through the fire station nearest you, the airport station with its air crash equipment, or the training center with its tower. Phone 458-8281. to arrange.

Tours: *By appointment 10am-noon, 4:30-9pm M-Sat. Groups of 1-25.*

You'll see all the trucks and equipment, where the firemen sleep, and the poles they slide down. Good for young children.

MEMPHIS LIGHT GAS & WATER DIVISION (MLGW)
528-4557.
Tours of:

Water Pumping Stations— Various locations throughout the city.

Tours: *By appointment 8:30-10am, noon-2pm M-F. Groups of 6-60.*

Workers will explain how Memphis gets its water. If you go to Sheahan

Pumping Station, 3941 Grandview, you'll also get to see the city's water lab.

Downtown Administration Bldg. - 200 S. Main.

Tours: *By appointment 9am-3:30pm M-F. Groups of 4 +. 30 minutes - 1 hour.*
Lunch: *Fifth floor sandwich shop.*
MATA: *Downtown buses.*
E&H: *Wheelchair accessible.*

You'll go through the control room, past the computers, to the executive areas, board room, and information center where customer calls come in and work crews are dispatched.

Liquified Natural Gas Plant - near Arlington, 11095 Millington/Arlington Rd.

Tours: *By appointment 9am-noon M-F. Groups of 4-12.*

You'll see the tanks and they'll explain the process. Gas is cooled to 230° and converted to a liquid state.

Chaperones are required for all school-age tours, one adult for each seven youngsters 3rd-6th grade, one for each 12 7th-9th grade, and one for each 15 10th-12th grade. Tours are most interesting for 6th grade +. Children under 3rd grade are not permitted.

MEMPHIS/SHELBY COUNTY PUBLIC LIBRARY, MAIN BRANCH
1850 Peabody. 528-2952.

Tours: *By appointment 9am-3pm M-F. Groups of 5-25. All ages.*
MATA: *#56, 50 (ex Sun).*
E&H: *Wheelchair accessible.*

Guides point out the different subject divisions and show you the Memphis Room*.

NAVAL AIR STATION/MILLINGTON
Main gate on Navy Rd., approximately three miles east of Hwy. 51, Millington. 872-5761.

Tours: *By appointment 10am M-F. Tours last about two hours and run through lunch. Groups of 10-40. Ages 6 +.*
Lunch: *Arrange for lunch in the enlisted men's dining room, $1.40 per person.*
Other: *You'll need your own bus/transportation for the tour.*
E&H: *Arrangements possible for those in wheelchairs.*

The tour begins with lots of action—you'll see a simulated airplane fire and rescue mission. Then on to the control tower and weather facility. After lunch you'll be guided around the base on your own bus. Those with a particular vocational interest can ask to see vocational training facilities.

Army pilots trained on old Park Field here during World War I. After the armistice, the field was abandoned until World War II when the area was reopened as Millington Naval Air Base.

Today the base is a vast complex covering 3400 acres. There are 24 different commands, including a naval air technical training center, naval hospital, and naval reserve training unit. The base is under the command of a two-star admiral who is in charge of all naval technical training in the U.S. About 15,000 military and civilian people work at the base which has the largest payroll in the state of Tennessee.

The town of Millington itself grew up around Millwood and Old Glencoe, two railroad stops on the Paducah and Memphis Railroad. In 1875 George Millington donated land for a depot and business district. The two stops merged to form Millington.

POST OFFICE
Main Branch, 555 S. 3rd. 521-3389.

Tours: By appointment 9:30am M-F. Groups of 1-50.
MATA: #39, 44 (ex Sun).
E&H: The building is wheelchair accessible, but the tour covers a large area.

There's a lot of activity here. Three year olds love it, but the best ages are probably 6-9. Bring along a letter and money for a stamp—you can follow your letter through the whole process.

SHELBY COUNTY PENAL FARM
1045 Mullins Station Rd. 386-4391 ext. 213.

Tours: By appointment 12:30pm Tu & Th. Groups of 10-25. High school age (with chaperones) or older. One hour.
MATA: #54 (ex Sat & Sun).
E&H: Not equipped for wheelchairs.

A slide show on prison programs, a talk about the justice system, and a 15-minute tour of the institution are in store.

TENNESSEE AIR NATIONAL GUARD
Democrat Rd. between Lamar & Airways. 363-1212.

Tours: By appointment 9:30am & 1pm Tu & Th. Groups of 1-25. 45 minutes.
Lunch: Ask about eating in the cafeteria.
MATA: #32, 30 (ex Sun).

E&H: *Airplane not accessible to wheelchairs.*

Inspect the inside of an airplane.

TENNESSEE HIGHWAY DEPARTMENT GARAGE
Hwy. 70, one block east of the caution light in Arlington. 867-2959.

Tours: *By appointment 8am-4:30pm M-F.*

Young children enjoy seeing large road equipment up close.

TENNESSEE HIGHWAY PATROL
6348 Hwy. 70 (Summer). 386-3831.

Hours: *8am-4pm M-F.*
Tours: *By appointment. Best for ages 8-14.*

Take a drivers' license test, see the radio room, and inspect a highway patrol car.

U.S. CORPS OF ENGINEERS RIVER EQUIPMENT
Ensley Engineer Yard on Mitchell Rd. at the River. 521-3348.

Tours: *By appointment 9am-2pm M-F, Dec-July best. Best for age 10+.*
MATA: *For the young and old, it's safer and easier to bring your own bus. A guide joins you for a tour of the boatyard.*

See barges and dredging and revetment equipment that help harness Old Man River.

MEDICAL FACILITIES

LE BONHEUR CHILDREN'S MEDICAL CENTER
848 Adams. 522-3392 (ask for patient service representative).

Tours: *By appointment 10-11am, 2-3pm M-F. Groups of 2-25. Ages 5+ (those under 14 not admitted to patient floors). 45 minutes. Geared to group's level of interest.*
Lunch: *Hospital cafeteria.*
MATA: *Showboat Bus or #53 (ex Sun).*
Other: *Groups often take favors or plan a program for patients.*
E&H: *Wheelchair accessible. Special tour for the hearing impaired possible.*

You'll first see the ground floor x-ray facilities, emergency room, lab, and day care areas. For those over 14, the tour then goes to a patient floor. You'll see a room, dietary facilities, and play room and have a chance to entertain or bring gifts to the patients.

Le Bonheur Club, a non-profit women's organization, founded the pediatric hospital in 1952. Members are hospital volunteers and have representatives on the hospital's board. The hospital was expanded in 1974 and again in 1977. Today it has 225 beds. The University of Tennessee Center for the Health Sciences* is affiliated with the hospital and trains its pediatric residents here.

ST. JUDE CHILDREN'S RESEARCH HOSPITAL
332 N. Lauderdale. 522-0300.

Tours: By appointment 10am-2pm M-F. Groups of 1-15 (larger groups can be divided). Age 12 + . One hour.
Cost: Free, but a group donation to the hospital would be welcomed.
Lunch: Make arrangements for cafeteria lunch.
MATA: #19 (ex Sun), 52.
Other: 1) You can plan a program to entertain the patients. 2) Special tour offered for visiting medical personnel.
E&H: Some places difficult for wheelchairs.

You'll visit the administrative offices, pharmacy, lab, chapel, and play area and see a typical patient's room. Most tours include a visit to a lab floor and blood bank. Tours are geared to a group's interest level.

Danny Thomas, the well known entertainer, helped found this hospital in 1958. Dedicated to the patron saint of the hopeless, St. Jude specializes in the treatment of catastrophic illness in children. It is the world's largest center for the study and treatment of leukemia and muscular dystrophy.

UNIVERSITY OF TENNESSEE CENTER FOR THE HEALTH SCIENCES*.

MISCELLANEOUS BUSINESSES

CLEO WRAP
4025 Viscount. 369-6300.

Tours: For accredited school groups only. By appointment 9am M-F Feb-Nov. Elementary-high school age. Call several weeks in advance to arrange. Groups of 25-50.
MATA: #20 (ex Sun).
E&H: No wheelchairs.

Manufactures bows and prints valentines and paper.

COLONIAL BAKING COMPANY
1340 Larkin Ave. 726-9104.

Tours: By appointment 11am-3pm M, W, Th, F, May-Sept. Groups of 10-25.
Ages 6 +. About 30 minutes.
MATA: #10 runs across Cleveland (ex Sun).
E&H: Wheelchair accessible.

You see bread and buns being made, and Colonial gives you a baker's hat to take home.

DECOR NOEL CORP.
265 E. Belz Blvd. 774-7050.

Tours: By appointment 9am-3pm M-F mid-Jan-Nov. Groups of 10-30. All ages
(young children, one adult per child). About 30 minutes.
MATA: #39, 44 (ex Sun) to 3rd & Belz.
E&H: No ramp; difficult maneuvering.

One of the biggest tinsel and garland companies in the U.S.

FEDERAL EXPRESS CORP.
Main facility on Sprankel near Memphis International Airport. 369-3613.

Tours: By appointment 9am-noon Tu-F, but to see the company in action go at
1am Sat. Groups of 1-25. Age 10 +. About 30 minutes.
MATA: #30 (ex Sun).
E&H: Difficult for wheelchairs.

Hear the success story of Federal Express, the national package airline started in 1973. Go inside an airplane, tour the package hub, and go home with your own styrofoam Federal Express plane.

GENERAL MOTORS TRAINING SCHOOL
4771 Summer. 685-5401.

Hours: 8am-5pm M-F.
Tours: By appointment for those with a special interest in automotive vocational
training. Groups of 1-30.
MATA: #53 (ex Sun).
E&H: Wheelchair accessible.

See classrooms where the area's GM technicians are trained in everything from automotive components to marketing.

GOODWILL INDUSTRIES REHABILITATION CENTER
2605 Chelsea Ave. 323-6221.

Tours: By appointment 9am-11am, 1:30-4pm Tu & Th. Groups of 1+. Ages 8+. About 30 minutes. (Special tours for those trained in rehabilitation.)
MATA: #19 (ex Sun), 8.
E&H: Wheelchair accessible. With advance notice, special arrangements possible for the visually handicapped.

See evaluation and rehabilitation programs and the plant where handicapped workers practice their skills.

HYATT REGENCY HOTEL
939 Ridge Lake Blvd. 761-1234.

Hours: 9am-5pm M-F.
Tours: By appointment. Groups of 8-20. Ages 16+.
Lunch: Make reservations for lunch at Ducks & Company (See American restaurants).
E&H: Wheelchair accessible.

Tours geared to a group's special interest. You'll see how a big hotel operates.

INTERNATIONAL HARVESTER CO.
3003 Harvester Lane. 357-5311.

Tours: By appointment 8am-2pm M-F. Groups of 1-45. Ages 12+. About 2 hours.
Lunch: Arrange for cafeteria lunch when you schedule tour.
MATA: #14 (ex Sun).
E&H: Small area accessible to wheelchairs.

You'll go through the factory where parts are made, assembled into farm equipment, and painted. And then to the shipping dock where the hay balers, cotton pickers and other farm machines are sent to dealers.

IVERS AND POND PIANO
2718 Pershing. 324-7351.

Hours: 8am-4pm M-F.
Tours: By appointment. Groups of 5-10. Ages 12+. 45 minutes.
MATA: #53 (ex Sun) to 2700 block of Summer, walk three blocks north to Pershing.
E&H: No wheelchairs.

See pianos made—from wood and ivory to finished instruments.

KIMBERLY-CLARK CORP.
400 Mahannah. 529-3800.

Hours: *8:30am-4pm M-F.*
Tours: *By appointment. Groups of 4-15 (larger group divided up). Ages 13 +*
Two hours.
MATA: *#14 (ex Sun).*
E&H: *Be ready for a long walk. The plant spans 40 acres under one roof.*

See paper pulp being made into such products as bathroom and facial tissue.

MEMPHIS PUBLISHING CO. (Publisher of Memphis' two major daily newspapers, "The Commercial Appeal" and "The Memphis Press-Scimitar.")
495 Union. 529-2218.

Tours: *By appointment 8:30-10:30am, 1-3:30pm M-F. Groups of 1-25. Chaperones required with school groups. Ages 11 +. 1½ hours.*
MATA: *#34 (ex Sat & Sun), 56, 20 (ex Sun), 9 (ex Sat & Sun), 43 (ex Sun).*
E&H: *Movie is wheelchair accessible, but tour is difficult.*

Tour begins with a film. Then you'll be guided through the plush new office building and warehouse to see the presses, mail room, and reporters at work.

NATIONAL HARDWOOD LUMBER ASSN. & INSPECTION SCHOOL
6830 Raleigh-La Grange Rd., near I-40 & Whitten Rd. 377-1818.

Hours: *8am-4:45pm M-F.*
Tours: *By appointment.*
E&H: *Wheelchair accessible.*

The association was formed in 1898 to set grading standards for hardwood lumber. The office building, completed in 1980, was designed to display different hardwoods. The inspection school trains 240 students each year.
At the end of the 19thc. Memphis was the largest hardwood lumber market in the world.

PLOUGH INC.
303 Jackson Ave. 320-2624.

Tours: *By appointment 10am-3pm (morning is best) Tu, W & F. Groups of 1-25.*
Ages 13 + (for younger groups, contact the personnel director). 45
minutes.
MATA: *#52.*
E&H: *Wheelchair accessible.*

You'll see the huge production line machinery make and package such products as Di-Gel and Aspirin. Abe Plough, the company's founder, is one of the city's largest donors to non-profit and charitable causes.

ROYAL CROWN CANADA DRY BOTTLING CO.
1695 Harbor (on President's Island). 947-1121.

Tours: By appointment 8am-3pm M-F. Groups of 5-10. All ages but remember machinery can be dangerous. 30 minutes.
MATA: #15 (ex Sun; morning and night only).
E&H: No wheelchairs.

Start at the empty bottles, see them washed and sanitized, watch them pass through the quality control laboratory, see the drink ingredients mixed, and then watch as Nehi's, Royal Crown Colas, and Canada Dry mixes are packaged and labeled.

RYDER TRUCK LINES INC.
4510 Getwell Rd. 365-2040.

Hours: 24 hours daily.
Tours: By appointment. Groups of 1-30. All ages (children must be well chaperoned).
E&H: Wheelchair accessible, but notify in advance.

Something here for all ages—young children like the big trucks and forklifts, older ones may enjoy seeing freight being loaded, and for teens and adults, information on the truck business and the handling of hazardous materials.

JOSEPH SCHLITZ BREWING CO.
5151 E. Raines Rd. 362-5450.

Hours: 8:30am-4:30pm M-F.
Tours: Regularly scheduled tours, 10:30am, 11:30am, 1:30pm, 2:30pm, & 3:30pm M-F. Only groups of 10 + need make reservations. Groups of 1 +. All ages. 30 minutes - 1 hour.
Lunch: Groups may use the Schlitz Belle, a riverboat replica, for meetings and/or luncheons. Phone for an application form. Schlitz provides a list of approved caterers.
E&H: Wheelchair accessible.

Watch Schlitz beer processed, bottled, and labeled. If you're of age, you can sample the results. Schlitz opened this plant in 1971.

Time was when Memphis had its own local beer, Goldcrest 51, brewed by the Tennessee Brewing Co. Tennessee Brewing was founded in 1885 and built its brewery at 477 Tennessee Ave. in 1890. It closed in 1954, but the building still stands.

SEARS ROEBUCK AND CO.
495 N. Watkins. 725-2180.

Tours: By appointment 9am-2pm M-F. Any size group. Ages 12+. 30 minutes -1 hour.
Lunch: Cafeteria.
MATA: #31 (ex Sun), 10 (ex Sun).
E&H: The building is wheelchair accessible, but the area covered on the tour is large.

You'll see how an order comes in and is processed and how merchandise is stored.

Sears built this building in 1927 to serve the Mid-South with its catalogue mail-order business. The 11-story structure handles mail orders from seven states.

SHARP MANUFACTURING CO. OF AMERICA
Sharp Plaza Blvd., near Raines & Mendenhall. 795-6510.

Hours: 7:30am-3:30pm M-F.
Tours: Only for those with a specialized interest in manufacturing or electronics and only by written request. Groups of 1-25. Age 16+.
E&H: Limited wheelchair access.

Manufacturing, inspection, and testing of color TV sets and microwave ovens are covered.

SHELBY COUNTY GROWERS/SCOTT STREET PRODUCE MARKET
814 Scott Street. 327-8828.

Hours: 4am-5pm winter, 3am-10pm summer daily.
Tours: None - just browse on your own.
Cost: Winter/free, June, July & Aug/25¢. Free for organized groups (schools, Cub Scouts,...) who call ahead.
MATA: #52, get off at Jackson & Scott and walk south.
E&H: Wheelchair accessible.

This retail and wholesale fresh produce market deals in bulk quantities, but in the summer, when local farmers sell their produce, you can buy in smaller amounts.

WONDER BREAD
400 Monroe. 525-8404.

Tours: By appointment 9am-noon W-F Feb-May. Groups of 10-40. One Hour.
MATA: #10 (ex Sun).
E&H: No wheelchairs.

See bread, hamburger and hot dog buns, cupcakes, and donuts being made.

RADIO & TV STATIONS

WHBQ-TV / CHANNEL 13
485 S. Highland, 323-7661.

Tours: *By appointment 9:45am-4pm Tu & W, 1-4pm M & F (summer & fall are best). Groups of 10-25. Ages 9+. 45 minutes.*
MATA: *#9 (ex Sat & Sun) and walk north three blocks.*
E&H: *Wheelchair accessible.*

The technical aspects of TV are emphasized (special effects, lighting and set design, but you'll also learn something about programming and the commercial aspects of the business.

WKNO TV & RADIO
900 Getwell Rd. 458-2521.

Hours: *8:30am-5pm M-F.*
Tours: *By appointment. Groups of 1-20. Ages 7+. 30-90 minutes.*
MATA: *#57 (ex Sun).*
E&H: *Wheelchair accessible.*

Memphis' public broadcasting station where Sesame Street, Electric Company, Masterpiece Theatre, and Dick Cavett come. Most of Channel 10's programs are on film or tape so you won't be able to watch a local show in progress, but you will see the studio and operations room and learn how a TV program is produced. You'll also see the radio studio.

WMC TV 5, RADIO 79 & FM 100
1960 Union. 726-0555.

Tours: *By appointment 8-11am, 1-3pm Th. Groups of 10-25. Ages 7+. One hour.*
MATA: *#20 (ex Sun), 34 (ex Sat & Sun).*
E&H: *Wheelchair accessible.*

You'll see a video tape on how TV works and visit the studios, newsroom, and master control room.

RADIO WDIA*.

RESTAURANTS

BURGER KING
All branches. Check phone directory for locations and phone numbers.

Tours: *By appointment 7-10am daily. Arrange with branch. Groups of 10 (larger groups can be divided); 1 adult per 5 children. All ages, but probably most fun for ages 7-12.*
Lunch: *Order a hamburger and fries, and your drink is free.*
E&H: *No space for wheelchairs.*

See burgers, shakes, and fries prepared. You'll get a coupon for free french fries.

JOHANN SEBASTIAN BAGEL
692 Mt. Moriah (Poplar at Mendenhall - across the tracks). 682-3057.

Tours: *By appointment 10am daily except W & Sun. Groups of 10-25.*
Lunch: *Stay for a bagel and....*
MATA: *#55 (ex Sun).*
E&H: *Wheelchair accessible.*

See the bagels being boiled and baked.

MCDONALD'S
All branches. Check phone book for addresses and phone numbers.

Tours: *By appointment 9-10:30am, 2-4pm M-F. Call the branch to arrange. Groups of 5-20 (larger groups will be divided). All ages 15-20 minutes.*
Lunch: *Big Macs, natch.*
E&H: *Wheelchair accessible.*

See how hamburgers, fries, soft drinks, and shakes are handled. Free soft drinks.

SHAKEY'S
All branches. Check phone book for addresses and phone numbers. 726-4301 main office.

Tours: *By appointment with branch 9-10am M-F. Groups of 10-100.*
Cost: *$1.25 per person.*
E&H: *Wheelchair accessible.*

Make and eat your own pizza. Free drinks.

THORNTON'S DONUTS
2229 Lamar. 324-2118.

Hours:	*Irregular, M-F.*
Tours:	*By appointment. Groups of 5-15. 30 minutes.*
Cost:	*Free.*
MATA:	*#56, 36 (ex Sun), 17 (ex Sun).*
E&H:	*Difficult for wheelchairs to maneuver, but you can see the process through a window.*

See donuts being made and get a free sample.

The Arts

Art show opening at Oates Gallery 1973.

William Eggleston

ART MUSEUMS

BROOKS MEMORIAL ART GALLERY
Overton Park* 38112. 726-5266.

Hours:	10am-5pm Tu-Sat; 1-5pm Sun.
Tours:	Scheduled tours 1:30 & 3:30pm Sun. Group tours (for 5+) by appointment; may be tailored to a specific topic and given in foreign languages.
Cost:	Free.
Lunch:	Bring your own and picnic in Overton Park. (No picnicking on museum grounds.) Museum's kitchen facilities available for special art meetings and receptions; arrange in advance.
MATA:	Showboat Bus. Or #5, 55 (ex Sun) to Poplar and Tucker, the Park's main entrance; walk north two blocks. Or #3 (ex Sat & Sun) to the zoo entrance; walk south about five blocks.
Other:	1) Gift shop, postcards and gifts. 2) Sunday Series: 2:30pm. Movies, poetry readings, musical presentations, or lectures. 3) Reference art library, open to museum members. 4) Two special tours, "About Faces" (a multi-media display) and "The Color Gypsy" (a color game for children). 5) Special art weekends for children, free educational programs. Child must be accompanied by an adult.
E&H:	1) Wheelchair accessible. Ring buzzer at north entrance. 2) Phone education office to arrange tours for the visually or hearing impaired. Special guides and signers available. Hour long tactile tours for visually handicapped, by appointment 9am-4pm M. 3) Senior citizen program, 1:30-3pm Th, features a film, short tour of one section of the museum, and tea and cookies. Individuals may drop by; larger groups should call in advance.

Brooks is the city's primary museum of the fine and decorative arts. It houses part of the Kress Collection of Renaissance paintings and permanent exhibits of 18th and 19thc. American, European, Egyptian, and Oriental painting, porcelain, furniture, silver, and glass. Major temporary and traveling loaned exhibits change often, four a month on the average.

Mrs. Bessie Vance Brooks built the museum in memory of her husband, Samuel Hamilton Brooks. In 1912 she gave it to the city. The original building was designed by James Gamble Rogers and resembles the Villa di Papa Guilio II near Rome. The museum's first director was Florence M. McIntyre, author of Art and Life. In 1972 a large two-level main exhibition area was added.

DIXON GALLERY AND GARDENS
4339 Park Ave. 38117. 761-5250.

Hours:	11am-5pm Tu-Sat, 1-5pm Sun. Closed M and major holidays.
Tours:	Docent guided group tours. Arrange in advance.
Cost:	Adults/$1; children 3-11, students & senior citizens/50¢; by appointment, non-profit groups, 50¢/person and organized school groups, free.

Free entry for everyone on Tu.
Lunch: Arrange in advance for group picnics on the terrace or catered receptions and luncheons.
MATA: #57, 52.
Other: 1) Films, 7pm the last Th of each month. 2) Occasional lectures, seminars and out-of-town tours. 3) Outdoor spring and summer concerts. 4) Drawing classes for children each summer.
E&H: Museum and gardens are accessible to the physically handicapped.

Margaret and Hugo Dixon left this lovely 1940s house, 17 acres of gardens, and their outstanding art collection to the public. The permanent collection is primarily 19thc. French and American Impressionists and related schools. There are also 18th and 19thc. British portraits and landscapes and British and French sculpture.

The house is filled with antique English furniture, silver, crystal, stoneware, porcelain, and rugs. The atmosphere is that of a private home rather than a museum.

NATIONAL ORNAMENTAL METAL MUSEUM
374 W. California (on the river, just south of Harahan, Frisco, and Memphis-Arkansas Bridges). 774-6380.

Hours: Noon-5pm Tu-Sun.
Tours: For groups of six or more, phone in advance.
Cost: Free.
Lunch: Picnic tables on the grounds. For large groups, arrange in advance and make a donation to the museum to cover clean-up costs.
MATA: No service.
Other: Bring your knives, axes, copper pots, wrought iron furniture—any metal item in need of repair—to the free "fix-it" held one weekend each year. They'll sharpen, solder, ... it. Entrance fee/$1. Donations are accepted.
E&H: Access to museum would be extremely difficult for those in wheelchairs.

The metal museum is located on three acres of parkland just north of DeSoto Park* in three 1930s buildings that once housed doctors and nurses from the Marine Hospital. The Marine Hospital itself was established in 1884 by the federal government to care for employees in marine or waterway jobs. The raised Victorian Italianate building was constructed about 1860.

The museum displays historical and contemporary work in both cast and wrought iron, brass, bronze, and copper. Demonstration/workshops are held periodically.

PINK PALACE*—Primarily a natural history and science museum, but the Pink Palace occasionally has temporary art exhibits ranging from decorative arts and crafts to photography.

ART GALLERIES & SHOWS

COMMERCIAL GALLERIES
Memphis has three full-time commercial galleries:

Alice Bingham Gallery—24 S. Cooper. 722-8665. Open 11am-5pm Tu&W, 11am-10pm Th-Sat. Primarily prints and posters by local and international artists.

Brad McMillan's Studio/Gallery—116A S. Front Str. at Gayoso. 522-9931. Open 11am-6pm M-Sat, 1-5pm Sun. His own cartoons and prints plus craft and commercial art shows.

Oates Gallery—97 Tillman. 323-5659. Open 10am-4pm M-Sat. Primarily current European paintings with occasional shows by local artists.

Many banks, stores, office and theatre lobbies, and community and religious centers have commercial gallery space. Current exhibits are listed in the monthly "Memphis Magazine", the Memphis "Commercial Appeal" Sunday Fanfare Section, and the "Memphis Press-Scimitar" Friday Showcase section.

Rose Long, Art Authenticator (725-1283), is an art dealer who buys, sells, and advises clients by appointment.

CLOUGH-HANSON GALLERY
Southwestern*, 2000 N. Parkway, Clough Hall (most modern building on campus, just northeast of library). 274-1800.

Hours: 9am-4pm M-F.
Tours: Browse around the tiny gallery on your own.
Cost: Free.
Lunch: School dining hall and snack bar, in nearby buildings, open during academic year.
MATA: Showboat Bus and #53 (ex Sun).
Other: Visitor parking in front of library. Enter campus off University Str.
E&H: Wheelchair accessible.

Exhibits here change monthly and might be works by visiting artists, faculty, or students or pieces from the university collection.

LEMOYNE-OWEN COLLEGE* EXHIBIT SPACE/LIBRARY
807 Walker. 774-9090 ext. 271.

Hours: 9am-4pm M-F. Space is sometimes used for meetings so phone ahead to *make sure it's open.*

Tours: Call to make arrangements for groups.
Cost: Free.
Lunch: School dining hall in the student center.
MATA: #4.
Other: 1) Starving Artist Sales, Aug & Dec. 2) Art festivals, March & June.

Exhibits change monthly. Loaned exhibits by both community and non-resident artists alternate with shows by faculty and students.

MEMPHIS ACADEMY OF ARTS*/GALLERY
Overton Park. 726-4085.

Hours: 9am-5pm M-F.
Cost: Free.
Lunch: Snack bar.
MATA: Showboat Bus and #5, 55 (ex Sun), or 3 (ex Sat & Sun), then about a three-block walk through Overton Park.
E&H: Wheelchair accessible through a ground floor entrance on the building's east side.

Faculty, student, and visiting artist shows throughout the year in the spacious lobby/gallery. You might want to commission a work of art.

THE UNIVERSITY GALLERY
Communication & Fine Arts Bldg, Rm. 142, Memphis State University*. 454-2224.

Hours: 10am-5pm Tu-F, 10am-6pm Sat, 1-5pm Sun.
Cost: Free.
Lunch: Campus cafeterias are open to the public. See MSU map for locations.
MATA: #50 (ex Sun).
Other: Closest parking lot is on Central across from the theatre complex.
E&H: Wheelchair accessible.

The gallery opened in 1981 and offers special exhibitions, group faculty and graduate student shows, and exhibits drawn from MSU's African, Egyptian, and print collections.

FILM

COMMERCIAL THEATRES
Most commercial theatres in the city show first-run feature movies. Tickets, about $4 with occasional 'til 2pm bargain matinees. Some feature special children's and classic series. Check ads in the local papers. A

listing and brief review appear in Friday's and Sunday's "Commercial Appeal" and in Friday's "Memphis Press-Scimitar". The Balmoral Cinema at 6080 Quince (683-8994) and the Memphian at 51 S. Cooper (272-9604) show occasional reruns and foreign films. The hearing impaired may enjoy shows with subtitles.

FILM SERIES

Film buffs, whatever their age or interest, can find a film series around town. The newspapers, "Memphis Magazine", and WKNO Radio usually announce the schedules.

Brooks Art Gallery* Sunday Programs—Museum's basement auditorium, Overton Park. 726-5266. Irregular schedule, movies share 2:30pm slot with other programs. Free

Chucalissa Indian Museum*—Museum's auditorium, off Highway 61 S. and Mitchell Rd. 785-3160. 30-45 minute documentaries on Indian history and culture. 2pm alternate Sun. Free.

Dixon Gallery and Gardens* Series—Gallery's auditorium, 4339 Park Ave. 761-5250. Popular films and classics. 7pm last Th each month. Adults/$2, children (5-12) & senior citizens/$1, members of gallery/free. Schedule included in member's newsletter; membership open to public.

Filmtrak—Jewish Community Center, auditorium, 6560 Poplar. 761-0810. Documentaries and classic and current foreign films. One per month, 7:30pm W Sept-Apr. Post-showing coffee and discussion. Tickets, $2.25 at the door or season ticket, public/$12, members of Center/$10.

Friday Flics—Memphis and Shelby County Public Library and Information Center, basement meeting rooms A & B in the main library, 1850 Peabody Ave. 528-2988. Everything from classics to documentaries. 3pm & 7:15pm F. In addition, comedies are shown outdoors in the parking lot during the summer, 7:15pm W. Children might enjoy this outdoors treat. A quarterly schedule, "Reel World" is available at the library. Monthly notice of films included in library's news pamphlet "Kaleidoscope". Free.

Goodwyn Institute Lectures and Films—Memphis State University*, University Center, main campus across from Administration Bldg, 3rd floor multi-purpose room. 454-2041 or 454-2040. Travel films and lectures 7:45pm 1st F each month. Free. Brochure available.

Images—Southwestern College, Frazier Jelke Science Center, auditorium, 2000 N. Parkway. 274-1800. Avant-garde international films.

Series of five films in the spring. 8pm Sun. Southwestern students/$1, others/$2.50. Schedule available in college's student center.

MAA Cinema—Memphis Academy of Arts, Overton Park, basement auditorium. 726-4085. Usually foreign art films. 8pm usually on F during school year. Free.

Memphis and Shelby County Public Library and Information Center*—The various branches offer scheduled free films. Many are for children—what a nice way to spend a rainy day! For schedule and information check with the branch nearest you or pick up a monthly "Kaleidoscope" at the library. See also Friday Flics.

University College Classic Film Series—Memphis State University*, Johnson Hall, Patterson Str, main campus, main floor auditorium. 454-2035 or 454-2079. Classics, documentaries, and a few popular films. 7:30pm at least one Th per month except summer & Dec. Tickets/ 75¢. Schedule available by phone or in 414 University Center.

University Program's Popular Film Series—Memphis State University*, University Center, main campus near Administration Bldg, 3rd floor ballroom, ticket office on main floor. 454-2035 or 454-2079. Fairly current full-length films. At least two per month, 12:30 & 7pm W, 12:30 & 9:30pm F except summer & Dec. Tickets/75¢. For schedule phone or go by 414 University Center.

Women's Resources Center of Memphis—499 Patterson. 458-1407. Occasional films by or about women. Usually 7:30pm Th. Free. Center's newsletter with information is available for $5.

SHOW YOUR OWN

The Films and Community Video Department of the main library on Peabody (528-2988) has a film loan program. Sixteen millimeter films varying from old features to travel and religious films may be borrowed for 24 hours by community and non-profit groups. Borrower must be issued a special library card and pay 75¢ per reel. The library has a catalogue of available films.

Wondering what to do for a child's birthday party? Eight millimeter films, usually cartoons and comedies, available for three days at 25¢ per reel. Art and travel related slides available for 10¢ per set.

The library has catalogued its films by special interest. Among the subjects available are Black history, business & management, travel, city life, and films for the hearing-impaired adult.

Projectors may be rented from audio-visual companies or rental services. See the yellow pages of the phone book.

DANCE

HARRY BRYCE DANCE COMPANY

Kuumba Work Shop, 1004 Miss. Blvd. 774-9119. Modern, Afro-Caribbean, and jazz dance are the specialties of this seven year old company. Public performances presented on an irregular basis. Tickets/$2.50-$3. Courses for ages 13 + in dance and theatre makeup, especially makeup for the black performer. Lecture demonstrations/mini-performances are offered to community groups, organizations, and schools for fees starting at $200.

MEMPHIS BALLET/BALLET SOUTH

P.O. Box 41741, 38104. 274-3970. Memphis' two major ballet companies merged in spring 1981 to form this single corporate structure. Each company remains a separate artistic entity, offering several performances in a joint season series. Memphis Ballet, organized in 1952, and now under the artistic direction of Michael and Judy Tevlin, has a repertoire ranging from classical full length productions to contemporary works by nationally recognized choreographers. Each Dec they perform the "Nutcracker Suite" with the Memphis Symphony Orchestra. A Christmas treat for all ages! Ballet South, formed in 1969 by its current artistic director George Latimer, offers original compositions and choreography and is the more urban oriented branch of the company. Each artistic director operates his own school. A season series ticket for four performances is $35, students $25. Individual tickets range from $7-$15. Lecture demonstrations and touring performances may be arranged.

YOUTH CONCERT BALLET, INC.

1904 Harbert. 276-6075. This is a children's performing ballet company, the first of its kind in the South. Children ages 10-18 present one major performance a year. The company is available for lecture demonstrations with at least one month advance notice. Dorothy Gunther Pugh is the artistic director.

MUSIC & OPERA

Brooks Art Museum*, Dixon Galleries and Gardens*, the Jewish Community Center, various school auditoriums, and churches feature occasional concerts and recitals.

Local and touring commercial concerts and performances are usually booked at the Coliseum*, Auditorium*, and Orpheum*.

For information on jazz, blues, rock & roll, and country & western music and on nightspots see the chapter Music/The Memphis Sound.

ARTIST CONCERT SERIES
Sponsored by the Beethoven Club, 263 S. McLean 38104. 274-2504.

Curtain: 8pm, nights vary, three to five major performances each year in the Auditorium.

Tickets: Single/$3-$15. Series/$12-$30, varies each year depending on number of performances.

Other: 1) Beethoven Club Boy Choir, elementary schoolboys participate. 2) Three free resident artist recitals each year.

Begun in 1888 as a small "music circle", the Beethoven Club has encouraged the arts in Memphis for 90 years and is the city's oldest cultural organization. It annually sponsors this concert series of performances by visiting professional artists. The programs include opera, ballet, symphony, and Broadway musicals.

GERMANTOWN SYMPHONY ORCHESTRA
Germantown Arts Council, 2381 Germantown Rd. S. 754-2528.

Curtain: Usually 8:15pm at various area theatres.
Tickets: Free.
Other: Occasional children's matinees.

The non-professional community orchestra's musical programs are designed to appeal to the whole family. Children are welcome. Aspiring musicians can audition for the orchestra in Aug & Jan.

MEMPHIS SYMPHONY ORCHESTRA
3100 Walnut Grove Rd, Suite 402, 38111. 324-3627.

Curtain: Nine major performances in Auditorium's Music Hall, 8pm Sat, repeated at 2:30pm Sun, Oct-Apr.

Tickets: 1) Series/$25-$62.50. Single/$3.50-$9.50; students under 24 years old get a 50% discount. 2) Pop Concerts, series/$8-$25.50, single/$3.50-$9.50. 3) "Nutcracker Suite" tickets, adults/$3.50-$9.50, children 12 and under/$3.50-$5.50. 4) Organizations and schools may buy blocks of seats for individual performances at reduced rates.

Other: 1) A 22-player little symphony, the Memphis Symphony Chamber Orchestra, goes into the schools as an educational program. The annual Children's Art Day combines their performance, a picnic, and tours/puppet shows/animal shows at the Pink Palace* for Mid-South and Memphis school children. 2) A 72-player Youth Symphony, composed of students, gives two or three concerts per year in Ridgeway School's auditorium. Tickets/$1. Membership, by audition. 3) Part-scholarships offered to a few children to Sewanee Music Camp.

In 1909 orchestral groups merged to form the core of Memphis' first symphony orchestra. It had its first season as a 21 person chamber orchestra in 1952 under the direction of Conductor Vincent de Frank. In 1960 the name became officially the Memphis Symphony Orchestra.

Vincent de Frank still conducts the symphony which is now all-professional. Major performances feature world-famous artists and conductors such as Lorin Hollander, Leontyne Price, Arthur Fiedler, Van Cliburn, and Pablo Casals. The symphony also plays a pop series yearly and performs a "Sunset Symphony" during Memphis in May* festivities. Each Christmas they stage "The Nutcracker Suite" with the Memphis Ballet.

METROPOLITAN OPERA COMPANY OF NEW YORK/MEMPHIS VISIT
Sponsored by Arts Appreciation Foundation, Southern Ave. 454-2074.

Curtain: 8pm, three nights each May in the Auditorium.
Tickets: Single/$10-$29. Series/$34-$78.

The Met comes to Memphis each May with three operas, one for each night of their visit. Bravissimo!

MUSIC DEPARTMENT, LEMOYNE-OWEN COLLEGE*
807 Walker. 775-9090. The humanities division sponsors jazz clinics, jazz concerts, gospel concerts, Christmas programs, and opera in the college's Little Theatre or gym, or at Second United and Second Congregational Churches. Admission, usually free.

MUSIC DEPARTMENT, MEMPHIS STATE UNIVERSITY*
Harris Auditorium, Central Ave. (parking lot across the street). 454-2043 (ticket information), 454-2557 (information and times). This is a very strong music department; the city is lucky! It sponsors the MSU Symphony Orchestra, Contemporary Chamber Players, Symphonic Wind Ensemble, String Quartet, Woodwind Quintet, jazz bands and combos, Percussion Ensemble, University Chorale, University Opera Theatre, Memphis Oratorio Society, University Concert Choir, Camerata Singers, and concert and varsity bands. There are also faculty, student, and guest recitals.

Performances are usually scheduled at 8:15pm in the campus' Harris Auditorium. Some performances are free, for others there is a charge, adults/$5, faculty, staff, & senior citizens/$3, students/$1.

For budding musicians—the university has a suzuki music program. And don't forget, during football season, children might enjoy watching the band practice near MLG&W on Zack Curlin Str.—just follow your ears.

MUSIC DEPARTMENT, SHELBY STATE COMMUNITY COLLEGE*

1588 Union Ave, P.O. Box 4568, 38104. 528-6841. Two programs annually, one during Christmas season and one during Spring Festival Week feature the Concert Band, Choir, Singers, and Jazz Band. Two student and faculty recitals are offered each year. Performances are free and usually held in the ground floor theatre of Building D (enter from Linden).

MUSIC DEPARTMENT, SOUTHWESTERN*

2000 N. Parkway. 274-1800. Two performances by the Southwestern Chamber Orchestra and Singers, one visiting artist concert, six faculty recitals, and a spring music festival are offered each year. Performances, usually free, are held in Hardie Auditorium in the campus' Administration Building (distinguished by its tower). Private music lessons may be arranged through the department.

OPERA MEMPHIS

Memphis State University, South Campus (Park & Getwell), 38152. 454-2043 (tickets and information), 454-2706 (information).

Curtain: 8pm Sat, four major performances yearly in Dixon Myers North Hall of the Auditorium.

Tickets: Series/$20-$70. Single/$5-$20. Faculty & student discounts with valid ID.

Other: Southern Opera Theatre is an adjunct of Opera Memphis. Members are graduate students at MSU. They perform lesser roles in Opera Memphis productions, put on productions for school groups, and tour in the spring.

A nationally acclaimed professional opera company, Opera Memphis presents four full-length operas and one recital each year. Guest conductors and singers appear with the company under the direction of Anne Randolph.

THEATRE

In addition to the following local theatre, many touring dramatic productions stop in Memphis, usually at the Auditorium* (523-7645) or the Orpheum* (523-6188).

CIRCUIT PLAYHOUSE

1705 Poplar, 38104. 726-5521.

Curtain: 8pm F, Sat, & Sun, June-Feb plus special summer shows.

Tickets: Season: adults/$25, students & senior citizens/$20. Single: adults/$5, *students & senior citizens/$4.*

E&H: 1) *No wheelchairs.* 2) *Theatre of the Deaf operates out of Circuit Play-house. It is a theatre for hearing-impaired adults and youth ages 12-18. The hearing-impaired take part in both technical and dramatic aspects of the performances which use sign language and pantomime as well as the spoken word and music.*

Avant-garde and popular plays. Circuit Playhouse is always looking for new ideas. This theatre, staffed entirely by volunteers, presents six plays a year, usually for five week runs.

GASLIGHT DINNER THEATRE
1110 E. Brooks Rd. 396-7474.

Curtain: *Cocktails 6:15pm, dinner 6:45-7:45pm, show 8pm Tu-Sat; cocktails 4:15pm, dinner 4:45-5:45pm, show 6pm Sun.*
Tickets: *$15/person, includes dinner, show, and tax. Group rates for 20+.*
E&H: *Wheelchair accessible.*

A package offering dinner and professional popular plays.

GERMANTOWN THEATRE
3037 Forest Hill Rd, Germantown, Tn. 38138. 754-2680.

Curtain: *8pm Th-Sat & 3pm Sun, Sept-June.*
Tickets: *Season/$25. Single: adults/$6, students/$4.50 for plays; adults/$7.50, students/$6 for musicals. Senior citizens tickets at student rates for matinees. Group discounts by arrangement.*
Other: *Germantown Children's Theatre is a drama company with three productions a year by and for children. Tickets, adults/$2, children/$1.*
E&H: *Wheelchair accessible.*

This volunteer community theatre presents five plays a year.

MAIN THEATRE and STUDIO THEATRE
Memphis State University*, Theatre and Communication Arts Bldg, Central. 454-2565 (show times), 454-2043 (ticket information).

Curtain: *8pm, days vary, Sept-June.*
Tours: *Given by graduate students during the school year. Call to arrange.*
Tickets: *Season: adults (10 tickets)/$25; students, MSU faculty & staff (5 tickets)/$7.50. Single tickets: for musicals, adults/$5, students & faculty/$3; for non-musicals, adults/$3.50, students & faculty/$2. Group discount rates available.*
Other: *Dance, mime, and chamber theatre troupes sponsored by MSU offer lectures, workshops, and performances for school and community groups Sept-June. They tour in the summer. Fees for a touring performance begin at $75 and go up depending on type of performance, audience size, and*

🚲 *your ability to pay. Occasional special shows geared to children are of-*
fered.
E&H: *Wheelchair accessible through side doors.*

Each year ten shows—plays, comedies, musicals, —are presented in the Main Theatre which seats 400 and in Studio Theatre which seats 125. Guest professionals occasionally take part in both the technical and dramatic aspects of productions.

🚲 MEMPHIS CHILDREN'S THEATRE
2635 Avery Ave. (behind Board of Education). 274-3611.

Curtain: *When active 7 or 7:30pm daily, 2:30 & 5:30pm Sat & Sun. Plays generally*
run for 12 performances.
Tickets: *50¢.*
Other: 1) Free classes for children ages 6-18 in acting, dance, voice, technical
aspects of theatre, 4-9pm M-F and all day Sat. 2) A children's summer
touring company performs at various parks and community centers during June & July.
E&H: *Wheelchair accessible.*

Children produce four to six major shows and several small ones each year. The plays are often adaptations of nursery and folk tales. Run by the Park Commission, the theatre has a professional staff that coordi-nates and directs the programs, but the actors, backstage crew, scenery painters, ... are children. Participation in the theatre is open to all in-terested children.

PLAYHOUSE ON THE SQUARE
2121 Madison, Overton Square, 38104. 726-4656 (box office), 725-0776 (business office).

Curtain: *8pm W-Sun, Sept-June.*
Tickets: *Season (7 performances): adults/$33-$38, students & senior citizens/*
$28. Single: $6-$7 for non-musicals, $7-$8 for musicals. Group discounts
available on W, Th, & Sun. Groups of 10-24 get 20% off.
Other: *1) Make a night of it in Overton Square*. With a season ticket you receive*
seven dinner discounts at many of the Square's restaurants. 2) Story hour,
an hour of stories, puppet shows, mime, and magic, 3pm Sat, Oct-Apr.
🚲 *Children/50¢, adults/free. 3) The Playhouse Conservatory Theatre pro-*
gram offers theatre classes for students aiming at a professional career,
9am-noon Sat.
E&H: *Wheelchair accessible.*

Memphis' only resident professional theatre has a repertoire ranging from classical to avant-garde. The atmosphere in the small theatre is much like that of a New York cabaret.

Playhouse on the Square is the professional theatre of Circuit Playhouse Inc.* The director is Jackie Nichols.

THEATRE DEPARTMENT, LEMOYNE-OWEN COLLEGE*
807 Walker Ave, Little Theatre in the Alma C. Hanson Student Center, 38126. 774-9090. The LeMoyne-Owen Players present three or four plays during the school year. Each runs for about four days in the Little Theatre, located in the student center basement. Admission, free for LeMoyne students, free or about $1 for visitors.

THEATRE DEPARTMENT, SHELBY STATE COMMUNITY COLLEGE*
1588 Union Ave, P.O. Box 4568, 38104. 528-6875 or 528-6733. Shelby State produces one or two plays each year. Performances are in the ground floor theatre of Building D Room 102 on the Linden side of the school. Admission, free for Shelby State students, other: adults/$2, children under 12/$1.50.

THEATRE DEPARTMENT, SOUTHWESTERN*
2000 N. Parkway. 274-1800. They produce about six plays a year, each running four to six nights. Plays are usually in Theatre Six, located in the basement of Palmer Hall (distinguished by its tower). Curtain times vary. Admission, free-$2.

THEATRE MEMPHIS
630 Perkins Ext. at Southern, 38117. 682-8323.

Curtain: 8pm Tu-Sun & 3pm Sun, Sept-June.

Tickets: Season (6 performances): adults/$22.50, students/$18. Single: musicals and guest star performances, adults/$8-$10, students/$5-$6; plays, adults/$6, students/$4. Group and senior citizen discounts available for previews.

Other: 1) Classes for all interest levels from four year olds to advanced drama students in dance, yoga, voice, lighting, design, and other theatre-related fields. 2) Free lectures and slide show for community organizations and groups. Arrange at least three to four weeks in advance. 3) Costumes and props may be rented by civic and educational organizations at low rates. 4) Lawrence Anthony's sculpted figures outside the theatre depict figures from theatrical history: Pulcinella, Sarah Bernhardt, Medea, Oscar Wilde's Ernest, Shakespeare's Cleopatra, Synge's Christie Mahon, and Beckett's Ham.

E&H: 1) Wheelchair accessible. 2) Classes in creative dramatics for the handicapped.

One of the country's oldest amateur community theatres, Theatre Memphis presents six major productions yearly. Its first was in 1921. From 1929-1975, Memphis Little Theatre, as it was then called, was housed in the Pink Palace*. In 1975 Memphis Little Theatre became Theatre Memphis and moved into its well-designed new home. The theatre's two stages, the main auditorium seating 435 and the Little Theatre seating 135 in the round, usually offer traditional plays by amateurs under professional direction.

SUMMERTIME TREATS

Arts in the Park—Overton Park* Shell. 454-5750. Spend a lovely summer night listening to music and star-gazing. Free summer outdoor programs, 8:15pm Tu&Th. Programs run the gamut from drama to ballet, bluegrass, gospel, jazz, children's theatre, and opera. They are sponsored by the Park Commission. Schedules available or check the local papers.

Blues Foundation Concerts—Beale Str.* 332-6459. Daily blues concerts around Handy's* statue, 4:30-8pm M-F, June-Aug.

Children's Theatre Bus Shows—274-3611. A small touring group from Children's Theatre* performs in city parks and community centers during June & July.

Downtown Dream Machine—Confederate Park*, Court at Front Str. 725-7836. Organized to promote both the arts and downtown, 18 different groups combined to make the dream come true. For two weeks during July a play is presented outdoors at 8:30pm Tu-Sun. Tickets, adults/$2, children/$1. Free lunchtime treats on the same stage, 12:15pm M-F, range from bluegrass and puppet shows to short plays and dance.

Jazz Concerts—Memphis/Shelby County Public Library and Information Center, main branch, Peabody at McLean. 528-2965. Three free jazz concerts by Memphis artists—one each month during the summer, 7:30pm Th.

Memphis Park Commission Music Classes—454-5750. Six weeks of free musical instruction for children ages 6-12 offered at selected community centers in June & July.

Red Balloon Players—454-2576. If you see bunches of kids in the park giggling and clapping, they're probably watching the Red Balloon Players, an adjunct of the Memphis State University* Speech and Drama Dept. The summertime-only pantomime shows are staged in different parks at 11am & 1:30pm M-W. Check local papers for park locations. Performances in Memphis State University's Studio Theatre, 10:30am & 1pm Th & F. Performances are free and almost as much fun for the grown-ups as for the children.

Summerband—Germantown High School. 754-9998 or 754-8380. Summerband is open to anyone who has ever played in a band before, youth or adult. It rehearses 7:30-10pm every Th night during the summer in the band room at Germantown High School. They present four free community concerts in the Germantown Municipal Park sponsored by First Tennessee Bank. Phone for dates.

INFORMATION

The Memphis Arts Council—P.O. Box 41682, 263 McLean Blvd, 38104. 278-2950. They offer current information on art events and Memphis teachers of the arts. The "Senior Arts Sampler" offers a transportation and discount ticket package to those 60 + .

FM-100 Concert Line—WMC-FM 100, 1960 Union 38104. 276-7881. A 24-hour daily recorded message lists upcoming musical concerts, performance dates, prices, and ticket sale locations.

Memphis State University Schedule & Information—454-2079. A 24-hour daily taped message lists art exhibits, concerts, theatre performances, lectures, and other university activities.

LINC (Library Information Center)—1850 Peabody 38104. 528-2999. Trying to find a place for your 12-year-old to study silk screening? LINC can refer you to their free pamphlet "Summer Survival Kit" or to classes sponsored by such organizations as the Germantown Arts Assn. LINC has current information on groups interested in folk dancing, square dancing, classical guitar, dulcimer, handloom weaving, writing, watercolor, crafts in general, and pottery in particular. Many of these art organizations offer lecture/demonstrations to interested groups.

They'll tell you that the Independent Political Action Committee provides drum and majorette corps for performances at Democratic rallies, that you can hire the International Brotherhood of Magicians to perform magic shows for birthday parties, that the Hobby Center of the Park Commission offers classes to those 18 + and provides speakers, demonstrations, and exhibits in various areas of arts and crafts, that the choral/drama group of the Peabody Center for Senior Citizens gives performances on a six-week notice and the band on a two-week notice, that the Pink Palace offers films, puppet shows, and activities for children at 2pm

Sat & Sun, Oct-May, that the Dental Society Auxiliary offers free puppet shows on dental hygiene for children 5-7 years old, that the 40-member Shelby State Metro Concert Band will play free at non-political group meetings or civic events with a two week notice, that the Stage Set Players may be hired to present plays for children, and that in addition to films, the library branches offer free storytelling and craft programs for children.

Just give them a call. Their service is free and very helpful.

"Program Resources and Techniques"—A pamphlet, compiled by the Memphis and Shelby County Public Library and Information Center is available from their education department for $1 and is worth ten times that.

The brochure is published each year and offers current information on available speakers. For instance, under Arts you'll find speakers on stained glass, art in the community today, communication and art, art objects as an investment, photography, literature, music, and many other specialties.

It will also refer you to the Art/Music/Recreation Department of the Main Library (Eileen Sheahan at 528-2976). Free lectures on a two to three week notice are offered on ceramics, art history and periods of art history, crafts, Memphis music, opera, history of theatre in Memphis, history of motion pictures, ...

Theatre Ticket Services

Goldsmith's Central Ticket Agency: Oakcourt, 4545 Poplar - 767-7495. Downtown, 123 S. Main - 527-3894.

Ticket Hub: 149 N. Angelus - 725-4822.

Tickets Now: Orpheum* - 523-6188.

Sports

Alan Floyd and Russell Rhodes, Bat Boys for the Chicks, July 1980.

SPORTS/TO DO

MEMPHIS PARK COMMISSION

2599 Avery Ave. 454-5759. The city's parks, including its four major ones — Overton, Audubon, McKellar, and Dr. Martin Luther King, Jr.- Riverside — and its 26 community centers are all operated by the Memphis Park commission. They offer a wide range of facilities and organized programs summer and winter.

The 26 **community centers** are scattered throughout the city and are designed as meeting places for all ages. In northwest Memphis:

Bickford	232 Bickford Ave.	527-8752
Dave Wells	915 Chelsea	526-7193
Ed Rice	2907 N. Watkins	357-6919
Hurt Village	582 Auction Ave.	525-4047
Katie Sexton	1235 Brown Ave.	272-1388
Greenlaw	—	—
North Frayser	2555 St. Elmo	—

In northeast:

Douglass	1616 Ash	327-6131
Gaisman	4221 Macon Rd.	682-6161
Hollywood	2499 Chelsea Ave.	458-6775
Lester	317 Tillman	324-2639
Raleigh	3678 Powers Rd.	372-2085

In southeast:

Bethel Labelle	2698 LaRose Ave.	743-6875
Davis	3371 Spottswood Ave.	323-8015
Hanley	680 Hanley Str.	323-8663
McFarland	4955 Cottonwood Rd.	362-8350
Willow	4791 Willow Rd.	685-8120

In southwest:

Gaston	1046 S. 3rd	774-4156
Glenview	1813 Southern Ave.	276-6180
Hamilton	1363 Dixie Ave.	947-6417
Magnolia	2130 Wabash	278-4944
Mitchell	602 W. Mitchell Rd.	789-2927
Pine Hill	973 Alice Ave.	774-7950
Riverview	1891 Kansas	774-3041
Westwood	810 Western Park	785-5975
Whitehaven	4318 Graceland Dr.	332-0783

From Sept-May the centers operate primarily indoor programs; June-Aug, they emphasize outdoor activities. Centers are open 2-10pm Tu-F, 9am-5pm Sat, Sept-May; 2-10pm M-F, June-Aug.

SPECIAL PROGRAMS are offered at certain centers: arts and crafts at Sue Hick Hobby Center (2635 Avery Ave, 324-7650), social, cultural, and recreational programs for those with mental or physical disabilities at Raymond Skinner Center for the Handicapped (712 Tanglewood, 272-2528), and special senior citizen programs at Lewis (1188 N. Parkway, 272-7408), Orange Mound (2569 Douglass Ave, 323-3662), and Peabody (1205 Peabody Ave, 726-6952) centers.

Church, business, and civic sponsored TEAMS, FOR MEN AND WOMEN OVER 18, are run city-wide by the Park Commission's adult athletic program. Fees per team are: basketball, touch football and rugby/$200, softball/$225, and baseball/$125-$325 depending on number of games. For information phone 454-5755.

For Memphis YOUTH, ages 6-18, the Park Commission runs baseball, basketball, boxing, touch football, rugby, soccer, softball, tennis, and volleyball programs. Leagues are organized for church, school, business, and civic sponsored teams. There is a $2 per person fee for team sports; soccer is the exception with a $1 per person fee. Youth programs are run out of four zone offices: Zone 1 (353-9532) serving northwest Memphis/Frayser, Zone 2 (388-5911) serving northeast Memphis and Raleigh, Zone 3 (767-4580) serving southeast Memphis, and Zone 4 (789-5665) serving southwest Memphis. For specific program information contact your zone.

The Park Commission operates several special SUMMER PROGRAMS for youth: track at Whitehaven and the Fairgrounds 4-10pm M-F; playground activities for ages 6-16, around the city, 9:30am-4:30pm M-F; day camps (274-8406) in two-week sessions for ages 6-16, 10am-3pm M-F; overnight camping sessions in July at Country Camp, Shelby County Penal Farm, three-day sessions include swimming, arts & crafts, fishing, hiking, and horseback riding, cost, $10; free music camps; special education day camp for children with physical and/or mental disabilities.

For more information about Park Commission programs get a copy of their two free booklets, "The Play Book" by Jimmy Ogle and "Memphis Recreation".

SHELBY COUNTY CONSERVATION BOARD
2599 Avery Ave, 38112. 454-5763. The Conservation Board is responsible for all parklands in Shelby County outside the Memphis city limits. It:

Sponsors SUMMER RECREATIONAL PROGRAMS in boxing, hockey, paddle tennis, volleyball, arts and crafts, and horseshoes.

Sponsors BASEBALL AND SOFTBALL PROGRAMS.

Maintains SHELBY-FARMS PLOUGH RECREATION AREA on Mullins Station Rd. Activities include fishing, horseback riding, hiking, picnicking, and playground. Open 8am-4:30pm M-F.

Operates the EQUESTRIAN CENTER, an outdoor arena located on Germantown Rd. at Walnut Grove. Available for horse shows.

Operates the MEMPHIS/SHELBY COUNTY BOXING ARENA in the Merchant Building at the Fairgrounds.

Maintains seven free TENNIS FACILITIES.

YMCA

Business office, 2670 Union Ave. Ext. 454-1201.
Branches:

Mason Branch/Northeast—3548 Walker. 323-4505. 8am-10pm daily. 24 hour information. Indoor swimming, full gym, rooming facilities, summer day camp.

Davis Branch—4727 Elvis Presley Blvd. 398-2366. 8:30am-9pm, M-Sat. Indoor and outdoor swimming, tennis, & some exercise equipment.

Stratton Branch/Downtown—245 Madison. 521-9622, 526-4421 (fitness center). 6:45am-9pm M-F. Indoor swimming, full gym + racketball & handball courts.

Quince Branch/East—5885 Quince. 767-9396. 8:30am-9pm M-Sat. Outdoor swimming.

Shady Grove Branch/East—5530 Shady Grove. 685-2898. 2-6pm M-F. Summer day camp.

The YMCA offers a wide variety of recreational and educational programs and classes, including swimming, youth sports, youth track, senior citizen programs, day care, nursery care, jogging, weight lifting, and physical fitness. Yearly membership rates for family or individual. Facilities and special programs vary among branches. For information call the individual branches or the main business office.

For out-of-town visitors, facilities are open on an individual fee basis. A swim or visit to the health club is in the $2 range. For specifics and arrangements call the main business office (454-1201).

ROOMS are available at the Mason Branch for men and women 18 years and older, $37.52 per week with a $15 deposit the first week.

SWIMMING CLASSES FOR THE MENTALLY/PHYSICALLY HANDI-CAPPED are offered each Sat. at the Mason Branch, $12 for a five week session.

PHYSICAL FITNESS PROGRAMS are designed at the Stratton and Mason Branches with testing and personalized exercise programs. At Stratton, gym and health club facilities for men only. Mason facilities, open to men and women.

SUMMER CAMPS for children 6-12, 9am-4:30pm M-F at Shady Grove and Mason Branches. Non-member fee, $37.50 a week. Early morning/late stay child çare program available for working parents.

SUMMER SWIMMING CLASSES at branches with pools. Two-week sessions with classes M-F. Ages three months +. Fee, members/$5, non-members/$35. Davis Branch also sponsors a swim team for member children 6+. Fee, first child/$25, each additional child in family/$10.

YWCA
Business office, 3387 Poplar. 323-2211.

Branches: **Germantown** (754-4356), **Raleigh-Bartlett** (382-3540), and **Sarah-Brown** (948-0493).

The local YWCA offers adult interest groups and educational programs, day and residential camps for girls, and a special one-week camp for handicapped girls.

LIBRARY INFORMATION CENTER (LINC)*
Memphis/Shelby County Public Library, McLean at Peabody. 528-2999. Contact LINC for current information and phone numbers. They can tell you about church and community sponsored programs and about local groups and clubs interested in particular sports. They have a list of summer camps and sports clinics. Don't miss getting a copy of their "Summer Survival Kit", free at library branches.

INDIVIDUAL SPORTS A—Z

Most individual sport listings have information for adults and youth.

ARCHERY
Archery ranges maintained by the Park Commission at Davy Crockett

Park (Range Line Rd. at Hawkins Mill Rd.) and at McKellar Park (on Airways, south of Wilson). Bring your own equipment. Open daily, daylight hours. Free.

Meeman-Shelby Forest State Park* does not maintain an archery range, but offers special summer archery lessons. For information phone 876-5201.

AUTOMOBILE AND MOTORCYCLE RACING

Races are held every Sat night Apr-Sept at Riverside International Speedway on Hwy. 70 E in West Memphis, Ark. Phone 735-8071 for information.

Two local clubs, the Delta Motorcycle Rider Club and the Mid-South Region Sports Car Club, sponsor local races, beer busts, and informational meetings.

Future racers will love driving go-carts around the track at Putt-Putt Sports Centers, 1401 Bartlett Rd., 386-2992.

BASEBALL

Both the Shelby County Conservation Board* and the Memphis Park Commission* sponsor amateur children's and adult's teams. The Jackson Park Sports Assn. (388-0284) organizes and sponsors baseball teams for youths 7½-15. Annual membership dues, family/$3.

BASKETBALL

The Memphis Park Commission* sponsors two basketball programs, one for those 6-18 and one for adults.

There are two local basketball teams for wheelchair participants, the Bluff City Wheelers (523-8990 ext. 5306) and the River City Rollers, Inc. (388-6936). The Wheelers train players free and furnish wheelchairs for new members when possible. The Rollers have weekly summer recreational activities in other sports also.

BICYCLING

Unfortunately for Memphians there is only one designated bikeway in the city, through the Vollintine-Evergreen neighborhood from University Park (University & Edward) and Gooch Park (University & Hunter) to the small commercial shopping district at Chelsea and Watkins.

In Meeman-Shelby Forest State Park* a new scenic six-mile bike trail and new bike rental facility have opened. Three-speed and 10-speed bikes may be rented for $1.25/hour 10am-6pm daily June-Labor Day and on weekends the rest of the year (weather permitting).

Residents of Frayser and Raleigh, local bicycle shops, and the Memphis Park Commission sponsor bicycle races for boys ages 6-17 at Kennedy Park (4575 Raleigh-LaGrange Rd., 382-4225). Races at 2pm on alternate Sun, late spring through early fall.

The Memphis Park Commission sponsors occasional bike trips. Call 454-5759 for information.

The Memphis Hightailers, a cycle association, organizes rides to places of interest around Memphis and sponsors a racing team. For current phone number contact LINC* (528-2999).

BOATING

The Mississippi River and McKellar Lake offer Memphians boating right in the heart of downtown. There is a public boat ramp at McKellar Lake located in Dr. Martin Luther King-Riverside Park off I-55 near President's Island. The Yacht Club*, on the downtown riverfront at Court, provides facilities for the moorage and service of sail and motor boats. Many lakes are within a two-hour drive of Memphis. Two of the largest and most popular are Pickwick* in Tennessee and Sardis Lake* in Mississippi.

Tennessee state parks* do not permit personally-owned boats and motors on small park lakes. Boat rental rates are:

Type	Hour	Day	Week
CANOES	$1.50	$5	$15
ROW BOATS	$1	$4	$13
FISHING BOATS			
Harrison Bay	$1	$4	
Meeman-Shelby		$2.25	
Paris Landing		$5	
Pickwick Landing		$5 (with motor $10)	
Reelfoot		$3 (with oars)	
		$5 (with small motor)	
		$7 (with large motor)	
PEDAL BOATS	$1.50		
YAK-YAK BOATS	$1		

For Power Boaters:

There is a local racing club, Memphis Power Boat Club, and Coast Guard Auxiliary classes on safety. For current phone numbers contact LINC* (528-2999).

For Canoers and Kayakers:

Outdoors Inc. (767-6790) is probably the best local source for gage readings on area rivers, for canoe and kayak rentals, and for all kinds of equipment.

The Bluff City Canoe Club (P.O. Box 4523, Memphis, 38104, 767-6790) conducts canoe and kayak floats for members, basic canoe training for anyone, and advanced canoe training for members. The club sells an excellent "Mid-South River Guide" for $1. Annual membership dues, single/$3, family/$5.

Two guidebooks recommended on this area are "Arkansas

Whitewater" by Tom Kennon and "Missouri Ozark Waterways" published by the Mo. Dept. of Conservation.

See also North Arkansas Rivers.

For Sailors:

Sailing is fairly new to the Mid-South but interest is growing. The Coast Guard Auxiliary offers fundamental sailing classes. The River City Sailing Club sponsors races and overnight cruises. The Delta Sailing Assn. sponsors races at 2pm Sat & Sun mid-March - late Oct at Arkabutla Lake*, less than an hour's drive south of Memphis in Mississippi. For current phone numbers phone LINC* (528-2999). One of the few places in the area to rent small sailboats is at Heber Springs*, Ark., about 150 miles from Memphis.

BOWLING

For information on all American Bowling Congress sanctioned tournaments and leagues, both men's and mixed, contact the Bowling Assn. Inc.

Cherokee Bowling Center, 2930 Lamar (774-7700) provides bowling instruction and organized league play for the visually, mentally, and physically handicapped for $2.75 per session. Rubaiyats, Inc. provides transportation to the special classes for visually handicapped youth. For current phone numbers contact LINC* (528-2999).

BOXING

The Memphis Park Commission* operates a free boxing program in the Merchant Building's arena at the Fairgrounds. Regulation rings, speed bags, dressing rooms, and other equipment and directors available for supervision and instruction 1-8pm M-F; summertime program 9am-4pm M-F. Anyone may participate. Contact the gym at 278-3493 for more information. After the planned destruction of the Merchant Building, the boxing program will be dispersed to various community centers. Two gyms have already opened, one at Community Center, 1048 S. 3rd (774-4156), the other at Raleigh Community Center, 3678 Powers Rd. (372-2085).

The Police Youth Activities Club at 243 Winchester Ave., 38105, (528-2086) offers a free boxing program for boys 10+.

The Fire Fighters (795-6191) operate free boxing programs in the Whitehaven Community Center, 4318 Graceland Dr. (332-0783), and in the Frayser Community Center, 2903 N. Watkins (357-6919).

The River City Boxing Club (346-KIRK) operates a program at 2nd and Union, over the Gridiron Restaurant.

CANOEING*.

FENCING

A local fencing club meets in the basement of Idlewild Presbyterian Church at 1750 Union (725-4165) and offers instruction at 25¢ per meeting to anyone over 16.

FISHING

The area's lakes and rivers have bass, crappie, bream, trout, catfish, and larger rough fish. Fishing is legal year round in the tri-states — Tennessee, Arkansas and Mississippi. Licenses may be purchased at most retail sporting goods stores.

In Tennessee licenses for residents are $5 a year or 50¢ a day. For non-residents licenses are the price of the applicant's home state license (minimum $5) a year, $1.50 for 3 days or $2 for 10 days. A $2 trout stamp is required for both residents and non-residents. Everyone 16-65 must have a license.

In Arkansas fishing licenses for residents are $3.50 a year. For non-residents they are $6 a year or $3.50 for 14 days. Those 16-65 must have licenses.

In Mississippi resident licenses are $5 a year for a combination hunting and fishing license, $3 a year for fishing, or $1 for a 3-day permit. Non-resident fishing licenses are $6 a year or $1.50 for 3 days. Those 14-65 must have licenses.

Each state has daily limits for various species of fish. For specifics on limits, fishing conditions, water levels, and effective types of bait and equipment contact: the sports departments at Memphis' major local papers, "The Commercial Appeal" (901-529-2361) and the "Memphis Press-Scimitar" (901-529-2540), the Tennessee Game and Fish commission in Nashville (615-741-1421), the Arkansas Game and Fish Commission in Little Rock (501-371-1025), or the Mississippi Game and Fish Commission in Jackson (601-354-7324).

Two free pamphlets are available on the area's fishing, "Fishing in Tennessee" from Tennessee Tourist Development, 505 Fesslers Ln, Nashville, 37201, and "Memphis Area Fishing Guide" from the Memphis Area Chamber of Commerce, P.O. Box 224, 38101. The latter lists 90 fishing spots near Memphis and cites the following 15 as "great": Bull Shoals Lake, Greers Ferry Lake, Horseshoe Lake, Norfolk Lake, and the White River in Arkansas; Enid Lake, Flower Lake, Grenada Lake, Lakeview (Horn Lake), Moon Lake, Sardis Lake, and Tunica Cut-Off in Mississippi; Kentucky Lake, Pickwick Lake, and Reelfoot Lake in Tennessee. See the chapter Worth the Drive.

Nearly all Tennessee State Parks* offer some type of fishing. In the small park-owned and operated lakes fees are about $1 for everyone 16+. All TVA and US Army Corps of Engineers lakes offer free fishing at all times.

In nearby Meeman-Shelby Forest State Park*, Poplar Tree and Piersol

Lakes offer fishing to those 16 + . You may fish from the bank or pier, or rent a boat ($2.25 per day). Fishing permits, $1.80/day or $7.80/year, sold at the lakes.

The County Conservation Board* maintains a free fishing area at Shelby Farms* for bank fishing.

The Memphis Park Commission* allows fishing only in McKellar Park and Audubon Park and only for those under 16 or over 65. State licenses are required at Audubon.

FOOTBALL

The Memphis Park Commission*, the Jackson Park Sports Assn. (388-0284), and the Collierville Optimist Club sponsor football programs for youth. The Park Commission also sponsors adult touch teams.

GOLF

According to Memphis sports writer Nash Buckingham, cottonmen assigned to Memphis from England established the city's first golf course before 1900. Courses have proliferated, and today the city has many, both public and private.

The Park Commission operates and maintains:

Audubon Golf Course	4160 Park	683-6941
Davy Crockett Park Golf Course	4380 Range Line Rd.	358-3375
Fox Meadows Golf Course	3064 Clarke Rd.	362-0232
Galloway Golf Course	3815 Walnut Grove Rd.	685-7805
McKellar Golf Course	Airways at Shelby Drive	346-0510
Edmund Orgill Golf Club	9080 Bethuel in Millington	872-3610
Overton Park Golf Course	Poplar at Parkway	725-9905
Pine Hill Golf Course	1005 Alice Ave.	775-9434
Riverside Golf Club	465 S. Parkway E.	774-4340

Except for the 9-hole Overton and Riverside courses, all are 18-hole regulation. Facilities at most include snack bars, showers, lockers, pro shops, clubs, and carts. Concession stands sell hamburgers, hot dogs, soft drinks, and beer.

Rules and rates are the same for all Park Commission courses. No one under nine is allowed on an 18-hole course; no one under six is allowed on any public course. Ages 9-12 must be accompanied by someone 13 + , tee off before noon and play at Audubon only on M, Fox Meadows on Th, and Pine Hill, Davy Crockett, & McKellar on M-F. Green fees, on 18-hole courses/$5 daily, on 9-hole courses/$3 daily. Senior citizens (62 +) may purchase a ticket for weekday play for $15/month or $150/year. Ho-Ho-Ho — play is free on Christmas day. During summer vacation, those 18 and under may play nine holes for $1. Cart rental fees, 18 holes/$10, 9 holes/$5. Courses open 6am-8:30pm summer and 7:30am-5pm winter. For additional information phone 274-5064.

The state maintains an 18-hole regulation course and facilities at T. O. Fuller State Park* (Mitchell Rd., west of U.S. Hwy. 61S, 785-3950). The course is open 6am-dark daily. Fees, 9 holes/$2.75, unlimited holes all day/$5.50 M-F; 9 holes/$3.25, 18 holes/$6.50 Sat., Sun., & holidays. Yearly permit/$200; yearly permit for senior citizens/$100. Seniors may play free M except holidays. Cart rental, $5 for 9 holes.

Two pay-as-you-go public golf courses are Holiday Golf Club at 11300 Goodman Rd. in Olive Branch, Miss. and the Brooks Rd. Golf Course near the airport at 1940 E. Brooks Rd. The latter is lighted and open daily until midnight.

Among the many private golf courses in the city are those at Bella Vista Country Club, Briargate Country Club, Chickasaw Country Club, Colonial Country Club, the Defense Depot, Farmington Country Club, Fox Meadows, Holly Hills Country Club, Houston Levee Golf Club, Memphis Country Club, Millington Naval Air Station, Olive Branch Country Club, Ridgeway Country Club, Stonebridge Country Club, Whitehaven Country Club, and Windyke Country Club.

For children, don't forget putt-putts. They're listed in the yellow pages under Golf-miniature. It's a fun way to practice your putting and a good place for birthday parties.

HANDBALL

Memphis is reputed to have more handball courts per person than any city in the South. The downtown YMCA*, many churches, private clubs, and public facilities have courts. For information contact Mid-South Handball Assn. or Tennessee Handball Assn. LINC* (528-2999) has current phone numbers.

HIKING

Several parks have marked hiking trails. Meeman-Shelby Forest State Park* has maps of trails available at the park office. T. O. Fuller State Park* maintains a hiking trail for blind persons marked with pebbles and Braille signs. Shelby Farms* has a trail designed for the handicapped.

The Memphis Park Commission* offers summer canoeing, backpacking, hiking, rock climbing, and tent camping programs for children ages 12-15. Fee, $25.

Other organizations also sponsor hiking and related outdoor activity programs. Mid-American Mountaineering (Memphis State University, Dept. of Health, Physical Education and Recreation, 454-2319) offers backpacking, canoeing, mountaineering, rock climbing, and spelunking classes and conducts outings. Yearly membership, individual/$6, family/$7.50. The Sierra Club sponsors hiking, climbing, and canoeing outings for members. Yearly membership, adult/$20, children & seniors (60 +)/$10. The Trail Club offers backpacking, rock climbing, caving, and riflery. The club builds and maintains the hiking trails at Meeman-Shelby Forest State Park.

HORSEBACK RIDING

There are more horses per capita in Shelby County than anywhere else in the U.S., or at least so says the U.T. Agricultural Extension Service.

Several private stables in the city offer riding classes and boarding for horses. Check the yellow pages under Horse-Breeders, Dealers, and Training. Two of the oldest are Jerome Robertson Stables and Hugh Frank Smith Horse and Pony Farm. Spring Creek Stables Inc. at 3322 Bobo Rd. in Germantown (754-6688) offers both an outdoor and indoor arena. There are also two hunt clubs, Oak Grove and Longreen, for fox hunters.

For those interested in a ride, the County Conservation Board* maintains a riding stable at Shelby Farms Plough Recreation Area* (382-4250) on Mullins Station Rd. for those five and older (ages 5-9 must be accompanied by an adult). Stables open 9am-7pm daily. Fee, $4.50 per hour; for groups of 10+, reduced rates possible.

Meeman-Shelby Forest State Park* has a new riding stable and marked trails. Usually open 9am-dark, but phone ahead (876-5756) to make sure someone is there. Rates, $4.50 per hour; for groups of 10+, $4 per hour. Children under nine must ride on the same horse with an adult — they are not charged. The stable offers a two-hour hayride and bonfire for a $50 minimum, 25 people or less; $2 for each additional person.

Several associations sponsor riding events, among them the Southern Amateur Saddle Clubs Assn. and the Mid-South Quarter Horse Assn. Get current phone numbers from LINC* (528-2999).

Having a child's birthday party? Col. Ken Herman will bring his pony to your backyard for rides, $35/hour. Upon request he also will bring cowboy and cowgirl clothes and a Polaroid camera. Phone The Colonel's Party Pony (458-2333).

HUNTING

The Memphis area has long been famous for its hunting. At the turn of the century Memphians took friends from New York, Liverpool, and Chicago hunting at any of a half dozen sporting lodges within a 100 mile radius. In the early 1900s, President Theodore Roosevelt came to hunt bear in Bobo, Miss. Sports write Nash Buckingham tells stories of duck shoots at such famous private hunting clubs as Wapanocca*, Beaver Dam, Claypool's, Greasy Slough, Murray's, and Section 16. Ducks and geese were so plentiful in the Mississippi River flyway that members at the Wapanocca club set a daily 50 duck per hunter limit before federal regulation began.

Today there are dove, squirrel, rabbit, quail, duck, geese, deer (archery and gun), turkey, raccoon, and oppossum seasons and limits in the tristate area. Each state has its own licensing and fee arrangements. Licenses are sold at most retail sporting goods stores. Rates vary for large and small game and for residents and non-residents licenses. For annual information contact the Jackson office of the Tennessee Game and Fish Commission (1-800-372-3928), the Mississippi Game and Fish Commission in Jackson, Miss. (601-354-7324), or the Arkansas Game and Fish Commission in Little Rock (501-371-1025).

Additional sources for hunting information are: the sports desks of Memphis' two major papers, "The Commercial Appeal" (529-2361) and "Memphis Press-Scimitar" (529-2540), the Arkansas State Parks Recreation and Travel Commission (State Capitol Building in Little Rock, 72201), the Travel Department/Mississippi Agricultural and Industrial Board (1504 State Office Building, Jackson, 39201), and the Tennessee Conservation Department (2611 West End Ave., Div. F, Nashville, 38203).

The Memphis Chamber of Commerce (P.O. Box 224, Memphis, 38101) prints a free pamphlet listing the annual calendar for the tri-states, license and fee rates, information on area animals, a list of nearby quail preserves, and a map of wildlife management areas and other nearby hunting preserves.

You're always sure to see some birds at the privately operated hunting preserves where birds are pen raised and released for shooting. The preserves are open to the public on a fee basis. Reservations are necessary.

Several nearby government owned wildlife management areas are opened to the public for hunting on a limited basis. These include White River National Wildlife Refuge near DeWitt, Ark, Hatchie River Wildlife Refuge near Bolivar, Tn, and Holly Springs National Forest near Holly Springs, Miss. For information and reservations contact the state's game and fish commission.

Meeman-Shelby Forest State Park* in Millington, right on the city's doorstep, allows hunting of all small game and waterfowl M, W, and Sat during the season. Turkey and deer hunting are permitted at special times. Check with the park headquarters (876-5201) for specifics. The West Tennessee Sportsman's Assn. conducts juvenile squirrel, deer, and turkey hunts in the park.

Hunters might be interested in subscribing to the monthly "Mid-South Sportsman" (P.O. Box 775, Clarksdale, Miss., 38614) and "Water Fowlers World Magazine" (3181 Ridgeway Rd., Memphis, 794-8589). Memphis author Nash Buckingham's historical hunting pieces are nationally recognized.

For gun safety courses and target practice information see Shooting.

RACQUETBALL

Racquetball is booming in Memphis, national headquarters of both the American Amateur Racquetball Assn. and the International Amateur Racquetball Federation. The city is also home to Sarah Green, the nation's 1977 #1 amateur and #4 professional women's player. From

1977 to 1981 Memphis State University has had the #1 men's and women's collegiate racquetball teams in the U.S.

Courts are available at:

Idlewild Presbyterian Church, 1750 Union (726-4165), non-regulation size courts, free

YMCA Stratton Branch, 245 Madison (521-9622), membership and public rates

Memphis Supreme Courts, 2611 S. Mendenhall (794-2288), membership and public rates

Memphis State University* (454-2801) for students and alumni only, alumni must reserve courts after 11am the day they wish to play and must pay a $1 fee each time

Bellevue Baptist Church, 70 N. Bellevue (725-1130), members only

Jewish Community Center, 6560 Poplar (761-0810), members only

Don Kessinger Court Club, 1010 June Rd. (682-6661), members only

Racquet Club of Memphis, 5111 Sanderlin Ave. (767-9235 or 767-6980), members only

RUGBY

Rugby, a fairly recent import to the South, is an increasingly popular sport. The Memphis Park Commission* sponsors adult and youth teams and tournaments as does the local Rugby Club. There are two seasons: Feb-Apr and Aug-Dec.

RUNNING

There's a place for every caliber of runner in Memphis' two track clubs, The Memphis/Shelby Track Foundation (MSTF) and the Memphis Runners' Track Club (MRTC).

MSTF is noted especially for its youth track program which has produced winners of the Girls National Track title and of state Junior Olympic boys and girls titles. In 1977 the club was ranked number one in the country by "Starting Line" magazine.

MRTC sponsors road races and track meets, events for beginners, and a team that competes with nearby colleges. Most members are non-competitive runners. They meet at 7pm Th at Southwestern's* track.

The sporting goods stores catering to joggers usually have bulletin boards full of notices and information on nearby runs. See Sporting Goods in the yellow pages of the phone directory.

If you're looking for more than a running place, try the Shelby County Penal Farms-Plough Recreation Area's* new 1½ mile exercise trail. The path is scenic and has 20 stop-'n-exercise points along the way. Each station has different instructions and equipment for the walker/jogger/runner to do calisthenic exercise. Financed by J. C. Penney, it's designed to tone muscles and build cardiovascular strength. It even sounds like fun for the whole family. Entrance to the park is on Mullins Station Rd, two miles east of the Penal Farm main building. Free.

SAILING*

SCUBA DIVING

In this area there's a real problem with underwater visibility, but, for the determined, Greer's Ferry, Norfork, and Ouachita lakes, all in Arkansas, are the most popular. For the very experienced diver there are sites in Greer's Ferry Lake and the Tennessee River near Shiloh* that offer underwater towns, Indian and early American artifacts, and the remains of 19thc. vessels. For information and places to take lessons, check with the diving shops listed under Divers' Equipment and Supplies in the phone directory's yellow pages.

SHOOTING

The Shelby County Penal Farm's Pistol and Rifle Range (1045 Mullins Station Rd., 38134, 386-4391 ext. 314) is just off Walnut Grove Rd. near Germantown Rd. Shooters must supply their own guns and ammunition. Facilities include a pistol and rifle range and a regulation trap field. Fees, per day for the pistol and rifle range/$3, clay targets/$2.75 per round. Range open, 8am-4pm W-Sun to those 16+.

The Gun Club shooting range (P.O. Box 11386, 38111, 386-0310) is on Appling Rd. off Hwy. 64. Open all day Sat & Sun March-Oct and from noon to dusk Sun Nov, Dec, & Feb. The Gun Club will arrange skeet and trap shooting lessons. Fees per round, members/$1.75, non-members/$2.75. Shooters must bring their own guns and shells.

The Indoor Shooting Center (3029 Bellbrook Dr, 38116, 396-2478) shares the premises with a retail store for ammunition, firearms, and accessories. The indoor shooting range is open 9:30am-11pm M-Sat and noon-8pm Sun. Persons under 18 must be accompanied by an adult. Rate, $3.75 per hour. The center sponsors league shooting for men and women. The range is accessible to the handicapped.

Robert Howard (P.O. Box 4282, 38104, 274-5026) offers instruction to classes of 10+ in firearm and hunting safety. The 10-hour course, which leads to a certificate, is offered at several locations including the Penal Farm, YMCAs, and various community centers. $1.75 charge for ammunition. Mr. Howard is active in the West Tennessee Sportsman's Assn.

SKATING

On Ice:

Memphis ponds rarely freeze. It is usually artificial ice that we skate on. The city has two indoor skating rinks, and both can be rented for parties.

Ice Capades at the Mall of Memphis* is the city's Olympic size indoor rink. It's open 11am-11pm daily with public sessions except when classes are being taught (5:15-7:30pm Tu, W, & Th and 9am-noon Sat). Skating rates for a day long session (you must stay within the skating area): those 13+/$3, children 12 and under/$2.50. Skate rental/$1. On Tu morning there is a women's skate and coffee club. $3.50 includes admission, coffee, and instruction. Special group rates and rink rental possible. Phone 362-8877 for information. Watch free skating exhibitions at 2pm Sat & Sun.

Libertyland Park* on E. Parkway between Central and Southern, offers winter ice skating under a bubble top. The season is limited, end of Nov-Feb, and the hours erratic, roughly 5-7pm M-Th, 5-11pm F, 1-11pm Sat, and 1-7pm Sun. Phone 274-8800 ext. 312/309 for a schedule and other information. The rink is 72' × 182'. Cost, Libertyland gate admission/50¢ plus skating charge for a 1¾ hour session/$2, skate rental fee/75¢. Spectators pay only the 50¢ park admission. Booked groups of 20+ pay no park admission. There are all sorts of promotional reduced "specials", but the best bet for saving is probably the $25 season pass. Skating lessons and private rink rental possible. Private parties after normal hours only. Cost $100 to rent the rink plus $1 per person with a minimum of 40 people. Concession stand available for hot dogs, pizza, and popcorn — no alcohol.

On Rollers:

Popular in the '50s, roller skating is "in" again, this time with a new beat — disco. Rinks listed in the phone directory's yellow pages under Skating Rinks. Hours, rates, and amenities vary, so shop around. If you're planning a child's birthday, a husband's 30th, a fund-raiser for the ballet, you can rent a rink.

Or what about skating in the park? Three miles of Overton Park* roads are barricaded to motor vehicles each weekend, and roller skates are for rent near the park's picnic pavilion on E. Parkway north of Poplar. Rentals, $2.50/hour, $5/day. Concession open noon-5pm Sat & Sun when weather is clear and temperature 50 degrees or warmer.

SKIING

For Water Skiers:

The closest spot is McKellar Lake, a loop off the Mississippi River (located off Riverside Dr. in Dr. Martin Luther King-Riverside Park*), but most of the area's nearby lakes allow skiing and have a ramp to launch your boat. For information check with sporting goods stores or the Water Skiing Club (LINC*, 528-2999 has the current phone number).

For Snow Skiers:

The Mid-South Ski Assn. is for snow skiers and gives information on snow skiing and charters to various skiing locations. The closest spot to ski is Cedar Cliff, Tn. (615) 676-5122, 125 miles northeast of Memphis in Wayne County. They make snow when it's cold enough. Cedar Cliff has slopes, a T-bar lift, lessons, equipment rental, and a snack bar. No sleeping accommodations, no dining lodge, no bar. Ski sessions, 9am-3pm and 4-10pm daily. Lift tickets, for 4 hours/$5, for 6 hours/$10, for 12 hours/$15. Equipment rental rates, $5 per day Sat & Sun, $4 per day M-F. Practice before you go — Alpine Sports, 1939 Poplar (722-1972) has a simulated slope.

SKY DIVING AND HANG GLIDING

High Adventure Sports (345-4404) maintains a drop zone at the Sardis, Miss. Airport for sky diving enthusiasts, weekends March - Dec. A parachute, plane, and instructor are available at a first jump rate of $65-90. Each additional jump, $15.

The Mid-South Hang Gliding Club gives instruction in gliding and maintains sites. Prospective members get a one time glide for $10. LINC* (528-2999) has current phone numbers.

SOCCER

Soccer is sweeping the South, and is especially popular with school age children. The Memphis Park Commission* sponsors youth and adult programs. The Soccer Assn. provides information on organized soccer teams in the Memphis area (adult leagues/525-1411, youth/372-1463). The city has two lighted soccer fields for league play, the Park Commission field on Willow Rd. and the Hyster Co. field and grandstand at 5511 E. Shelby Dr. The Americans, the city's professional indoor soccer team, plans to make their facility at 2500 Mt. Moriah open afternoons and nights daily for a fee to adult and youth league teams.

SOFTBALL

The Memphis Park Commission* and the Shelby County Conservation Board* sponsor softball teams and programs for youth and adults.

SWIMMING

Memphis summers are torrid. A splash brings welcome relief. The Memphis Park Commission has been operating pools in the city since 1922, when it opened a pool at the Fairgrounds. The large pool, surrounded by sand beaches, had a dressing room for 2,000. Since then many pools have been added. Today the city operates:

Douglas	1616 Ash	Malone	580 N. Main
Fairgrounds	811 Alabama	Orange Mound	2430 Carnes
Fox Meadows	3064 Clark	Pine Hill	973 Alice
Frayser	2907 N. Watkins	Raleigh	3678 Powers
Gaisman	4223 Macon	Riverview	182 Joubert
Gooch	1974 Hunter at University	Tom Lee	920 Peach
L. E. Brown	617 S. Orleans	Washington	1072 N. 2nd
Lester	317 Tillman	Westwood	810 Western Park
		Willow	4777 Willow Rd.

City pools are open for eight weeks, from early June to early Aug. Hours are noon-7pm M-Sat and 1-7pm Sun. Each pool has one "dry day" per week, either M or W. Entrance fees, adults/$1, ages 17 and under/ 50¢. Free swimming lessons, in the morning for children six and older, at night for adults. Classes run in two-week sessions and are taught by the Red Cross. Sign up at the pools. Classes in life saving and baby swimming also offered. Phone 388-5911 for more information. Park Commission pools may be rented for private parties for about $50.

Youth Services in Memphis gives free swimming instruction for teenagers (13-17). For specifics phone 452-5600.

Handicapped take note — The Park Commission* in conjunction with Handicapped Inc. offers free therapeutic swimming classes to the physically and mentally handicapped at Raymond Skinner Handicapped Recreation Center, 712 Tanglewood. Call 272-2528 for information.

The various YMCA* branches offer swimming programs—the best bet for indoor facilities. For information phone the branches.

T. O. Fuller State Park's* (3269 Boxtown, 38109, 785-3950) swimming pool is open noon-8pm W-Sun in summer. Admission, $1.35 per person.

Meeman-Shelby Forest State Park's* pool (Millington, 876-5824) is open 10am-6pm daily in summer. Fees, $1.35 per person.

Two swimming facilities are open to the public for a fee: Maywood, across the Mississippi state line, open mid-May-Aug, 9am-7pm daily. Fees, ages 13+/$3.50, ages 5-12/$1.75, under 5/free; includes access to pool, picnic areas, and pavilion. Groups of 25+ eligible for reduced group rates. Adult women may get in for $1.75 Tu & F and the driver of a car with a Maywood sticker free on Th. Drive east out Lamar to Craft Rd. exit and follow the signs. Phone (601) 895-2777.

Lakeland Campground, 3970 Canada Rd. at I-40, 386-4881, opens its swimming lake to the public 10am-7pm daily June-mid Aug, 10am-7pm Sat & Sun mid-Aug-Labor Day. $3 per person to swim and picnic.

TENNIS

The city's tennis courts are run by the Memphis Park Commission.

There are eight tennis centers directed by pros. Each center has several courts, is usually open 9am-10pm daily Mar-Nov and 9am-5pm daily Dec-Feb, charges $2 per person for 1½ hours on the court, offers lessons, and accepts phone reservations up to a week in advance. If you're looking for a bargain: free play 9am-noon W; those 12 or under can play free when a court is available; senior citizens (62+), youths (17 and under), and students may play for ½ price; weekly contract rates; individual yearly rate/$72 and family yearly rate/$144 available. Centers are open year round:

| Audubon/Leftwich | 4145 Southern at Goodlett | 685-7907 |
| Bellevue | 1310 S. Bellevue at Parkway | 774-7199 |

Frayser	2907 N. Watkins	357-5417
Raleigh	3680 Powers Rd	372-2032
Riverside	435 S. Parkway W.	774-4340
John Rodgers	1123 Jefferson	523-0094
Whitehaven/Eldon Roark	1500 Finley Rd.	332-0546
Wooddale	3391 Castleman Ave	794-5045

Only Leftwich Center in Audubon Park and Eldon Roark Center in Whitehaven have indoor courts. The indoor courts at Roark are open year-round, at Leftwich only Oct-May. Hours, 9am-10pm daily; prime time, weekday nights 5:30-10pm and weekend days 9am-5:30pm. Rates per court for 1½ hours, prime time: summer/$10, winter/$14, non-prime time: summer/$7, winter/$11.

The Park Commission also operates free courts, open daylight hours daily, no reservations, at:

Audubon	Goodlett at Park	Glenview	1141 S. Barksdale
Cherokee	2940 Filmore	Gooch	1235 University
Coleman	3210 Raleigh-Millington	Havenview	1481 Hester
Davis	3371 Spottswood	McKellar	4955 S. Airways
Egypt-Central	4001 Egypt-Central	John Rodgers	1123 Jefferson
Gaisman	4235 Macon	Sherwood	Rhodes at Prescott
		Southside	640 S. Parkway E.

The Shelby County Conservation Board maintains free tennis facilities, open daylight to 11pm daily, no reservations, at:

Ellendale	7266 3rd Rd, Ellendale
Farmington	Cordes at Farmington, Germantown
George R. James	2050 Collierville/Arlington/Eads
Northaven	855 N. Circle, Benjestown
Peterson Lake	3414 Peterson Lake, Collierville
Riverdale	7345 Neshoba, Germantown
Whitten	1348 Whitten Rd, Bartlett

Several private clubs are geared mainly to tennis: the Racquet Club of Memphis, Shelby Tennis Club, and Wimbleton Racquet Club. If you're interested, phone them for membership information.

There are several tennis related associations in Memphis. The Ladies Doubles League (388-5482) organizes four doubles tennis tournaments for women each year. The Southern Tennis Assn. Inc. (P.O. Box 11063, 38111, 458-8030) sponsors tennis clinics, tournaments, and a film library. The Tennis Assn. (P.O. Box 11422, 38111, 682-7579) provides umpires for matches, group instruction, and information on tennis instructors. They also work with the Memphis Park Commission to upgrade the city's tennis courts and to sponsor tennis tournaments.

If lethargy sets in, your feet get blistered, or ... consider table tennis.

The Bluff City Table Tennis Club operates in a warehouse at 283½ Union Ave. 7:30-10pm Tu & Th and 3:30-7pm Sat & Sun. Dues, $90/year, $9/month, or $2/day. Family memberships available. Phone 523-9871.

VOLLEYBALL
Both the Memphis Park Commission* and the Shelby County Conservation Board* have youth volleyball programs. The Delta Region of the U.S. Volleyball Assn. conducts $1 clinics on playing and officiating. Some of the city's churches and community centers* have adult volleyball programs.

SPORTS/TO WATCH

AUTOMOBILE AND MOTORCYCLE RACING
All kinds of races are held at Riverside International Speedway on Hwy 70E in West Memphis, Ark. Races every Sat night Apr-Sept. Gate opens at 5pm. General admission from $6 up, depending on the race. Phone 735-8071 for information.

BASEBALL

Professional Baseball:
Memphis is historically a baseball town. Teams were first organized in the 1870s, and by the 1880s the first professional team was playing. On and off since 1915 the professional Memphis Chickasaws "Chicks" have played here. In 1960 the team was disbanded after its stadium, Russwood Park, burned to the ground and was replaced by a parking lot for Baptist Hospital. Today fans of the rejuvenated Chicks are clammering for enlargements to the present Tim McCarver Stadium at the fairgrounds. A class AA Southern League team, the Chicks are a locally owned professional farm team for the Montreal Expos. The Apr-Sept season is spiced with such special events as two-bit beer night and local companies' nights. You can arrange children's birthday parties with hot dogs, cokes, an autographed baseball, and happy birthday sung over the loudspeaker. General admission, adults/$2.25, students, military, & senior citizens/$1.75, children under 12/$1.25. Boxes, adults/$3.25, children/$2.75. Single games start at 7:30pm, doubleheaders at 7pm. For a schedule and information phone 272-1687.

Memphis has seen other professional teams come and go. The Memphis Blues folded in 1976 and the Memphis Red Sox vanished in 1958-59. The Red Sox, founded in the '20s, became one of the nation's top ten black baseball teams. They were a charter member of the Negro American League in 1937 and won the championship in 1938. After

1947 when major league baseball began opening up for black players, the Red Sox began their decline. The first black pitcher to sign with the majors was the Red Sox's Dan Bankhead who went with the Brooklyn Dodgers. Kenneth Neill wrote a good article on the Red Sox in "Memphis Magazine's" June 1979 issue.

College Baseball:

The Memphis State University* Tigers play at Nat Buring Field on the campus, south of the railroad tracks near the other athletic facilities. Admission, $1. For schedule information phone the recorded calendar 454-2079 or sports 454-2331.

Southwestern's* games at Stauffer Field on its campus are free. For information phone 274-1800.

Shelby State Community College* plays at Tony Gagliano Field, Mendenhall at Mt. Moriah Rd. Free. Phone 528-6754 for information.

LeMoyne-Owen's* games are played at Bellevue Park on Elvis Presley Blvd. at S. Parkway. Free. Phone 774-9090 for schedule information.

Christian Brothers College's* men's and women's games are played on campus at Hollywood and Avery Rd. Free. 278-0100.

BASKETBALL

Professional basketball tried briefly to make a go of it here in the 1970s. The team played in the old American Basketball Assn. under three names — Pros, Tams, and Sounds — until the ABA ceased to exist. Today the city relies on college basketball.

College Basketball:

The Memphis State University* Tigers belong to the Metro Seven Athletic Conference. Home games are in the 11,200 seat Mid-South Coliseum*. Season tickets range from $82-$100; part-time student tickets, $3 per game. The only individual game tickets available to the public are unpurchased student tickets. These vary in price and go on sale at the Coliseum the day of the game. For the recorded school calendar phone 454-2079; for more detailed information phone 454-2331.

Southwestern* plays in Mallory Gymnasium on its campus. Admission, adults/$2, students/$1, children/50¢.

LeMoyne-Owen* is in the Volunteer State Athletic Conference and plays its games in Bruce Hall on the campus at Neptune and Walker Strs. Tickets, adults/$2, students with a school ID and children/50¢. Tickets on sale at the gate. Phone 774-9090 for information.

Shelby State Community College* sponsors men's and women's teams in both the Tennessee and National Junior College Athletic Assn. Games are played in the campus gym at Linden and Walnut Strs. No admission charge for the women's games. For the men's it is adults/$2, students/$1. Tickets on sale at the door. Phone 528-6754 for information.

Christian Brothers College's* men's and women's teams play in the Volunteer State Athletic Conference. Its games are in the school's DeLaSalle Gymnasium, E. Parkway at Central Ave. Admission, adults/ $2, students/$1. 278-0100 for schedule.

High School Basketball:

For an excellent high school game, see the West Memphis Blue Devils. They've won 60 straight games and were ranked the #2 U.S. high school team in 1980 and '81 by UPI.

BOATING

The Kilowatt Marine Stadium at McLean and Chelsea is a secured race course for power boats. Five or six races are held each summer. For most races admission is adults/$3, children under 12/free. Phone 327-6121 (Haynes Electric) for schedule information.

BOXING

Tennessee legislators outlawed prizefighting in 1901 but changed their minds and re-legalized it in 1909. Memphis' biggest promoter, Billy Haack, made Memphis a fight town. He is credited with developing Gorilla Jones, winner of the middleweight title in 1931. Haack brought heavyweight champion Jack Dempsey to Memphis three times and Gene Tunney to town twice.

Today the Mid-South Professional Boxing Assn. (358-0386) sponsors monthly fights usually at 8pm Tu in Cook Convention Center. They are looking for a new home, so be sure to check before you go. General admission, $8 at the door, $7 in advance; ringside seats, $10. Tickets at Goldsmith's department stores' ticket offices.

DOG RACING

Dogs have run at Southland Greyhound Park (735-3670) in West Memphis, Ark. since the track's opening in 1956. Gamblers flock to the parimutuel betting windows M, Tu, Th, F, & Sat in July & Aug and M, Th, F, & Sat in May, June, Sept, & Oct. Races begin at 8pm; extra day races at 1:30pm on Sat and holidays.

Adults only. To enter, downstairs/50¢, air-conditioned upstairs section/$1.50; fee for seats upstairs/50¢, 75¢, or $1. Food and soft drinks available from concession stands and in the TV monitor room. For alcohol you must be a member of the private Greyhound Kennel Club. The club has race course seating and a dining area/bar with a view of the track. Membership applications available at the track; membership fee, about $100.

To get there, take either I-55 or I-40 across the river and exit at Ingram Blvd. in West Memphis. Free and pay parking. When the dogs are in action, Bridge Transit buses* run to and from the track every thirty minutes. You can catch the buses at MATA stops along a route beginning at 3rd and Union, going north to Madison, west on Madison to 2nd, south on 2nd to McCall, west to Main, south on Main to Crump, and west to the track.

FOOTBALL

Football has always been a Memphis favorite, but only briefly has the city had professional football. In the late 1920s, Clarence Saunders* sponsored a local independent football team, the Tigers, who were paid to play a limited schedule of games. In 1929, 8,000 fans at Hodges Field cheered them to a 20-6 victory over the year's national professional football champions, the Green Bay Packers. In the 1970s Memphis again had professional football. In 1974 and '75 the Grizzlies played in the now defunct World Football League.

College Football:

The enthusiasm and allegiance engendered by local college teams can match that generated by the pros elsewhere. In the 1920s the medical college* sponsored a team, the Doctors, that received national acclaim. Historically the Ole Miss Rebels (University of Mississippi) have been a local favorite and have played many home games in Memphis. Of late, Ole Miss has reduced the number of games in the city and fans have been turning their allegiance to Memphis State University's* Tigers. The Tigers, an independent team, Division 1 of the NCAA, play teams in various conferences including the SEC. Home games are in 50,000 -seat Liberty Bowl Stadium at the Fairgrounds. Tickets: Season/$47; single game, general public/$10-$11, part-time students and guests/$3, full-time students/free. For information and tickets, phone 454-2331. The recorded calendar of events (454-2079) gives the schedule.

Southwestern* plays in the College Athletic Conference. Games are at Fargason Field on the campus. Admission, adults/$2, students/$1, children/50¢.

Each year in Dec, two nationally top-ranked college teams compete here in the Liberty Bowl. The bowl was organized in Philadelphia in 1959. Five years later it moved to the Atlantic City, N.J. Convention Hall, where it became the first bowl game ever to be played indoors. The next year, 1965, the Liberty Bowl moved to Memphis. Reserved tickets, about $15, and box tickets, about $20, go on sale in Oct at the Liberty Bowl Stadium office in the Fairgrounds complex, 335 S. Hollywood.

GOLF

Each June golf's greatest professionals compete in the Danny Thomas Memphis Golf Classic. Mason Rudolph has been a contender each year since the tournament's beginning in 1958. In 1977 Al Geiberger scored a 59 here, the lowest score ever recorded in a PGA tournament. Lee

Trevino, a three time DTMC winner, is the all-time Memphis money winner. The Classic's Pro-Am draws celebrities and a big crowd. In 1978 former President Gerald Ford thrilled the crowd with a hole-in-one. The tournament is held on Colonial Country Club's par-72 course at 2736 Countrywood Parkway off I-40 E at Exit 16 (388-5370). Season tickets, adults/$25, children under 14/$5. Single tickets, $3 for Pro-Am and qualifying days, $6 for W, Th, & F of the tournament, and $12.50 for the finals on Sat & Sun. Tickets are sold at Goldsmith's department stores, Stamm's stores, and tournament headquarters at Colonial. Proceeds go to St. Jude Children's Research Hospital*.

MATA runs shuttle buses to the tournament from Handy City (Summer at I-240), Eastgate Shopping Center (Park at White Station Rd), and Mendenhall Square Mall (Winchester at Mendenhall). Roundtrip bus fare, $3.

Leave your camera, radio, cooler, step-ladder, and golf clubs at home. They are not allowed.

A salute here to Cary Middlecoff—Memphis' own, who won the Masters Tournament in 1955 with a score of 279, a seven stroke victory over Ben Hogan. It was the widest margin ever at the Masters. Dr. Middlecoff also won the U.S. Open in 1949 and 1956 and the Western Open in 1955.

HORSEBACK RIDING

In 1905 Tennessee legislators outlawed horse racing, a vote which many blame for a cultural and economic decline in Memphis. At the turn of the century the Memphis Driving Park, Thomas at Firestone Str., had harness racing, and Montgomery Park, where the fairgrounds is today, had thoroughbred racing. The famous Tennessee Derby was run at Montgomery Park from 1884 to 1905. From 1901 to 1904 the Memphis Trotting Assn.'s course was reputed to be the fastest in the world. Private railroad cars brought wealthy visitors to the city for the races, many of whom stayed at the luxurious, now defunct, Luehrmann Hotel.

Today racing is limited to the dog track in West Memphis, but polo matches, horse shows, and rodeos abound for horse aficionados.

Polo games are played at 2pm Sat & Sun May-Oct at Wildwood Farms in Germantown, Sat's games on Cottonplant Rd. at Quince, Sun's on Germantown Rd. at Winchester. Games are cancelled if it rains. Admission, free except for occasional benefit games. There are no bleachers, so bring a blanket or chairs. A picnic hamper might be fun too.

The Germantown Charity Horse Show, started in 1948, is an annual event for gaited horses and hunters and jumpers. Each June there are over 100 events in five days of competition. Tickets, reserved seats/$3.50, box with eight seats/$75, general admission: in advance/$2, at the gate/$2.50. Free parking on the Germantown Horse Show Grounds, 7745 Old Poplar Pike, just east of Germantown High School.

For information write P.O. Box 38102, 38138.

The annual Memphis Hunter-Jumper Classic, a nationally "A" rated horse show, is held in July at the Shelby County Equestrian Center, 171 S. Germantown Rd, just south of Walnut Grove Rd. Admission at the gate, adults/$2, children under eight/free. Free parking. For additional information phone 528-3279.

Summertime is rodeo time — the Southern Amateur Saddle Clubs sponsor lots of rodeo-type events, the WW Ranch in Arlington holds several rodeos for high school age riders, and the International Rodeo Assn. sponsors rodeos all over the South.

In early Sept, the Mid-South Fair* brings the professional World Championship Rodeo to the Mid-South Coliseum at the Fairgrounds for four days. Shows are usually at 8:30pm F, at 1, 4:30, & 8:30pm Sat, at 2:30 & 5:30pm Sun, and at 1 & 8pm M. Tickets, which include entry to the Fairgrounds, range from about $3.50 to $7.50. Phone 274-8800 for information.

A cheer for Memphian Melanie Smith — in 1978 Lady Rider of the Year and Grand Prix Rider of the Year, in 1979 member of the U.S. team that won the Gold Medal Pan-American Games, in 1980 America's Horsewoman of the Year and U.S. Equestrian Team Horsewoman of the Year, and in 1981 Silver Medalist in the World Cup Competition!!!

HUNTING

A fantastic chance to enjoy the countryside and watch some of the nation's finest bird dogs — the Grand National Bird Dog Field Trials. They have been held each Feb since 1900 at Ames Plantation in Grand Junction*, Tn. About an hour's drive — follow Hwys. 72 and 57 to Hwy. 18 just north of La Grange; go north on Hwy. 18 about 1½ miles to Buford Ellington Rd; turn left and the stables are several miles ahead. The trials usually last ten days, 8-11am and 1-4pm daily. Free admission. Daily noon lunch at the plantation's assembly hall, $4. You can visit the barns, watch the dogs and riders head out, or bring your own horse and follow the dogs. Some horses are available for rent. Riding the course is recommended for the skilled only. For more information write Ames Plantation, Rt. 1, Box 100 Grand Junction, Tn. 38039, or phone (901) 764-2167.

RACQUETBALL

Twelve racquetball tournaments are held in Memphis each year including the National Inter-Collegiate Racquetball Tournament held each Apr at the Racquet Club of Memphis.

Most professional tournaments are held at Memphis State University's* field house. Some are free; some charge admission. For information check at the university (454-2040 or 454-2801).

For more information check with the American Amateur Racquetball

Assn. or the International Amateur Racquetball Federation, both nationally headquartered at 5545 Murray Rd, 761-1172.

SOCCER

Professional Soccer:
Arizonan Ray Kuns purchased the Hartford Hellions of the Major Indoor Soccer League in 1981, transformed the team into the Memphis Americans, and brought professional soccer back to Memphis. Hurray! The city sadly had lost the Rogues of the North American League to Montreal in 1980.

The Memphis Americans, 2771 Clarke Rd, 795-7113, play 22 home games each year in the Mid-South Coliseum. Their season runs Nov-Apr. Games are at 7:30pm Tu, F, & Sat and 2pm Sun. Prices, adults/$4-$8, children (under 16)/$2. A good family outing!

College Soccer:
Intercollegiate soccer games are played at Memphis State University* (454-2321) and Southwestern* (274-1800). Games on the respective campuses are free.

SOFTBALL

Amateur softball blazed during the 1930s, '40s, and '50s, its golden age in Memphis. There were nine diamonds at the Fairgrounds alone. According to David Tankersley's article for "Memphis Magazine", 10,000 fans would show up for a game. About 30 class A teams played in the city. Today there are only seven local class A teams, but one of these, the Franklin Enterprises, was ranked in the top AA category in 1980.

In all, about 1200 amateur teams now play in city parks. Some of the best games are played at Willow Field on Willow Rd, near Mt. Moriah. To see some good women's teams, go to Tobey Park behind the Board of Education Bldg. on Hollywood. Games are free.

TENNIS

Cotton magnate Billy Dunavant and his Racquet Club of Memphis have brought big time tennis to Memphis. Each Feb since 1976, they have hosted the country's oldest indoor tennis tournament, the U.S. National Indoor Tennis Championships. The tournament is a six-star Grand Prix event and the richest indoor tournament in the world. It's the city's chance to see John McEnroe, Jimmy Connors, Arthur Ashe, Vitas Gerulaitis, ... Tickets: series/$75-$110, single/$6-$25. Available through the Racquet Club (5111 Sanderlin Rd. 767-6980).

The Racquet Club has also been the scene of the USTA Girls 18-and-Under National Clay Court Championship, the American zone finals of the Davis Cup, and the Southern Senior Women's Tournament.

Christian Brothers College* (278-0100), Memphis State University* (454-2346), Shelby State Community College* (528-6754), and South-western* (274-1800) all play intercollegiate tennis. Games on the respective campuses are free.

For city tournament information and schedules, phone the Memphis Park Commission* (454-5755).

WRESTLING

Every M night at 8pm Jerry Lawler fans gather for professional wrestling at the Mid-South Coliseum at the Fairgrounds (274-7402). Tickets range from $3 to $5 and can be bought at the gate or picked up at the Mid-South Coliseum box office F, Sat, or M before the fight. On Sat, from 11am-12:30pm, promotional events are televised. Call WMC-Channel 5 to request studio tickets.

Restaurants

Lisa Snowden

A tempting display by some of Overton Square's restaurants, 1981. Robert Moye, Public Eye; Lorenzo Sanchez, Gonzales and Gertrude's; Robert Arder, Bombay Bicycle Club; James "Chef" Myles, Friday's; Garnet Foster, Paulette's.

At the turn of the century Memphis was known to the super-rich as the home of Luehrmann's and Gaston's restaurants/hotels. Luehrmann's served fine German cuisine and Gaston's, classical French. Actors, opera singers, sportsmen, and financiers came by private railroad cars to dine sumptuously on duck from Michigan, partridges from the Argentine, and good wines. The waiters wore tails, and napkins were of linen. The prohibition of race track betting in 1905 and liquor in 1909 spelled doom for these elegant restaurant/hotels. From the 1930s through the '50s, the Peabody Skyway, a chic rooftop nightclub, was the "in" spot; now in the '80s it's being revived. The city is much larger today, and the number and variety of restaurants greater.

The following are our personal favorites. Memphis has many other pleasant restaurants. For fuller listings, check "Memphis Magazine", "Key", and the yellow pages of the phone directory. For new finds, read Andy Hill's excellent monthly reviews in "Memphis Magazine".

KEY TO ABBREVIATIONS

Credit cards

AE American Express
CB Carte Blanche
DC Diner's Club
MC Master Card
Visa

Meals

B Breakfast
L Lunch
D Dinner

Prices

Classified on the basis of dinner for two, including an inexpensive bottle of wine, tax, and tip.

$ under $15
$$ $15-$30
$$$ $30-$45
$$$$ $45 +

Many restaurants have lower priced lunch menus.

AMERICAN & CONTINENTAL

Anderton's Restaurant
1901 Madison, 726-4010. A step into the 1950s. Try the oysters-on-the-

half-shell ($2.10/½doz.) L ex Sat, D 11am-10pm M-Th, 11am-11pm F, 4-11pm Sat. Closed Sun. Full bar. AE, DC, MC, Visa. Reservations. $$

Bill's

Highway 77 in Arkansas, betweeen Memphis and Marion, 735-1357. About one mile north of West Memphis, this roadhouse is worth the drive. Features esoteric offerings like rooster dainties (they're what you imagine, but taste much better), frog legs, quail, barbecued beef stew. BLD 6:30am-10pm Tu-Sat. Beer only. No cards. No reservations. $$

Bombay Bicycle Club

2120 Madison in Overton Square, 726-6055. The "in" spot among young professionals for food, drink, backgammon, and jazz. Happy hour, 4-6:30pm M-F; backgammon played constantly, weekly tournament 6:30pm Sun; live jazz 9:30pm-1:30am F&Sat; popular lunch spot; special brunch Sat & Sun with complimentary champagne mimosas. LD 11:30am-11pm daily. Bar 'til 1am Sun-Th; 'til 2am F&Sat. Full bar. AE, DC, MC, Visa. Reservations. $$

Boston Sea Party

1575 E. Brooks Rd, 345-1771. An all-you-can-eat franchised buffet, but if you like non-fried seafood, try it. Caviar, oysters, shrimp, lobster, ... in a candlelit, New England atmosphere. They also have steak for non-sea-fooders. Upstairs dining room available for private parties. D 6-10pm M-Th, 5-11pm F&Sat, 4:30-9pm Sun. Full bar. AE, DC, MC, Visa. Reservations. $$$$

The Carriage House

680 Adams (rear), 525-1170. A renovated carriage house in historic Victorian Village*, romantic and charming. Originally the Lee* family's carriage house. L 11:30am-2pm M-F; D 6:30-10pm Tu-Sat. Wine and whiskey, no beer. AE, DC, MC, Visa. Dinner reservations. Private parties, up to 150. $$$

Diane's Restaurant

100 N. Main, 523-2098. The view of the river and city as you circle the 38th floor of Memphis' tallest building is fabulous. L 11am-2pm. Available for private parties at night. Full bar. AE, MC, Visa. Reservations for large groups. $

Ducks & Company

939 Ridge Lake Blvd, ground floor Hyatt Regency, 761-1234. Duck is the specialty. Different menus for different times of day. Take the kids along for a view of the duck pond and a ride in the glass enclosed elevator. Good buffet 10:30am-2:30pm Sun, $8.25/adults, $4.50/children under

13. BLD 6:30am-midnight daily. Full bar. AE, CB, DC, MC, Visa. Reservations. $$$

élan. See Nightspots/Without Live Music.

Fantasia. See Nightspots/With Live Music.

Folk's Folly Restaurant
551 S. Mendenhall, 767-2877. Unquestionably the best steaks in town. Served in a small converted house. D 6-11pm M-F, 6-12pm Sat, 6-10pm Sun. Full bar. AE, DC, MC, Visa. Reservations. $$$$

Jim's Place East
5560 Shelby Oaks Drive, 388-7200. A few Greek dishes spice up the fare. L 11am-2pm M-F; D 5-9:30pm M-Th, 5-10 F&Sat. Full bar. AE, MC, Visa. No reservations on weekends. $$

Knickerbocker
4699 Poplar, 683-2717. Go for their homemade soup of the day and cornbread, they're the bargain on the menu. LD 11am-10pm daily. Full bar. AE, MC, Visa. Reservations. $$

La Montagne
3550 Park, 458-1060. Fresh natural foods. The mood is casual and relaxed. Live music Tu night. Juice, tea, beer and wine; no liquor. L 11:30am-2:30pm M-Sat, 9am-2:30pm Sun; D 5:30-10pm Sun-Th, 5:30-11pm F&Sat. MC, Visa. No reservations. Back room seats 30 for private parties. $

Mr. "B"
4632 Winchester, 362-1345. The decor is plain, but the seafood is super! Gumbo and fried shrimp always; crayfish, oysters, and fresh fish when available. Packed on weekends. Casual. LD 11am-11pm M-F, 5-11pm Sat. Beer only. MC, Visa. No reservations. $$

91st Bomb Group
2561 Democrat, 346-1260. The World War II nostalgia and taped music are fun. The food is well-seasoned and good. Beware: there's a long wait for a table and drinks are $2 each. Happy hour: 4-7pm M-F. L 11am-2:30pm M-F; 11:30am-2:30pm Sat & Sun; D 5-10pm Sun-Th, 5-12pm F&Sat. Full bar. AE, MC, Visa. Reservations for 9+. $$$

Number One Beale Street Bar and Restaurant
1 Beale, 525-1116. The atmosphere is renovated/contemporary. Live soft jazz Tu-Sat. $5.95 cold buffet and champagne Sun brunch. 3 for 1

happy hour: 4-6:30pm M-F. L 11:30am-2pm M-Sat, 11am-3pm Sun; D 5:30-11pm M-Th, 5:30-12pm F&Sat. Full bar. AE, MC, Visa. Reservations for groups of 8+. $$

Shanti Steak House
5500 Hwy. 70 (Summer - just beyond I-240 & I-55 intersection), 386-9117. Roadhouse wallpapered with newspapers and business cards, and tables decorated with checkered cloths and candles in chianti bottles. You get a choice between steak and frog legs. **Conestoga's Ashlar Hall** (1397 Central, 272-9595) is a mid-town version. D 6-11pm, M-Th, 5-11pm F&Sat. BYOB. AE, MC, Visa. Reservations on weekend. $

Shelby Restaurant
6807 Hwy 70, 386-3922. Plain roadside-motel restaurant. Offers some of the city's best food — small fresh catfish. Just past the beltway, it's well worth the drive. BLD 6am-10pm M-Sat. Beer only. No cards. Reservations on weekends. $$

Swiss Manor
3165 Forest Hill Rd, east of Germantown, 755-6710. Continental cuisine; contemporary elegance; marvelous bread. Piano music live in the bar nightly. D 6-10pm Tu-Sun. Full bar. AE, DC, MC, Visa. Reservations. $$$$

The Unicorn
7691 Poplar, in the Pines, 754-0170. Country tea room in a small converted house. Daily specialties, many are Greek. L 11am-2:30pm M-Sat, D 5-9pm M-Sat. BYOB. MC, Visa. Reservations. $

Western Steakhouse and Lounge
1298 Madison, 725-9896. The real thing — a country-and-western gathering spot with good steaks. Top quality live music and dancing. D 4pm-1am M-Sat. Live music: 8pm-1am Tu-Sat. Beer or BYOB. AE, DC, MC, Visa. Reservations F&Sat. $$

Windows on the River
Atop the Holiday Inn-Rivermont, Riverside Dr. at Georgia St, 525-0121. Spectacular view of the river, elegant Art Deco furnishings, and continental cuisine. Complimentary antipasto and fruit courses. The dry ice volcano finale adds just the right touch of spoof. L 11am-2pm Sun only, D 6-11pm M-Sat. Full bar. AE, CB, MC, Visa. Reservations. $$$$

Woman's Exchange of Memphis
88 Racine, 327-5681. A mother's and grandmother's delight. Browse before and after lunch in the shop* filled with homemade gifts and

children's clothes. Two luncheon choices offered each day in a tea-shop/ courtyard setting, $3.75/person noon-2pm M-F; tea $1/person 2:45-4:15pm M-F. No tipping. No alcohol. No cards. No reservations. $

BARBECUE

In Memphis barbecue means pork. The city boasts it offers the world's best and has an annual barbecue contest each May to prove it. Cooks attribute their success to different things: sauce, quality of the pig and butchering, green hickory wood, design of pit, ...
Some of the best places to sample this native specialty are known as barbecue joints, and the name fits. They're usually small, have counter and to-go service, serve no alcohol, and accept no credit cards.
"Memphis Magazine" and the newspapers run occasional surveys of local joints. Here are a few of our favorites.

Blues Alley. See Nightspots/With Live Music.

Brady and Lil's Real Bar-B-Q
601 S. Parkway E, 942-9023. Don't claim to have had "real" bar-b-q until you've been here. It's divine. LD 11:30am-8pm Tu-Th; 11:30am-11pm F&Sat. No alcohol, but BYOB. No cards. $

Germantown Commissary
2290 Germantown Rd, Germantown, 754-5540. In the back of the small grocery/commissary. Good barbecue sandwiches and special rib plates to-go. You can eat on picnic tables outside. BLD 7am-7pm M-Sat, 12-7pm Sun. The store sells beer and soft drinks. Catering service available. MC, Visa. $

Gridley's
4101 Summer, 452-4057. And a new, bigger branch, 6065 Old Macon, 388-7003. Excellent ribs and sandwiches. A to-go counter and dining room area. Gridley's will cater, and the new branch will book weekday private parties. For breakfast they offer biscuits, eggs, ... BLD 6am-11pm Sun-Th, 6am-12pm F&Sat. Full bar. No cards. No reservations. $

Lamb's Eat Shop
232 N. Cleveland, 725-6640. There's not much overhead here, and the sandwiches are good and a bargain. Located in the now run-down curb market, the Lamb family has run it since 1922. BLD 8am-6pm M-Sat. No alcohol. No cards. No reservations. $

Payne's
1762 Lamar, 274-9823. Converted gas station with booths and a cold drink machine. Perhaps the best barbecue in town. In-house and take-out service. Try their barbecued sausage, too. Will cater. LD 11am-9pm M, Tu, & Th, 11am-6:30pm W, 11am-11pm F&Sat. No alcohol. No cards. No reservations. $

Public Eye
17 S. Cooper in Overton Square, 726-4040. 2655 Mt. Moriah Rd, 365-8620. Good ribs and icy beer. LD 11:30am-10:30pm M-Th, 11:30am-12:30am F&Sat, 3-10:30pm Sun. Full bar. AE, DC, MC. $$

Rendezvous
52 S. 2nd, 523-2746. A Memphis landmark. Dry spicy barbecue served in a cave-like atmosphere. Walls covered with an eclectic collection — everything from bottles to street signs. More Michelob draft beer is sold here than anywhere else in the South. L Sat only, opens 12:30pm; D 4:30pm-1am Tu-Sat. Beer or BYOB. AE, DC, MC, Visa. Reservations on week nights only. $$

Rib Rack
9102 Poplar Pike, east of Germantown, 754-7001. Sit on the front porch and munch on juicy ribs. Happy hour: 4:30-6:30pm Tu-F. LD 11am-10pm Tu-Th & Sun, 11am-11pm F&Sat. Beer only. MC, Visa. $

See Mason, Tn./Bozo's.

BEER & BURGERS

Bennigan's Tavern
5336 Poplar, 685-2088. An east Memphis spot for quiche, nachos, salads, and burgers. LD 11am-11pm Sun-Th, 11am-1am F&Sat. Bar 'til 2:30am. Happy hour: 11am-7pm M-F. Full bar. AE, MC, Visa. Reservations accepted only for 11am-noon; preferred seating if you call ahead. $

Circle Cafe
680 W. Brookhaven Cl, 767-5708. Big juicy burgers. Good bar. Popular. LD 11:30am-midnight M-Sat, 4pm-midnight Sun. Bar 'til 2:30am daily. Happy hour: 4-7pm M-F, 11:30am-7pm Sat. Full bar. AE, MC, Visa. $

Cockeyed Camel
5871 Poplar next to the Quality Inn, 767-9616. Lattice work and ceiling fans, relaxed atmosphere. D 4pm-2am daily. Happy hour: 4-7pm. Bar 'til 3am. Full bar. MC, Visa. $

Danver's

Part of the fast food hamburger and salad bar chain founded in Memphis. 10 local outlets: 3495 Austin Peay Hwy. (377-1987), 911 Estate Dr. (683-5835), 2238 Frayser Blvd. (353-5577), 757 S. Highland (327-3581), 7575 Hwy. 72 Germantown (754-6946), 2871 Perkins Rd. (794-9993), 910 W. State Line Rd. Southaven (342-0503), 1610 Sycamore View Rd. (382-4670), 1468 Union at McNeil (274-3233), 1635 Winchester Rd. (345-8611), 4299 Winchester Rd. (365-8515). The burgers are big and juicy and you can fix them up just the way you like with trimmings from the salad bar. Beer. LD 10:30am-closing (times vary from 10pm-midnight). $

T.G.I. Friday's

2115 Madison in Overton Square, 725-7737. There's always something happening at Friday's: rock'n roll/M, country and western/Tu, reduced prices on steaks/W, noisemakers and half-priced drinks from midnight 'til closing/Th, and a champagne brunch 11:30am-3pm Sun. It's loud and fun. The front windows open for alfresco dining on pretty days. Happy hour: 4-6:30pm at the bar (ladies always ½ price at the bar). LD 11:30am-1am daily. Bar 'til 3am. Full bar. AE, DC, MC, Visa. Reservations for 10 + . $

The Half Shell

4970 Poplar, 767-9828. A lot of east Memphians are regulars here. Popular, crowded, and noisy. Good fried oyster and steak sandwiches. D 4pm-1am M-Sat, 5pm-midnight Sun. Bar 'til 2am. Full bar. AE, MC, Visa. $

Huey's

1927 Madison, 726-4372. Huey's also has an out-East branch called **Louie's** located in a converted Dairy Queen at 5355 Poplar (685-9340), but we'll stick with the old place. Good burgers and chili. On Sun live jazz 3:30-6:30pm and live bluegrass, progressive, or ... 9:30-midnight. (Louie's features live pop & oldies Sun afternoons.) LD 11:30am-2am M-F, noon-2am Sat & Sun. Bar 'til 3am. Happy hour: 4-7pm M-F. Full bar. AE, MC, Visa. No reservations. $

Jefferson Square Restaurant. See Nightspots/With Live Music.

The London Transport

3595 Southern, 452-6648. A MSU area bar. The crowd is young, the burgers delicious and the patio fun. Live music on M, F, & Sat nights. Keith Sykes plays here! $1 cover occasionally. LD 11:30am-midnight M-F, 6pm-1am Sat, 6pm-midnight Sun. Bar 'til 1am M-F, 3am Sat & Sun. Happy hour: 11:30am-7:30pm M-F, 6-7:30pm Sat & Sun. Full bar. AE, MC, Visa. You can arrange private afternoon parties when the bar is otherwise closed. $

Varsity Inn
762 S. Highland, 452-9225. A MSU hang-out. Cheap beer, good gyros sandwiches, backgammon, cable TV, machines, and a loud juke-box. They also have a year-round outdoor patio and a seven day a week, 4-7pm happy hour. Live jazz on W. LD 11am-midnight daily. Bar 'til 3am. Beer only. No cards. $

Zinnie's
1688 Madison, 726-5004. A neighborhood bar with the city's best reubens. LD 11:30am-1am M-Sat, noon-1am Sun. Bar 'til 3am. Full bar. AE, MC, Visa. $

BLUE PLATE SPECIALS

In other cities these restaurants might be known as soul-food restaurants, but in Memphis they're neighborhood cafes. The food is "down home" Southern turnip greens and cornbread. A daily special offers your choice of a meat and three vegetables. They usually close early, are inexpensive, serve no alcohol, accept no cards or reservations, and are decorated plainly.

This list is by no means all inclusive.

The Blackeyed Pea
1782 Madison, 725-4150. 3500 Park, 324-3644. 3143 Austin Peay, next door to Raleigh Springs Mall, 377-2104. All have good vegetables and a salad of blackeyed peas. Cheerful tea shop atmosphere. Prices seem a little higher than at other blue plate spots. LD 11am-9pm Sun-Th,11am-10pm F&Sat. Full bar. AE, MC, Visa. $

Buntyn Restaurant
3070 Southern, 458-8776. We know people who go every day, but we think it's too expensive. Try the homemade rolls and coconut pie. LD 11am-8pm M-F. No alcohol. No reservations. $

The Cottage
3297 Summer, 454-9277. Possibly the best cornbread in town. BLD 10:30am-8pm M-F. No alcohol. No cards. $

The Cupboard
1495 Union, 276-6577. A very popular old standby. Delicious vegetables, especialy the baked eggplant. LD 11am-7:45pm M-F. No alcohol. No cards. No reservations. $

Dino's Southwestern Grill

645 N. McLean Blvd, 278-9127. A favorite with Southwestern faculty and students. Unlike most blue plate special spots, Dino's also offers spaghetti and Italian sausage. BLD 7am-8pm Tu-Sun. Beer only. No cards. No reservations. $

Fourway Grill

998 Mississippi Blvd, 775-9384. Started by the late Clint Cleaves, chauffeur to Memphis' famous political boss, E. H. Crump*. Booths in the front room, or enter through the back off Walker, and you'll find private dining rooms. BLD 7am-11pm daily. Beer only. No cards. No reservations. $

Kennedy View Restaurant

4002 Park, 452-9193. We like to go for breakfast. BLD 6am-8pm Tu-Sun. No alcohol. No cards. No reservations. $

Pearl's Sandwich Shop

67 Madison at Front (basement of UP Bank bldg.), 527-0680. At about $2 the lunch is probably the most reasonable in town. They offer special Greek dishes on W. BL 5am-3pm M-F. No alcohol. No cards. $

Sam's Restaurant

1802 Elvis Presley Blvd, 947-3710. You have to try their lemon icebox pie!!! BL 6am-3:30pm M-F. No alcohol. No cards. $

The Stacked Deck

5545 Murray Rd (1st floor of office building), 767-9659. Hard to find, but this tiny cafeteria is worth the search. Daily specials plus sandwiches and salads. You can get orders to-go. BLD 8:30am-8pm M-F. No alcohol. No cards. $

Sunset Motel

144 Hwy. 72 E, Collierville, 853-9523. If you're out this way try the cobbler and cornbread. BLD 5am-10pm M-Sat, 6am-3pm Sun. Beer only. No cards. No reservations. $

CHINESE

Most of the city's Chinese restaurants offer Mandarin and Szechuan food. They are usually small, plain, and relatively inexpensive. Most don't have liquor or beer licenses, so you must take your own (BYOB).

Only a few prepare Peking duck, and they require 24-hour notice. Call ahead. Memphis is lucky; it has lots of good Chinese restaurants. Here are a few of our favorites.

Formosa
3307 Summer, 323-4819. An extensive menu of Szechuan and Mandarin foods featuring Formosa duck and sesame chicken. Only a few tables. D 4:30-9:30pm Sun-Th, 4:30-10:30pm F&Sat. No alcohol. BYOB. MC, Visa. No reservations on the weekend. $

Hunan
4941 Summer, 685-0679. The food is good. Spicy dishes are quite hot. For the uninitiated, Hunan, like Szuchuan, is a province in southwestern China. The cooking in these regions shares a similar arsenal of peppery dishes cooked in oil; Hunanese cooks use chili and vinegar with even greater abandon. Country and western musak incongruously filters through the red and yellow dining room. Historical note: Hunan is located in part of what was the first Holiday Inn* in the U.S., now the Royal Oaks Motel. LD 11:30am-10pm Tu-Sun. No alcohol. BYOB. MC, Visa. Reservations. $

Jimmy Tin's Port Shanghai
2725 S. Mendenhall Rd, 794-4134. Mandarin and Cantonese cuisine. Nice decor. No fortune cookies. LD 11am-10pm Sun-F, 5-10pm Sat. Full bar. AE, MC, Visa. $$

Ming House
4222 Winchester, 362-1384. The atmosphere seems almost Japanese in its quietness and simplicity, but the food is divinely Chinese. Mandarin and Hunan dishes, unusual ones for the knowledgeable or adventuresome. 11am-2pm Sun buffet and dim sum (Mandarin pastries). If you haven't tried dim sum, you're missing a real treat. LD 11:30am-9:30pm Sun-Th, 11:30am-11pm F&Sat. Beer only. AE, DC, MC, Visa. Reservations. $

Peking Restaurant
Northwest corner of Poplar Plaza shopping center, Poplar & Highland, 327-1677. We like their hot and spicy dishes, especially the bean curd. City's best mai tais. LD 11:30am-10pm M-Th, 11:30am-11pm F, 4-11pm Sat, noon-10pm Sun. Full bar. AE, MC, Visa. Reservations 5+. $$

Wah Nam
4375 Stage Rd, 388-8430. Perhaps the best Chinese food in town. Marvelous crisp vegetables. Success has hurt their service. D 4:30-9:30pm M-Sat. BYOB. MC, Visa. No reservations. $

FRENCH

Cafe Du Louvre
2125 Madison in Overton Square, 276-4780. Excellent and imaginative French cuisine. Lovely intimate setting. D 6-11pm Tu-Sat. Wine and whiskey, no beer. AE, MC, Visa. Reservations. $$$$

Justine's
919 Coward Place, 527-3815. They have won the Holiday Magazine dining award every year since 1959. Elegant and formal atmosphere in the lovely converted Old Coward Place*. Live piano music ex Tu & Th. D 5:30-10pm M-Sat. Full bar. AE, DC, MC, Visa. Reservations recommended. Courtyard, wine cellar, and upstairs room available for private parties. $$$$

La Baguette French Bread and Pastry Shop
3088 Poplar, 458-0900. Mainly a retail bakery, but there are a few tables where you can lunch on limited sandwiches, quiche, and pastries. Catering service operates out of this shop. Open, 7:30am-7pm M-Sat.
567 Erin Dr, 761-4150. Tea shop and retail bakery. Open, 9:30am-5pm M-Sat.
4310 Summer (inside Stein Mart), 683-6866. Tea shop and retail bakery. Open, 10am-6pm M-Sat, 1-5:30pm Sun.
All branches: No alcohol. No cards. $

La Tourelle
2146 Monroe, just east of Cooper, 726-5771. In a small converted house near Overton Square, this provincial French restaurant offers a prix fixe dinner menu, varying with entrees from $16-$19; changes weekly. D 6-9:30pm Tu-Sun. Full bar. No cards. Reservations required. $$$

The Magic Pan Creperie
Germantown Village Square Mall, Poplar at Germantown Rd, 754-0820. It's fun to watch the crepes made, and the atmosphere is light and airy. Take the children along. Special Sat & Sun brunch. L 11am-4pm daily. D 4-9pm Sun-Th, 4-11pm F&Sat. Full bar. AE, MC, Visa. Reservations for 6+. $$

Paulette's
2110 Madison, 726-5128. Dependably good food in a French/Hungarian inn atmosphere. Live piano 7-11pm F&Sat, 5-9pm Sun. LD 11am-11pm M-Th, 11am-midnight F&Sat, 11am-9pm Sun. Full bar. AE, MC, Visa. Reservations ex Sun lunch/brunch. $$

GERMAN

Erika's German Restaurant
52 S. 2nd, 526-5522. This pleasant quiet restaurant offers authentic bratwurst, schnitzel, and sauerbraten. L 11am-2pm M-F, D 5-10pm F&Sat. Beer or BYOB. AE, CB, DC, MC, Visa. Reservations for groups of 5 + . $$

Fritzie's
Hickory Ridge Mall, 362-8705. German deli; to-go, counter, and limited table service. It's got a big-city downtown feeling. Open: 10am-9:30pm M-Sat, 1-6pm Sun. Beer only. MC, Visa. $

Lieselotte's Delikatessen
693 Avon Rd, 685-8602. Wonderful German sausages, breads, potato salad, cakes — to eat here or to take home. L 10am-6pm Tu-Sat. No beer. No cards. $

ITALIAN

Broadway Pizza House
2581 Broad, 454-7930. Frequented by everybody from neighborhood motorcycle gangs to junior executives, this pizzeria serves good pizza and beer. Elvis memorabilia on the walls, pinball machines, and a juke box. LD 10am-11pm Sun and Tu-Th, 10am-1am F&Sat. Beer only. No cards. No reservations. $

Chicago Pizza Factory
2059 Madison, 725-7020. Delicious deep-dish Chicago pizza. Eat on the patio in warm weather. You can reserve the downstairs room for private parties. LD 11am-11pm Sun-Th, 11am-1am F&Sat. Full bar. AE, MC, Visa. No reservations. $

Garibaldi's Pizza
3530 Walker, 327-6111. LD 11am-midnight Sun-Th, 11am-1am F&Sat. 6195 Macon Rd, 382-0110. LD 11am-11pm Sun-Th, 11am-1am F&Sat. Pizza to-go or eat-in. The juke box is loud. It's fun to watch the cook toss pizza dough in the air. Room available for parties. Beer. No cards. $

Giovanni's
282 N. Cleveland, 725-6660. It's dark, and Frank Sinatra plays in the background. They like garlic and so do we. D 4-10:30pm Tu-Sun. Full bar. AE, DC, MC, Visa. Reservations. $$

Grisanti's

1489 Airways Blvd, 458-2648. Owner John Grisanti is a flamboyant Memphis personality. He does everything from teach cooking classes to arrange benefits for St. Jude's Hospital. His restaurant captures his sense of fun and flamboyance. LD 11am-11pm M-Th, 11am-midnight F & Sat. Full bar. AE, DC, MC, Visa. No reservations except for large groups in the party room or groups of 4-10 in the gourmet room where special dinners are served on a 24-hour notice ($25 charge to reserve the gourmet room). $$

Marco's Fine Foods

5469 Poplar, 683-2990. With a name like Marco's Fine Foods, the interior is a pleasant surprise — white table cloths, fresh flowers, good food, and espresso and cappucino. LD 11am-9:30pm M-Th, 11am-midnight F, 5pm-midnight Sat. Full bar. AE, MC, Visa. No reservations, but call as you're leaving home to see if there's a wait. $$

Ronnie Grisanti & Sons

710 Union Ave (next door to Sun Studio*), 527-7668. Small neighborhood family restaurant. Friendly and fun. Limited menu and specials. BL 7am-3pm M-F. D 6-10:30pm Th-Sat. Beer or BYOB. MC, Visa. No reservations. Available for parties M-W nights. $$

Two Brothers' Italian Restaurant

3735 Summer, 458-2138. Two brothers opened this take-out or eat-in spot in a vacant fast-food restaurant. LD 11am-11pm M-Th, 11am-midnight F & Sat, 4-11pm Sun. Beer or BYOB. MC, Visa. Reservations for big groups. $

Vito's. See Ice Cream &/or Sandwiches.

ICE CREAM AND/OR SANDWICHES

See also Beer & Burger and Barbecue restaurants and Health Foods shops.

Abraham's Deli

338 N. Main at N. Jackson, 527-3659. One of the few reminders that Pinch* was once a bustling Jewish neighborhood. Mrs. Abraham's family, the Schneiders, has been on this corner about 70 years. Deli favorites are Hungarian meatball and corned beef sandwiches, kosher pickles, and carrot cake. To-go or small eat-in area. BL 6am-4pm M-F. Imported and local beer. No cards. $

Berclair Drug Store
4468 Summer, 683-2464. Good sodas. Small friendly neighborhood drug store with counter and table service. BL 8am-6pm M-Sat (grill off about 4:30 pm). $

The Candy Store
Overton Square*. 726-6073. This candy store sells homemade ice cream sandwiches — any flavor ice cream between two chocolate wafer cookies. A real treat! Open: 11am-9pm Sun-Th, 11am-11pm F&Sat.

Cheese on the Square
2090 Overton Square* (downstairs, behind the Sycamore), 722-8774. Small part-restaurant, part-market. Serves delicious sandwiches and sells coffees, teas, spices, cheeses, and gifts for the gourmet. You can order homemade rolls to go, but be sure to call several days ahead to place your order. L and snacks. 10am-5pm M-W, 10am-8pm Th-Sat, noon-3pm Sun. Beer only. DC, MC, Visa. $

Dixie Ice Cream Parlor
4599 Elvis Presley Blvd, 396-0055. It's so camp—if it were in L.A. crowds with roller skates on would be fighting to get in. Sandwiches and gooey ice cream fantasies. Hot pink and green carousel decor with an old Wurlitzer juke box in one corner. Homemade ice cream. Try one of the bargain sandwich/drink/sundae specials. LD Summer: 11am-11pm Sun-Th, 11am-midnight F&Sat. Winter: 11am-10pm Sun-Th, 11am-11pm F&Sat. No alcohol. MC, Visa. Phone to arrange birthday parties. $

Front Street Deli
77 S. Front, 522-8943. Tiny storefront sandwich shop. To-go or limited counter space. BL 8am-4pm M-F. Beer. No cards. $

Halpern's Kosher Delicatessen-Restaurant
280 N. Cleveland, 725-6039. It's the real thing. Sells retail, and lots of regular lunch customers take home meats, homemade pickles, ...You can easily pack a good picnic from here. Park in the bank lot next door. L 9am-4:30pm Sun-F. Beer only. No cards. No reservations. $

Harrell Drug Store
132 E. Mulberry, Collierville, 853-2201. The soda fountain offers good sodas and ice cream dishes, but no food. 8am-7pm M-Sat. No alcohol. No cards. $

Johann Sebastian Bagel*
692 Mt. Moriah (Poplar & Mendenhall, across the tracks), 682-3057. This retail deli has tables for about 30. You can see bagels being made

through the window. BLD 9am-6pm M-F, 8am-6pm Sat, 8am-5pm Sun. No alcohol. No cards. No reservations. $

La Baguette. See French restaurants.

Lieselotte's Delikatessen. See German restaurants.

Old Tyme Frozen Custard
5740 Mt. Moriah Rd. Ext, 794-7650. Frozen custard and sandwiches to-go or eat here. Fast food atmosphere. LD 10am-10pm Sun-Th, 10am-11pm F&Sat. No alcohol. No cards. $

Schiekle's Old Tyme Delicatessen
1301 Winchester (one block east of Elvis Presley Blvd.), 396-1191. Park Place Mall, 682-2002. Excellent sandwiches plus red cabbage, Greek olives, kosher pickles, hot tamales,.... Eat-in or carry-out. Cheese and meats by the pound to-go. Catering. LD 10am-6:30pm M-Sat. Imported and local beer. No cards. $

Sno Cream Castle
1650 Getwell Rd, 743-5570. You can get chocolate dip-top soft-custard cones, thousands of varieties of sno cones, pronto pups, and other old-time delights at this carry-out snack bar. LD and snacks daily, wintertime: 10am-10pm, summertime: 10am-11:30pm. No cards. $

Spotts Drug Store
108 E. Broadway, West Memphis, Ark, 735-1634. The soda fountain serves sandwiches, homemade soups and chili, and super sodas. BLD 8am-9pm daily. No alcohol. No cards. $

Swensen's Ice Cream Parlor
2109 Madison in Overton Square, 726-9721. LD 11:30am-10pm Sun-Th, 11:30-midnight F&Sat. 2518 Mt. Moriah, 794-0600. LD 11:30am-10:30pm Sun-Th, 11:30am-11:30pm F&Sat. Sandwiches and ice cream treats in a neo-soda fountain atmosphere. Prices seem a bit high. No alcohol. Arrangements may be made for birthday parties. No cards. $

Vito's
3024 Covington Pike, 372-1773. Italian sandwiches to-go or eat-in. Homemade sausage and pasta to-go. LD 10am-6:30pm Tu-Sat. Imported and local beer. MC, Visa. $

Wall Street Deli-Midtown Edition
911 Union, 525-3354. A good place to get a sandwich and beer near Bap-

tist Hospital. Fast-food atmosphere. BLD 6am-10pm M-W, 6am-midnight Th-Sat, 8am-10pm Sun. Beer only. No cards. $

Wiles-Smith Drug Store
1635 Union, 278-6416. The soda fountain's chili-dogs have a large regular following. Counter and table service. BL 8am-5pm M-F, ice cream 8am-10pm daily. No alcohol. No cards. $

JAPANESE

Unfortunately none of Memphis' Japanese restaurants serve sushi or sashimi.

Benihana of Tokyo
900 Ridge Lake Blvd. (at Poplar & I-240), 683-7390. Steak, chicken, lobster, and shrimp plus sprouts, onions, peppers grilled before you on your teppanyaki table for 8. Delicious and fun. The Japanese-style building is lovely. L 11:30am-2pm Sun-F. D 5-10pm M-Th, 5-11pm F&Sat. Full bar. AE, CB, DC, MC, Visa. Reservations. $$$

Edo Japanese Restaurant
4792 Summer, 767-7096. Small, quiet, authentic, and delicious. L 11:30am-2:30pm Tu-F&Sun. D 5-10pm Tu-Th&Sun, 5:30-11pm F&Sat. Beer only. AE, MC, Visa. Reservations 5+. $$

MEXICAN

Gonzales and Gertrude's
35 S. Cooper in Overton Square, 725-0005. Ole! Marvelous food and giant margueritas. Good bar. Patio for warm weather. LD 11:30am-11pm daily. Happy hour: 4-7pm daily. Full bar. AE, MC, Visa. No reservations. $$

RUSSIAN

Samovar Old World Eatery
10 N. Main (first floor of Porter Building*), 527-4570. Order and pick-up fast food style, but here you eat piroshkes, blintzes, knishes, soups, salads, and homemade breads in the Porter Building's old world splendor. Kosher. L 11am-5pm M-F. No alcohol. No cards. $

GOOD SUNDAY BRUNCH SPOTS

Bennigan's—Beer & Burgers*.

Bombay Bicycle Club—American & Continental*.

Carriage House—American & Continental*.

T.G.I. Friday's—Beer & Burgers*.

Ducks & Company—American & Continental*.

Magic Pan Creperie—French*.

Paulette's—French*.

Windows on the River—American & Continental*.

SUGGESTIONS FOR CHILDREN

Ice cream and sandwich spots and blue plate special restaurants are always good bets. Or you might want to introduce your youngster to tacos from **Pancho's** (5464 Fox Plaza 795-1600, 1850 Union 274-1311, 4404 Elvis Presley Blvd. 332-5115), or **El Chapo** (2439 Summer 323-8116). Or let them try chopsticks at one of the city's family oriented Chinese* restaurants.

Burger King, Johann Sebastian Bagel, McDonald's, Shakey's, and **Thornton's Donuts** give tours. See Memphis At Work/Restaurants. The magician, organ player, balloon twister, and movies are special treats at **Shakey's.** They have six locations here: 665 Mendenhall 683-6381, 1134 E. Brooks Rd. 396-4691, 1674 Poplar 726-4301, 2707 S. Perkins 365-8231, 3347 Austin Peay Hwy. 382-0155, and 570 W. State Line Rd. 342-1390. **Chuck E. Cheese Pizza Time Theatre** (5016 Park Ave. in Eastgate, 682-8190) is even more of an "happening". They have pizza, hot dogs, salad and sundae bars, electronic games and rides (tokens come with food), performing robots, and a lion impersonating Elvis. They're in action 11am-10pm daily. No cards. Beer only. Their specialty is birthday parties; arrange in advance.

At some restaurants the decor is especially fascinating to children. **The Hungry Fisherman** (I-40 & E. Macon Rd, 388-5057, and I-55 S. at Horn Lake, 393-0314) is designed like a boat and sits on a lake with ducks and a playground. **Victoria Station** (2734 S. Mendenhall, 365-7967) is not designed for children, but they're bound to be fascinated by dining in railroad cars. These two offer special reduced rate dinners for children. **Jade East** (3695 Austin Peay Hwy, 388-3955) is an eye catcher. Just past Raleigh Springs Mall is the red pagoda. Open for D daily, they have super specials and a helpful staff. A good place to try chopsticks!

And don't forget cafeterias. Everyone gets their choice, and the food is reasonable. **Britling, Wilmoth's, Robilio, S&S, Morrison's**, and **Mark Twain** are scattered throughout the city. They're usually open for BLD seven days a week from about 7am-8pm.

Picnics are a perennial treat for all ages. Where to pick up goodies? See listings under food shops and sandwich, French, and German restaurants for suggestions, or just visit your own grocery store's deli section.

24 HOUR SPOTS

Late night or early morning, try these 24 hour places. They're not necessarily known for their food or decor. Most serve no alcohol and accept no cards. Check the yellow pages of the phone directory for branch addresses and phone numbers; call ahead to make sure they're open.

Big Daddy's Sandwich Shop—Several branches.

Coach and Four Motor Lodge Restaurant—1318 Lamar, 726-5000.

Coleman's Barbeque—Several branches.

Denny's—Several branches.

Earl's Hot Biscuits—179 E.H. Crump Blvd, 775-9318. Try the country ham. They sell beer.

Gridiron Restaurants—Many branches.

Jojo's—50 S. Camilla at Union, 522-1877. They accept MC and Visa and serve liquor, beer, and wine.

Sambo's—Several branches.

Silky Sullivan's—2080 Madison (lower level), 725-0650. 11pm-7am Tu-Th, 11pm-2pm F&Sat. Ham, sausage, eggs, grits and red-eye gravy.

Steak 'n Egg—Many branches. Our favorite.

Super Sub Shop—4587 Elvis Presley Blvd, 332-2546. F&Sat only.

Toddle House Coffee Shop—5370 Winchester at Mendenhall, 362-6376. Good hamburgers and breakfasts. The hash-browns and black bottom pie are musts. The precursor of today's fast food hamburger chains, Toddle House, though started in Houston by J.C. Stedman in 1931, is claimed by Memphis as one of our success stories. In the early 1930s Stedman moved to Memphis and joined with W.E.B. Johnson, the founder of Britlings Cafeterias who had just moved to Memphis from Birmingham, to build and open the first Memphis Toddle House in 1934. Such successful Memphis businessmen as Fred Smith, James K. Dobbs, and Horace Hull were involved in the booming restaurant business. In the 1950s Toddle House was purchased by Dobbs House. Successive acquisition found the company part of Beechnut in 1966, Squibb in 1968, and Carson Pirie Scott in 1980.

Shopping

Interior of York Arms' sporting goods store at 162 S. Main Street 1968.

William Eggleston

This chapter is dedicated to the stumped shopper—the husband whose anniversary is today, the houseguest who still hasn't found the right gift for her hostess, the out-of-towner who wants something to take home, the Godmother for her just christened Goddaughter, or the newcomer. Here's how to send flowers by the month or a singing telegram or where to find an hour's decorating advice or cooking lessons.

Hours vary, and some stores are open different hours on different days. Stores are generally open 10am-5pm M-Sat. Large department and discount stores often are open until 9pm M-Sat and from 1-5pm Sun. Where the hours are particularly odd, they're listed. If in doubt, phone ahead.

Tennessee state sales tax is 4.5% and city tax is 1.5% for a total of 6% local sales tax. Very few items are exempt.

This list of shops is limited. Whole categories are left out. Best tip — let your fingers do the walking. Also see ads in the local papers and "Memphis Magazine". Looking for second-hand merchandise, check the two weekly newspapers that are 90+% classified ads —"East Memphis Shoppers News" (622 S. Highland, 458-8030) and "Memphis Shopper's Guide" (1535 E. Brooks Rd, 345-8000). *The Penny Pincher* by Barbara Blockman and Bettye Campbell is a small guide to discount shopping in the area.

SHOPPING CENTERS

The shopping centers listed have building areas of 100,000 square feet or more. Most offer drugstores, grocery stores, and discount or variety stores. Those with special amenities are described. For further information see a brochure, "Shopping Centers" put out by the Memphis Area Chamber of Commerce, P.O. Box 224, 38101, 523-2322.

1 AMERICAN WAY SHOPPING CENTER
Perkins & American Way at I-240. *MATA: Park & Ride Blazer.*

2 BROOKHAVEN CIRCLE
Off Poplar, east of Mendenhall. *MATA: #50 (ex Sun), 22 (ex Sun).* Small houses converted to specialty shopping.

3 CENTER CITY SHOPPING CENTER
Poplar & Avalon. *MATA: #5, 55 (ex Sun), 22 (ex Sun).*

4 CHICKASAW OAKS PLAZA & VILLAGE 1776.
Between Poplar & Walnut Grove, just east of Tillman. *MATA: #55 (ex Sun), 41 (ex Sat & Sun), 22 (ex Sun).* Small, chic enclosed mall. Specialty shops and restaurants.

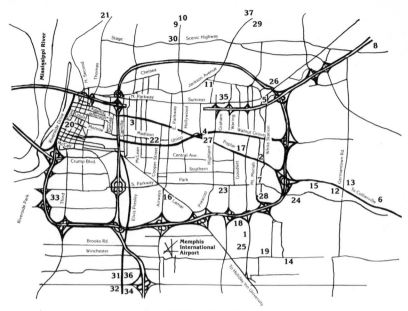

5 CLOVERLEAF SHOPPING CENTER

Summer & White Station. *MATA: #53 (ex Sun).*

6 COLLIERVILLE CITY CENTER

Hwy. 72 & Hwy. 57, Collierville. *MATA: #41 (ex Sat & Sun).*

7 EASTGATE SHOPPING CENTER

Park & White Station Rd. *MATA: #19 (ex Sun), 57.* Julius Lewis, Shainberg's, Woolco, a movie theatre, and many smaller shops are in the 364,000-square foot shopping center.

8 FACTORY OUTLET MALL

Canada Rd. & I-40. This enclosed mall opened in 1980 and is the first mall in the nation built exclusively for factory outlets. Prices seem higher than wholesale. Cosco, Country Miss, Kids Port USA, Carters, and Brand Name Fashions are among the outlets.

9 FRAYSER PLAZA

Frayser Blvd. & Overton Crossing. *MATA: #11 (ex Sat & Sun).*

10 FRAYSER VILLAGE

Frayser Blvd. & Rangeline Rd. *MATA: #11 (ex Sat & Sun), 10 (ex Sun).*

11 GATEWAY SHOPPING CENTER

Jackson & Macon Rd. *MATA: #52.*

12 GERMANTOWN RD.

Germantown Rd. going south off Poplar. *MATA: #41 (ex Sat & Sun)*.
Beginning with a wooded area called the Pines on Poplar and continuing
southward are occasional houses converted to antique and gift shops.

13 GERMANTOWN VILLAGE SQUARE MALL

Poplar just east of Germantown Rd. *MATA: #41*. Enclosed mall with
fashionable boutiques, gift stores, Helen of Memphis, M.M. Cohn, and
the Magic Pan Restaurant. Two levels of underground parking.

14 HICKORY RIDGE MALL

Winchester between Hickory Hill & Ridgeway. *MATA: Blue Blazer*.
1,140,000 square foot regional enclosed mall opened fall 1981. It's sleek
and fun. Goldsmith's, Sears & Roebuck, Julius Lewis, M.M. Cohn, plus
over 100 smaller shops like The Limited, Forty Carrots, and Chandlers
Shoes. Restaurants, cookie stores, and ethnic round-the-world fast food
court named The Patio, four movie theatres, fresh produce stalls, an amphitheatre with live free performances (often for children),....

15 KIRBY WOODS MALL

6675 Poplar (Hwy. 72). *MATA: #41, 22*. Enclosed mall with fountains and
skylights. Opened in 1973. Twenty-nine stores on two levels. Among the
excellent clothing stores and boutiques are Gus Mayer and Woolf Bros.
More specialty shopping across Poplar.

16 LAMAR-AIRWAYS

Lamar Ave. & Airways Blvd. *MATA: #56, 20, 32*.

17 LAURELWOOD

Poplar & Perkins Rd. Ext. *MATA: #55, 22, 50, 57, 19, 41, 59, 23*. Sears
& M.M. Cohn are the large stores here with many specialty shops and fine
boutiques in the surrounding area. Across Poplar is Goldsmith's Oak
Court store.

18 MALL OF MEMPHIS

I-240, Perkins Rd., & American Way. *MATA: Park & Ride Blazer*.
1,100,000 square foot two-level regional enclosed mall. Opened fall
1981. Lowenstein's/Maison Blanche, J.C. Penney, Dillard's department
store, Wilson's catalogue order store, Thalhimer's clothing store, an
Olympic size ice skating* rink, 160 specialty shops, an international fast
food court, a five screen movie theatre, and a play area for children.

19 MENDENHALL SQUARE MALL

Mendenhall & Winchester. *MATA: Blue Blazer*. Partially enclosed mall.

Has 21 stores, among them Central Hardware. The exterior is marked by a giant clock with exposed workings from an Oregon county courthouse.

20 MID-AMERICA MALL*

MATA: Downtown buses. Once the city's Main Street, now one of the longest pedestrian malls in the U.S. Fountains, trees, and benches entice downtown office workers and other shoppers. Goldsmith's, Shainberg's, Lowenstein's/Maison Blanche, Woolworth's, Royal Furniture, and Haverty's are among the stores along the walkway.

21 NORTHGATE SHOPPING CENTER

Thomas Str. at Whitney. *MATA: #11 (ex Sat & Sun).*

22 OVERTON SQUARE

Madison at Cooper. *MATA: Showboat Bus.* More than a shopping center, it's a revitalized area of Memphis with boutiques, gift shops, and restaurants centered around a courtyard gourmet market and bar. You'll find the unusual here. Many shops stay open until 9pm W & weekends. The Square makes shopping fun. A kiosk, run by the Convention & Tourist Bureau, open 11am-4pm daily (726-9422), sells tickets for current events and gives free information. Special events and Sat. story hour for children.

23 PARK CENTER

Park & Getwell Rd. *MATA: #9 (ex Sat & Sun), 57.* Hancock Fabric and Peaches.

24 PARK PLACE MALL

Park & Ridgeway. *MATA: #57, 41 (ex Sat & Sun).* An enclosed mall and open-air plaza. Opened fall 1981. Loehmann's is here selling discounted women's clothing. Other specialty stores include James Davis for Women, Oak Hall, Vance Boyd, John Simmons Entertains, Raiford's, B. Dalton Booksellers, and Oshman's sporting goods. Also here, Houlihan's restaurant and Schielke's Old Tyme Delicatessen.

25 PARKWAY VILLAGE

Perkins Rd. & Knight Arnold. *MATA: #36 (ex Sun).* Sears.

26 PERIMETER MALL

Summer & I-240. *MATA: #54 (ex Sun).* A Raw Furniture store and Toy City.

27 POPLAR PLAZA

Poplar & Highland. *MATA: #55 (ex Sun), 22 (ex Sun), 41 (ex Sat & Sun).* Built in 1949, this was the city's first big suburban shopping center. Lowenstein's/Maison Blanche, Penney's, and Gus Mayer plus many specialty shops like The Shop of John Simmons, Youngtown, The Book Shelf, McCrory's, and the Fun Shop are here. Across Poplar is Dillard Square with more specialty shopping.

28 QUINCE STATION
Quince Rd. & White Station. *MATA: #50 (ex Sun).*

29 RALEIGH SPRINGS MALL
Austin Peay Hwy., Yale Rd. & Scheibler Rd. *MATA: #52, 11 (ex Sat & Sun).* 880,000 square feet of enclosed mall and 75 stores. Many special activities such as Shelby State Community College* satellite classes. Goldsmith's, Lowenstein's, Penney's, and Sears have branches here. Children's strollers rented near the main entrance. Yale Plaza shopping center next door.

30 SKYLAKE SHOPPING CENTER
N. Hollywood & James Rd. *MATA: #40 (ex Sat & Sun).*

31 SOUTH PLAZA
Elvis Presley Blvd. & Raines Rd. *MATA: #43 (ex Sun), 48 (ex Sat & Sun).* Western Auto and Hancock Fabric. Whitehaven Plaza next door.

32 SOUTHBROOK MALL
Shelby Dr. & Elvis Presley Blvd. *MATA: #43 (ex Sun), 48 (ex Sat & Sun).* Service Merchandise, Pier 1 Imports, Fred Montesi's Supermarket, and a six-screen movie theatre. Southland Mall next door.

33 SOUTHGATE & WOOLCO SHOPPING CENTERS
Southwest and northwest corners of S. 3rd and Belz Blvd. *MATA: #39, 35 (ex Sat & Sun), 44 (ex Sun).* Mostly discount stores.

34 SOUTHLAND MALL
Shelby Dr. & Elvis Presley Blvd. *MATA: #43 (ex Sun), 48 (ex Sat & Sun).* The city's first enclosed mall, it opened in 1966. Its 500,000 square feet of shopping space includes southern branches of Goldsmith's, M.M. Cohn, and Sears. Many small specialty stores. Easy access to I-55; many visitors from Mississippi go no further. Southbrook Mall next door.

35 SUMMER CENTER
Summer & Waring Rd. *MATA: #53 (ex Sun), 54 (ex Sun).* TG&Y, Ace Hardware and other stores. The big draw is Stein Mart, a large store with reduced rates on quality men's and women's clothing and household goods. Worth a visit.

36 WHITEHAVEN PLAZA
Elvis Presley Blvd. & Raines Rd. *MATA: #43 (ex Sun), 48 (ex Sat & Sun).*

Lowenstein's, Fred's, Kent's, and Youngtown, South Plaza next door.

37 YALE PLAZA
Yale & Austin Peay Hwy.*MATA: #52, 11 (ex Sat & Sun)*. Service Merchandise and Seessel's Supermarket. Raleigh Springs Mall next door.

DEPARTMENT STORES

M.M. Cohn
Laurelwood, 767-6200. Southland Mall, 346-1212. Germantown Village Square Mall, 754-2150. Hickory Ridge Mall, 794-9999. Men's and women's clothing. Moderately priced.

Dillard's
Mall of Memphis, 363-0063. Here from Little Rock.

Goldsmith's
Mid-America Mall, 123 S. Main. Oak Court, 4545 Poplar. Raleigh Springs Mall. Southland Mall. Hickory Ridge Mall. Branch and department phone numbers are in the white pages. For 24 hour telephone ordering call 529-5000. To inqure about hours at all store locations call 529-4600. It's Memphis' Bloomingdale's — as a matter of fact, in the U.S. the Oak Court store is second only to Bloomingdale's in sales per square foot. Wares range from Godiva chocolates to antique Oriental rugs (766-2361). A personal shopping consultant will do your browsing for you (766-2357). Moderate to expensive.

Helen of Memphis
1808 Union, 274-0867. Germantown Villege Square Mall, 754-4100. Women's clothing. Nice bridal department.

Julius Lewis
1460 Union, 725-1144. Eastgate, 685-5116. Hickory Ridge Mall, 794-1144. Men's and women's up-to-date fashions. We like their midtown store best.

Lowenstein's/Maison Blanche
Mid-America Mall, 85 N. Main, 526-7711. Poplar Plaza, 526-8471. Whitehaven Plaza, 526-7731. Raleigh Springs Mall, 526-7741. Mall of Memphis. Full-service department store. Moderately priced clothing. You may order 24 hours a day (526-7711).

Gus Mayer
Poplar Plaza, 324-7366. Kirby Woods Mall, 754-9470. Women's clothing. Excellent designer shoe department. Good children's boutique at Kirby Woods; they even carry English button shoes for little girls.

J. C. Penney Co.
Raleigh Springs Mall, 388-1600, catalogue shopping - 388-3510. Poplar Plaza, 327-5625, catalogue shopping - 324-6633. Southgate, 948-1554, catalogue shopping - 774-4050. Mall of Memphis, 794-4163. The Raleigh store is their pace-setter and a complete full-service department store. The other branches carry mostly clothing. Good children's departments and catalogue shopping.

Sears Roebuck and Co.
495 N. Watkins, retail sale and catalogue merchandise distribution center. Laurelwood. Raleigh Springs Mall. Southland Mall. Collierville City Center. 7885 Hwy. 51 N. & Navy Rd, Millington. Parkway Village. 304 E. Broadway, West Memphis, Ark. Hickory Ridge Mall. Branch and department phone numbers in the white pages. All stores have catalogue telephone shopping and pick-up. Surplus stores at 495 N. Watkins, 5130 Old Summer, 938 E. Brooks Rd, 3456 Meyers, and 2164 Frayser Blvd. Retail outlet store at 2648 Broad. Sears is the world's largest retailer. Tool freaks swear by their Craftsman brand.

Woolf Bros.
Kirby Woods Mall, 754-2010. Primarily clothing. Quality sportswear to elegant designer clothing. Moderate to expensive. Good men's department.

DISCOUNT STORES

The merchandise at these stores runs the gamut from housewares to clothing unless otherwise specified.

Bargain Center USA
Frayser Plaza, 353-3353. Mid-America Mall, 82 S. Main, 522-9177. Factory Outlet Mall. 1175 S. Bellevue Blvd, 775-2089.

Fred's Discount Stores
Whitehaven Plaza, 332-6437. 2833 Lamar, 743-7321. 8912 Northwest Dr, 342-1805. 4589 Quince Rd, 682-4516. 6064 Stage Rd, 388-4810 (has pharmacy). 4321 Summer, 682-3708 (has pharmacy). Northgate, 358-0363. Frayser Plaza, 358-2231. 4280 Getwell, 794-9420 (their

premier store — three times as large as the others, much larger selection, plus a pharmacy). Fred's used to be known as Fred's Dollar Store. You can still find good bargains here. Also catalogue shopping.

Fred P. Gattas Distributors Co.
Parkway Village, 794-9900. 5000 Summer, 767-2930. No clothes.

Jefferson Ward
3030 Poplar, 458-2541. Frayser Village, 353-6552, South Plaza, 332-5050. Department stores and catalogue shopping.

Kent's Stores
1107 S. Bellevue Blvd, 946-5223. Southgate, 942-4483. Whitehaven Plaza, 398-8039. 721 N. Parkway, 527-3797. 3975 Jackson Ave, 388-2001. Lamar-Airways, 323-8064. 3512 Park Ave, 458-2676. 3237 Summer, 323-4888. Northgate, 357-1339. 408 E. Crump Blvd, 775-0020. 1230 N. Watkins, 276-3708. 5475 Elvis Presley Blvd, 398-4558. 4400 Summer, 683-2491.

Loehmann's
Park Place Mall, 767-1500. New women's furs, suits, coats, sportswear, rainwear, and dresses for ½ to ⅓ off.

Marshall's
4685 American Way. 363-7840.

T. J. Maxx
4659 Knight-Arnold Rd. 362-5610. Clothes and housewares at bargain prices.

Service Merchandise
Yale Plaza, 382-0200. Southbrook Mall, 332-1260. 584 S. Mendenhall Rd, 767-3780. No clothes.

Shainberg's
Mid-America Mall, 128 S. Main, 525-5481. Eastgate, 683-5266. 3217 Austin Peay Hwy, 386-2478. Southgate, 774-0501.

Stein Mart
Summer Center, 683-7304. Discounted better women's clothing, men's clothing, shoes, housewares, fabric, and a La Baguette outlet for croissants, quiche, ...(see French restaurants).

Target Stores
601 Colonial Rd, 685-9240. 1251 Wesley Dr, 332-2270. 4991 Stage Rd,

372-9090. 3700 Hickory Hill Rd, 363-0070. Their advertised bargains are truly that.

Wilson's
Mall of Memphis. Branch of country's largest catalogue order store.

Woolco Department Store
Eastgate, 683-4521. Southgate, 948-3451. Gateway Mall, 452-7391. See phone book for major department listings.

Zayre
Summer Center, 682-4616. Center City, 725-4515. Northgate, 358-5645.

SPECIALTY SHOPPING — A to Z

ANTIQUES, HOUSEWARES, FURNISHINGS, & GIFTS

See also Hardware & House Parts.

Accurate Engraving Service
339 Madison, 526-0491. Custom-made acrylic boxes, placemats, notions.

Anderson & Mulkins Treasure House of Antiques
9336 Hwy. 72, Germantown (between Forest Hill and Collierville), 754-7909. This has been a mother-daughter operation since 1906. Fine antiques.

Art galleries*.

Babcock Galleries
2262 S. Germantown Rd. 754-7950. English antiques, reproduction furniture, and gifts.

Barzizza's Estate Sales
1981 Union, 726-0800. Appraisals, liquidations, consignment sales. Antiques and used furniture. Open W only 9am-4pm or by appointment.

Alice Bingham Gallery. See Art Galleries & Shows. Nice custom framing.

Bradford Showroom Inc.
3860 S. Perkins Rd, 362-1740. Tremendous stock of high quality furniture. You might be lucky and hit a sale.

Carruthers Estate Sales
682-1255. By appointment only.

The China Mater
685-6983. Mrs. Eska Lee Cole matches discontinued or heirloom Lenox, Syracuse, English, and German china. Sets for sale. By appointment only.

Walter J. Cline. See Shopping/Jewelry. Antique clocks and watches. They repair.

Concrete Block & Ornamental Works
711 Scott, 458-8606. Molded concrete garden sculpture.

Contemporary Quilts
3466 Summer, 454-7063. Marilyn Califf, Art Academy graduate, designs and makes marvelous quilts.

Robert Crump's Hancock House
430 Perkins Rd Ext, 767-3050. Traditional fine silver, china, and crystal. Also a limited number of English antiques.

Economy Furniture & Antique Center
3632 Summer, 327-8485. Lots and lots of camp.

Flicker Street Market
46 Flicker Str, 454-9452. Flea market. Open 1-6pm F, 10am-6pm Sat & Sun. Browsing is free.

Frame Factory
3207 Austin Peay Hwy, 372-2962. 4858 Poplar, 682-9901. U-do-it-yourself, but they help you. A cost cutter.

Frames 'N Things
2346 S. Germantown Rd, 754-5640. Good custom framing.

Gift & Art Shop
4704 Poplar, 682-1621. Traditional wedding gifts are their specialty.

Goldsmith's Department Store* - Oak Court location. Oriental rug department.

Graham's Lighting Fixtures
550 S. Cooper, 274-6780. Large selection of fixtures, some made here.

Haas Furniture Showroom
Laurelwood, 682-7877. Large furniture showroom. Good quality.

Habitare
American Way, 794-3700. Simple, clean-line architectural furniture and accessories. Memphis' answer to Design Research. Stackables, clip on lights... at moderate prices.

Hyatt-Mummert, Ltd.
Overton Square, 274-6784. Decorative accessories, gifts, and some contemporary furniture. Lovely weather vanes.

The Idlewild House
1044 S. Yates Rd, 682-1165. English antiques, gifts, and accessories.

Interior designers*.

Zavan A. Kish - Oriental Rugs
2186 Central, 274-0997. For years at Goldsmith's, he's now on his own. Marvelous antique and semi-antique rugs. Reliable. Expensive.

The Lamplighter
2107 Union, 276-2766. Custom lamps and shades. Will wire anything. Good selection of lampshades.

Lamp Shade House
4286 Summer, 767-3220. Custom lamps and shades. Will paint bases and shades.

Masterpiece Galleries
2266 Central, 272-1804. Antiques, fine furniture, decorative accessories. Reasonable.

The Matchers
683-1337. Old patterns of Noritake china. Sets, fill-in pieces. By appointment only.

Memphis Potters's Guild Workshop
2492 Summer, 327-0908. The potters work here and have some of their work displayed for sale.

Mid-South Flea Market
Shelby County Bldg. at Fairgrounds (between Central and Southern, east

of Parkway), (615) 799-8184. 9am-7pm Sat, noon-6pm Sun, some weekends (check newspaper listings of things to do). Coleman-Simmons usually runs a flea market in one building the 1st, 2nd, & 4th weekends of the month. Hicks runs a three building market the 3rd weekend of the month. Entrance, 50¢.

Mike's Antiques & Refinishing
3703 Summer, 458-0434. Junque.

Jans Nicole Midtown Galleries
1876 Union, 278-4291. English and American antiques. Chinese export porcelain.

Oates Gallery. See Art Galleries. They handle woven Romanian rugs.

Marjorie H. Phelan
682-5166 or 682-0284. By appointment only. Estate and household sales.

Shop of John Simmons
Poplar Plaza, 458-5757. Germantown Village Square, 754-8000. John Simmons is a pace setter in the gift business. He opened his first shop in 1959 and today has franchises across the country. His key to success is making shopping fun. The new Poplar Plaza shop offers the best of everything: furniture, kitchen gadgets, whimsical gifts, jewelry, high-style women's clothing, interior designers, catering, ... even a beauty salon (David Johnson's). Plus lunch with live music. Memphis' own Scruples.

John Simmons Entertains
Park Place Mall, 685-8655. Everything for parties — readymade or custom invitations, paper goods, books on table settings, and plants and tablesettings for sale or lease. They'll recommend bartenders, caterers, musicians, and servers. Or they'll do the whole party for you.

Sisters Antiques & Gift Shop
1971 Madison, 725-4820. English, American, and a smattering of French antiques.

The Spider's Web
2330 S. Germantown Rd, 754-5111. Imaginative yet traditional. Gifts, antiques, and a few clothes. Baskets filled with goodies for thank-yous, Christmas, Easter, any occasion. Everything here has a special flair.

The Sporting Life
Chickasaw Oaks, 324-2383. The perfect place to find a duck print, desk set, or cocktail glasses for the man in your life. They also carry a few slacks and sweaters for men and women.

Springer Antiques
1712 Madison, 726-4585. Antiques and reproductions. Reasonable prices.

Sprott Antiques
5668 S. Rex Rd. off Brookfield at Poplar & I-240, 685-1088. China, furniture, silver, miscellaneous items. Mrs. Sprott also handles cotton boll totes, a fund-raising project for the East Memphis Quota Club, good "souvenir" gifts.

Studio of Jack & Eva Grauer
1261 W. Perkins Rd, 683-9540. Original and molded concrete statuary—interior and exterior. By appointment only.

SuJaCe Antiques
399 College, Collierville, 853-8369. Sue and Jane Cowan have a shop full of fine American antique furniture and accessories.

Summer Trading Post
3570 Summer, 324-4746. Junque.

Sycamore
Overton Square, 726-6781. The unusual in gifts, housewares, and furniture. Williamsburg candles, marvelous handmade pottery, unusual costume jewelry, and lots of whimsy.

Town & Country Antiques
2294 S. Germantown Rd, 754-1428. Primitives and country antiques.

Tuesday Morning
4651 Knight Arnold Rd. at Perkins, 363-4481. Discounted glass, linens, ceramics, household accessories. Not open year round, so phone ahead.

The Unicorn
4726 Poplar, 683-0627. Traditional decorative accessories and furniture. Good selection of beeswax candles and finials.

Victorian Keepsakes
1465 Yorkshire Dr, 683-8284. Handmade lace pillows, English smocking, silk wreaths and nosegays, all reminiscent of the turn-of-the-century.

What-Not Shop
2607 Broad, 327-8551. Piles of antiques and junque. Lots of antique clothing. Strictly for the adventurer. Open M, Th, and Sat only.

Workshop of Steve Crump
2002 Harbert. 276-6918. A local wood master, Steve designs and crafts contemporary wood furnishings and furniture. Phone for appointment.

Yesteryear Furniture & Gifts and The Sunparlor
7691 Hwy. 72, The Pines, 754-8361. The Germantown branch carries furniture, accessories, and gifts, all in a converted house. It's fun browsing. Everything from "early plank" furniture to unusual finials for your lamps and wicker rockers for your children. Decorating service also.

AUTOMOBILES & PARTS

Hubcap Annie
1450 Getwell, 743-2457. Replace your lost hubcaps here.

Madison Cadillac Body Shop
440 Beale, 526-2787. Custom "pimp-mobiles".

Parts for Imported Cars
904 E. Brooks Rd, 332-4760. Tremendous stock of foreign car parts. You can join the 15% discount club.

Wholesale House
1013 S. East Parkway, 274-5676. New and rebuilt foreign car parts.

BOOK STORES & NEWSSTANDS

B. Dalton Booksellers
Park Place Mall, 761-4600. Mall of Memphis, 794-1566. Paper and hardback bestsellers, children's,... plus discounted new books.

Blue and Gray Book Shop
3546 Walker Ave, 323-4591. Excellent paperback selection and helpful staff. Lots of classics in stock.

The Book Cottage
Overton Square, 726-5857. 7691 Poplar, The Pines, Germantown, 754-0809. Comfortable atmosphere for poking around. Chairs and tables so you can sit and read the "N.Y. Times" or listen to records you might want to buy. Small, eclectic stock.

The Book Inn
Chickasaw Oaks, 452-2168. Primarily best seller hardbacks.

Book Shelf
Poplar Plaza, 324-8891. Mostly hardbacks, new offerings. Good staff. Try the book club — a $10 family fee offers 10% discount on all books for one year. Also handles Crane's stationery.

Burke's Book Store
634 Poplar, 527-7484. If you're looking for a book on Memphis or Tennessee, this is the place to go. Handles hardback, used, and rare books. Has a search and special order service. Southern history is its specialty.

The Carpenter's Shop
767 Brookhaven Cl, 767-6766. A small religious book store in a boutique setting. There are also many excellent large religious book stores in the city. Check the yellow pages.

Ex Libris Book Shop
6686 Poplar, 755-3500. Good selection of hardcover and paperback books. Also carries out-of-town newspapers.

Pinocchio's. See Children's Stores. Well-written children's books.

Round Table Book Store
557 Erin, 761-0512. Chic atmosphere with a fireplace, sofas, and a good selection of books. Some of the city's most avid readers swear by it. Also books on tape for adults and children.

Tobacco Corner Newsroom
669 S. Mendenhall Rd, 682-3326. The staff is a bit brusque, but there is a wide selection of hard-to-find magazines and out-of-town Sunday newspapers. You can pick up a Sunday "N.Y. Times" around noon; it's best to reserve ahead.

Waldenbooks
Raleigh Springs Mall, 388-6012. Southland Mall, 346-5550. Hickory Ridge Mall, 795-0636. Part of a nationwide chain. Large inventory, good selection, and a dedicated staff. If you're gift shopping, both branches occasionally have good sales of "coffee table" books.

World News Company
124 Monroe, 523-9970. For the homesick — mecca. This source for out-of-town newspapers and hard-to-find magazines began in 1904 as a corner newsstand. Since then Maurice Hammett has stopped carrying

Greek, Italian, Spanish, and French papers, but he still carries Little Rock, St. Louis, Chicago, Nashville,... dailies. Sunday's "N.Y. Times", "Washington Post", and "L.A. Times" available Monday. Open 364 days a year and half-day on Christmas.

🚲 CHILDREN'S STORES

See also Fabric & Needlework.

Apron Strings
Chickasaw Oaks, 324-8223. Very special clothes, girls/infant -14, boys/infant -4T. English button shoes for little girls.

Babyland
671 Avon Rd, 767-4350. Toys, infant furniture and equipment. Clothes, infant - 4T.

Baby Time
3086 Norbrook Dr, 332-BABY. Baby furniture and supplies at warehouse prices.

Camper's Corner. See Sporting Goods. Seersucker and corduroy snuglies, marvelous infant pouches.

Children's Clothing Exchange of Memphis
Phone in July & Feb to find out where and when. Two enterprising women, Dee Dyer (452-5267) and Jamie Simmons (452-3938), operate this exchange out of their home. Twice a year, in the spring before Easter and in the fall before school, Memphis parents sell and buy good quality used clothing. Clothes must be clean and in good condition.

Chocolate Soup
Germantown Village Mall, 754-7157. Children's clothes. Specialty is appliqued animals and scenes on smocks and overalls.

The Country Bunny
4726 Poplar, 683-6810. The stuff dreams are made of. Special clothes, gifts, and accessories, girls/infant - 14, boys/infant - 4 T.

C. Robin Ltd.
Chickasaw Oaks, 323-2341. Toys from around the world. Enough to make even adults have visions of sugarplums.

C. Robin Miniatures
Chickasaw Oaks, 323-9829. Teeny everythings for the serious dollhouse collector.

The Dollmaker's Shoppe
683-2749. Dolls and their paraphernalia for the collector. Sylvia Cochran, doll surgeon and make-up artist, will fix up your "baby". Phone for new address.

Al Graci Educational Service
1225 Getwell, 324-9251. Educational toys and teaching equipment.

Layman's Games
964 June Rd, 683-3541. 7672 Hwy. 72 Germantown, 754-2957. Toys, games, puzzles for the young at heart.

Natie's
4691 Poplar, 685-8208. Germantown Village Square Mall, 754-2866. Hickory Ridge Mall, 362-0791. Clothes, infants-pre-teens. Good boys' department.

Pinky's Children Toggery
696 Brookhaven Cl, 761-0415. Special clothing, stationery, and a few toys.

Pinocchio's Children's Book Store
688 Brookhaven Cl, 767-6586. Started by three ex-teachers, they carry books about parenting, well-written old favorites, and new books for children. It's a fun place with a playroom, story hour for 3-5 year olds, and lots of good advice for shoppers.

Raiford's
4697 Poplar, 682-3737. Southbrook Mall, 398-5209. 111 Madison, 527-9458. 1022 Madison, 523-7181. Yale Plaza, 388-7480. Germantown Village Square Mall, 754-6520. Park Place Mall. Children's and adult's shoes. Regular and orthopedic.

Toy City
1056 E. Raines Rd, 332-0171. Perimeter Mall, 761-4162. A whole warehouse full of toys.

The Toy Exchange
6465 May Creek, 683-5078. For one week each Oct, two enterprising women give parents an opportunity to buy and sell good-condition second-hand toys. It usually runs W-W the second week of Oct; check the newspapers or phone before you go.

Woman's Exchange of Memphis
88 Racine St, 327-5681. Exquisite handmade children's clothing. Expen-

sive, so take your grandmother along. Handmade toys and gifts. Lunch is served in a garden room noon-2pm, tea 2:45-4:15pm, M-F.

Yesteryear Furniture & Gifts
7691 Hwy. 72, The Pines, Germantown, 754-8361. Overton Square, 726-1111. Dollhouses and the makings for them. Antique dolls. Child-size furniture.

Youngtown
Poplar Plaza, 458-3322. Whitehaven Plaza, 398-9201. Children's clothes, toys, equipment, and shoes — a department store for children.

CLOTHING — MEN'S & WOMEN'S

Alfred's
6327 Poplar, 767-6054. Executives young and old shop at Alfred's. Traditional menswear. Good tie selection. Expensive.

Amethyst Inc.
Peabody Hotel, 527-8228. Unique and sophisticated ladies accessories plus some children's toys and antiques. Small stock.

Anastasia
Park Place Mall, 767-1554. High Fashion European women's clothing.

Bending "B" Western Store
1084 Brooks Rd. (one block west of Elvis Presley Blvd.), 396-7684. Everything for the urban or rural cowboy and girl. Good boot selection. Yee-Haw!!!

Carlye's Fashions & Fabric Boutique. See Fabric & Needlework.
Custom designed women's clothes.

Casual Corner
1711 Union, 272-7501. 1269 Southland Mall, 346-3240. 3475 Summer Ave, 452-3300. Raleigh Springs Mall, 388-0147. Kirby Woods Mall, 754-2370. 4625 Poplar, 761-2650. Hickory Ridge Mall, 365-1548. National chain catering to teenage and college women. Fun.

Chelsea Ltd.
2075 Madison, 726-4493. Lots of music stars, male and female, go here for their clothes.

Collectibles
4726 Poplar (drive around to side), 682-1330. You'll find the unusual here. Lots of separates and super accessories for women.

100% Cotton
4717 Poplar, 682-9139. The name is a misnomer, but clothes here are part cotton. Preppy styles for the high school and college set.

Christopher's
Kirby Woods Mall, 754-9280. Trendy fun imported women's shoes.

Department stores*.

Discount stores*.

Do-Si-Do Shop
1138 Mosby Rd, 398-4953. Crinolines by the ton and 45s for square dancing. Men's and women's duds. Mail order service and a toll free number: 800-238-2490.

Dottie's
4830 Summer, 685-8317. 4690 Knight Arnold, 362-9660. 4115 Elvis Presley Blvd, 398-1546. Discounted brand name men's and women's shoes.

Frances Wright
1789 Kirby Parkway, 754-9440. Fabulous women's clothing. Everything from belts to ball gowns. Very expensive.

James Davis
Laurelwood, 767-4640. Germantown Village Mall, 755-3232. Top quality men's clothing and a few tweed skirts and things for women.

James Davis for Women
Park Place Mall, 761-5224. Tailored traditional high quality clothes and shoes for women.

Jewell Meyers
420 S. Perkins Ext, 682-1605. Expensive designer clothes for women.

La Boutique
Chickasaw Oaks, 324-7101. The creme de la creme. Once a spot to find beautiful nightgowns and lingerie, now it's expanded into a select women's boutique with clothes and accessories as well. Ask the sales staff for advice; they've got impeccable taste and creative ideas. We want everything in the shop. New branch in the Peabody Hotel.

Lily Pulitzer Shop of Memphis
Chickasaw Oaks, 458-2643. If you want to hide in the shadows, don't go. Otherwise do. Bright flowered clothes with a Florida flair for men and women.

The Limited
Southland Mall, 346-8170. Kirby Woods Mall, 754-2564. Raleigh Springs Mall, 377-1551. Hickory Ridge Mall, 795-2110. Mall of Memphis, 795-2996. National chain. Women's clothes. Trendy knock-offs of European separates. Inexpensive.

Linda's Love Lace
4964 Poplar, 761-5610. 1970 Madison, 726-5201. Risqué lingerie. A real traffic stopper — live models in Poplar store's window on Sat.

Loehmann's. See Discount Stores.

The Mad Hatter
Overton Square, 726-5079. Right inside the door at Tallulah's. Fantastic hats with a flair for all occasions.

Mam'selle
1543 Union, 274-5440. Kirby Woods Mall, 754-1617. Hickory Ridge Mall, 794-1677. Mall of Memphis, 794-0786. For the young minded woman, clothes with a flair. Especially good selection for small sizes.

Maternity Clothing:
Lady Madonna. Germantown Village Square, 754-5724.
Mothercare. Mall of Memphis, 794-0662.
Mother To Be. Raleigh Springs Mall, 388-2530.
Motherhood Maternity Shops. Southland Mall, 346-9152. Kirby Woods Mall, Germantown, 754-9149. Mall of Memphis, 795-4281.

Merle Norman Cosmetic Studios
Laurelwood, 767-4720. Raleigh Springs Mall, 386-0770. 3179 Poplar, 327-7336. Hickory Ridge Mall, 362-2187. Make-up, clothes, and accessories for women.

Mine
Boutique in John Simmons at Poplar Plaza, 323-3200. Sophisticated chic women's clothing and accessories. Top quality and design.

Minor Frances
Chickasaw Oaks, 452-7381. Top quality women's sportswear and separates.

Oak Hall
555 Perkins Ext, 761-3580. Park Place Mall, 685-1420. Good selection of quality men's clothing.

Pappagallo
I, 59 S. Idlewild, 726-4422. II, 569 Erin Dr, 761-4430. Shoes, shoes, shoes — purses and clothes. Fun, bright, and young.

Plantation House Inc.
Box 17366, 38117. Mail order. Beautiful 100% linen blouses imported from China. Reasonable.

Progressive Shoe Store
Pontotoc, Miss. (601) 489-3342. Men's brand name shoes. 20-30% off. They have a catalogue and will mail.

Reminiscence
28 S. Idlewild, 272-2820. Nostalgic clothing displayed with a flair.

Sara Fredericks of Memphis
Laurelwood, 682-1614. Expensive designer clothes for women.

The Social Heel
4726 Poplar, 767-5403. High-fashion designer shoes for women.

Sporting Life. See Antiques...Gifts. Traditional sports clothes.

Sportsman's One Stop. See Sporting Goods. Down jackets and vests.

Stein Mart. See Discount Stores.

Tallulah's
Overton Square, 725-9455. For women. Young and trendy. Reasonable prices. We particularly like the shoes and costume jewelry.

Timothy's
Hickory Ridge Mall, 365-3080. High style shoes and stockings for women.

Trousseau
1775 Union, 272-7579. Historically known for their lingerie and towels, they also have nice skirts, blouses, and gift items for the traveler.

Wardrobe consultants: The Butler Did It (726-5920) and Ainslie Todd (324-8683).

What-Not Shop. See Antiques. Antique clothing.

Whitfield & Co.
Chickasaw Oaks, 324-4469. Preppy clothes. Frequented by the college and young executive set. Men's attire and women's slacks, skirts, and blazers.

FABRIC & NEEDLEWORK

Broom Corn
5826 Stage Rd, 377-0584. 426 N. Front, 526-0153. Bolts and bolts of decorator fabrics — a warehouse full. Some housewares in the back.

Calico Corners
985 S. Yates Rd, 767-8780. "Seconds" of decorator fabrics at a 50% price saving. Makes referrals to decorators and upholsterers.

Carlye's Fashions & Fabric Boutique
713 W. Brookhaven Cl, 683-3337. Designer and imported fabrics plus custom designed clothes.

Genie Fabrics
3758 Summer, 452-7033. Fine dress fabrics and Bernina sewing machines. Classes.

Indie
3549 Southern, 327-0179. Fine yarns, custom designed needlepoint canvases. Classes.

Julie's Needle Art Shop
Chickasaw Oaks, 454-7019. Equipment, instruction, and finishing for all kinds of needlework.

Martha's Fine Fabrics
Chickasaw Oaks, 452-2259. Fine dress fabrics for adults and children. Classes.

Normandy Lace Shop
751 Brookhaven Cl, 761-4144. Fine fabrics, laces, and threads for hand-work on children's clothes. Classes.

The Ribbon Room
712 Brookhaven Cl, 761-3900. Every kind of ribbon you can imagine.

FLORISTS & NURSERIES

Flowers By Sandy
2029 Union, 276-4495. Fine flowers and arrangements with a flair. Citywide delivery.

The Flower Service
1591 Carr, 276-5374 (answering tape) or 278-6829. Betsy McStay buys at wholesale and sells to you at a slight mark-up. Tu & F only. Phone before 9am to order. Pick up after 11am. Slight charge for deliveries. Ms. McStay accepts standing orders for F, cost, $5/weekly — a good birthday or Christmas idea!

Four Fives Nursery
5555 Summer, 382-3411. Excellent plants and advice.

Gallery Greenhouse
2206 Union, 278-9940. Good selection of healthy, reasonably priced potted plants.

Green Earth Garden Center
5512 Stage Rd, 382-1810. Full service garden center.

Lawnscapes
442 Lookout Dr, 853-7810. Landscape design. They'll spruce up your old or design a new.

Rachel's Flower Shop
262 S. Highland, 324-2137. Buy a bunch of daisies here or potted plants, silk flowers, ribbons.

Stroud Garden Center and Nursery
2631 Jackson Ave, 452-2137. Excellent plants and advice.

Sweetpeas
Chickasaw Oaks, 324-6873. Silks only.

Tablescapes
Mrs. Robert Snowden, 323-1044. If you're having a party, she'll do the flower arrangements and decorations even down to tablecloths and china.

Trees By Touliatos
2018 E. Brooks Rd, 346-8065. This nursery handles uncommon plants.

Tropical Plant Leasing
4619 Monaco Rd, 761-2376. Rent plants by the month for your office.

Dan West Garden Center
4763 Poplar, 767-6743. 3641 Austin Peay Hwy, 388-0438. Limited plant supply; sells lawn mowers, sprays, pots, ... and, at Christmas, marvelous ribbons and decorations for trees and doors. Poplar store personnel are especially good at diagnosing what ails your plants.

FOOD, DRINK, & THINGS FOR THE KITCHEN

Barzizza's Gifts
4780 Summer, 683-4571. An emporium full of imported foods and housewares from the Orient.

Beverage Barn
2502 Jackson, 458-5794. 3085 Summer, 324-8706. Sells all kinds of "long necks", and the prices are good.

Big Star Supermarket Quon's #117
1470 Wells Station Rd, 767-5843. Complete line of Chinese items.

Braden's Products
Judy Maynard, 276-2152. Marvelous canned goods handled through a local distributor. Expensive.

Buster's Liquors
3493 Poplar, 458-0929. Large selection of imported beers and California wines. Specials are hard to beat.

Cheese on the Square
Overton Square, 722-8774. Cheeses, crackers, teas,..., but the homemade rolls to-go steal the show. Order several days in advance.

Coffee Connection
563 Erin Dr, 683-1009. Everything for coffee and tea lovers.

Delectables Ltd.
4741 Poplar, 767-1987. Uniquely packaged jelly beans and nuts. Whimsy. Delivery and mailing service available.

Dinstuhl's Candies
Laurelwood, 682-3373. 4466 Elvis Presley Blvd, 398-0729. 3616-1 Austin Peay Hwy, 382-4657. Germantown Village Square, 754-4810. A

sweet tooth's must. If strawberries are in season, try the chocolate covered ones.

Dixie Meat Co.
239 Jefferson, 527-7536. Greeks run this wholesale meat market; marvelous feta cheese, Greek olives, whole lambs....

Easy Way Markets & Market Baskets
Outlets around the city. For vegetable and fruit lovers.

El-Ranchito Tamales
348 Vance, 526-1704. Tamale factory where Mexican tamales are still rolled in corn husks.

Forty Carrots
Overton Square, 726-1667. Hickory Ridge Mall, 795-3505. Marvelous things for your kitchen and table. Cooking lessons too.

Frank's Liquor Store
327 S. Main, 526-5811. Super bargains.

Gaslight Liquor Shoppe
4177 Summer, 452-8743. Good prices.

Health Foods. Reputable health food shops ⋯⁺ᴸ small snack bars usually serving L only:
Good Life-Natural Health Foods. 3119 Poplar, 327-9755.
Healthy Trading. 1783 Union (behind Trousseau Shop), 278-6444.
Honeysuckle Health Foods, Inc. 4713 Poplar, 682-6255. Cooking classes.
Norris Health Foods, Inc. 4624 Poplar, 683-3984.
Squash Blossom Natural Foods. Overton Square, 725-4823.
Whole Foods. 1779 Kirby Pkwy, 755-3700.

Hickory Farms of Ohio
4620 Poplar, 767-0777. Mall of Memphis, 794-0777. National chain featuring cheeses and sausages.

Jones Orchards
6824 Big Creek Church Rd, Millington (off Raleigh-Millington Rd.), 872-2923. Pick your own peaches. Best in July.

Kroger
6660 Poplar, 754-0354. Poplar Plaza, 323-0191. Branches all over the city, but people rave about these two. Fresh fish. Open 24 hours a day except Sun morning.

La Baguette French Bread & Pastry Shop. See French restaurants. Tempting French pastries and bread baked fresh each day.

Lieselotte's Delikatessen. See German restaurants.

Lipscomb Country Hams
7537 Summer (Hwy. 70), 388-0617. Cures and sells its own country ham, sausage, and bacon.

Lipsey Fish Co.
1877 Union, 274-7080. 5041 Summer, 767-8531. Fresh fish. Most trucks come in on W or Th.

Marvels Cakes & Candies
6686 Poplar. 754-1994. They'll make any shape, any size for any occasion. Expensive but special.

Mid South Pecan Co.
303 N. 7, West Memphis, Ark, 735-1050. Shelled pecans, 5 lbs. for about $16.

Montesi's Supermarkets
1620 Madison, 726-4311. 5014 Poplar, 682-1618. Southbrook Mall, 332-5843. 3545 Austin Peay Hwy, 388-1703. Fred Montesi's has everything. Open 24 hours a day, M-Sat.

Oriental Center - Park & Shop
3664 Summer, 327-9756. Small Oriental grocery.

Overton Square*. Courtyard with gourmet market.

Planters Peanut Shop
24 S. Main, 525-1115. 4305 Summer. 682-1404. Let them eat roasted chestnuts elsewhere. The downtown store is something of a landmark to locals.

Sampietro & Co.
550 Poplar, 526-3286. Homemade Italian sausage. Call ahead to place your order.

Scott Street Market
814 Scott, 327-8828. Farmer's market. Fresh fruits and vegetables.

Seessel's Supermarkets Bakery & Delicatessen
1761 Union, 272-1771. 576 S. Perkins, 683-8244. 4485 Elvis Presley

Blvd. (Hwy. 51 S.), 332-3820. Yale Plaza, 386-0221. 2085 S. Germantown Rd, Germantown, 754-8030. 6100 Quince, 682-1590. Memphis based grocery chain with good deli, bakery, and cheese sections.

Shalom Bakery
Eastgate Shopping Center (in alley beside Woolco), 761-2898. Good dark breads.

John Simmons
Poplar Plaza, 458-5757. Joel's Gourmet-to-Go (323-JOEL) offers hors d'oeuvres, quiches, mousses, soups, salads, entrees, and desserts — a life-saver for the harried hostess. Catering too; they'll even deliver breakfast in bed. Buckingham Palate sells marvelous jams and preserves. And then there's china, glassware, cookware,....

Sulkin-Tate
485 N. Hollywood, 458-2503. Restaurant equipment that you might want in your own kitchen.

Vito's Deli & Imported Foods
3024 Covington Pike, 372-1773. Frozen homemade ravioli and fettucini to-go.

Weona #106
3151 Poplar, 458-6630. A small expensive store with an excellent prime meat department. Phone in for delivery.

Winery of Overton Square
60 S. Cooper, 278-2682. Brew your own. Everything for the wine or beer maker.

HARDWARE & HOUSE PARTS

Chandler Wrecking Co.
1223 N. Watkins, 276-5459. If you're searching for a 1940s cold water spigot, this is the place to rummage. Best to go with a friend, not alone.

Coopertown Chimney Sweeps
2511 Broad, 323-0002. Inspects, cleans, and caps chimneys.

The Craftsman Plumbing & Heating Supply & Parts
1380 Jackson, 274-3437. 2749 Park, 452-2651 or 452-2659. Everything to solve your plumbing problems.

W.B. Davis Electric Supply Co. Inc.
527 N. Hollywood, 452-7363. 2519 Elvis Presley Blvd, 946-2521. Everything from wire to light bulbs.

Gate City Hardware & Paint Co.
2500 Summer, 458-3050. Every size nut and bolt, and solid brass keys for just 50¢.

Hardwoods of Memphis
2667 Jackson, 452-9663. Rare and special woods. Custom cut.

Kelley Wrecking Co.
326 Vance, 527-5785. Architectural finds. Go with a friend.

Marine Supply Co.
255 Union, 527-8396. Brass fittings. Everything for your boat.

Morris Hardware
549 S. Highland, 324-5531. This neighborhood hardware store will fix your lawn mower and answer all your questions.

Old World Tiles & The Common Market
364 S. Front, 526-4501. Imported tiles and architectural finds.

Rainbow Studio
242 S. Cooper, 726-1378. Stained glass.

Shop of Tut-Uncommon
116A S. Front Str, 522-9931. Victorian woodwork.

Stewart Brothers Hardware Co.
1340 Madison, 726-1922. 7715 Hwy. 70, 377-1234. Old timey, neighborhood hardware store. Lots of knobs, drawer pulls, fireplace equipment....

Tennessee Fabricating Co.
2366 Prospect, 948-3354. Missing cast-iron parts for old houses.

INTERIOR DESIGNERS

Individual decorators stock various types and periods of furniture and accessories and have access to additional fabrics and household furnishings through custom ordering. Phone ahead for an appointment. See the yellow pages under Interior Decorators and Designers for a full listing. These are some of the people whose work we've seen and liked.

Michelle B. Babcock & Associates

1716 Lockett Place, 725-1647. Traditional English and early American. Sells antiques.

Denaux-Kimbrough

1723 Union, 274-0037. Well-established decorating firm with a wide variety of talent. Sells antiques and custom built furniture.

Lynn Field Interiors

2262 S. Germantown Rd, 754-7950. Colorful and eclectic. Uses a lot of local artisans.

Jim Goldate Inc.

709 S. Mendenhall Rd, 682-7611. Fresh gardeny feel.

Jimmy Graham Interior Design

657 Adams, 527-0633. An antique old-world country French flair. Antiques sold.

Isbell Gerhardt Wolfe

162 S. McLean, 278-2290. Varied. Own workrooms.

Mary H. Johnson & Associates

263 Court Ave, 522-1259. Commercial interiors.

McCormick-Eubanks

1793 Union, 274-6518. The youngest design firm in town; its style reflects it. Contemporary and quality reproductions. Marvelous lamps.

James F. Ruffin Interiors

2906 Poplar, 324-4922. Quietly and elegantly understated. Traditional. Sells antiques.

John Simmons Interior Design

Poplar Plaza, 458-4455. Colorful and contemporary.

Slenker & Kirkpatrick

1500 Union, 278-1700. A blend. Sells antiques and custom built furniture.

Margie Vanlandingham

707 Adams, 527-5479. She loves antiques.

Tom Wells Interior Design

Peabody Hotel, 526-2010. Commercial; residential; eclectic.

Woodward & Fooks Inc.
7528 2nd, Germantown, 754-0212. Eclectic.

JEWELRY

The real things. For costume jewelry check clothing and gift shop listings.

Vance Boyd & Son
Park Place Mall, 683-2469. Peabody Hotel, 529-8050. A girl's best friend.

Broadnax Jewelers
Laurelwood, 767-8920. Germantown Village Square, 754-0110. Poplar Plaza, 327-1633. Southland Mall, 346-4380. Raleigh Springs Mall, 388-5610. Hickory Ridge Mall, 794-2794. Mall of Memphis, 794-4277. Established 1897. Nice things.

Brown-Wright Jewelers
Chickasaw Oaks, 454-1434. It glitters.

Walter J. Cline
80 N. Tillman, 323-1326. Watches and clocks, sale and repair.

Endicott Nelson & Sons
9 N. 2nd, 525-5726. Suite 500, Clark Towers, 5100 Poplar, 767-3320. Especially noted for repairing, appraising, and remounting.

Julius Goodman & Son
113 Madison, 526-8528. Antique silver and jewelry.

Hays Jewelers Inc.
1750 Madison, 726-0220. Jewelry manufacturer.

MISCELLANEOUS SHOPPING

The Balloon Man
725-5379. Employees come to parties, homes, offices...dressed in clown costumes bearing nosegays of helium balloons. 1 doz/about $15, 2 doz/ about $18. Weekly specials.

Carter Seed Co.
85 S. Front, 527-8856. Old clothes, baskets, seeds, pecans by the pound,....

Carter's High Grade Seed & Supply
3072 Southern, 323-2989. Same things as Carter Seed Co. plus pottery and little pets.

City Beautiful Commission
125 N. Main, Rm. 605 City Hall, 528-2718. Will arrange to have trees planted in memory of deceased persons, birthdays, weddings,...., on city property of course. $15 minimum.

Coopertown Sing-A-Gram
2511 Broad, 323-9495. Will deliver the song-in-your-heart for you. Singers arrive dressed in red bellhop uniforms (or gorilla costumes for an extra $10) and croon such messages as "Happy Birthday", "I Love You" or "How About A Date". Rates vary according to time of day: 9am-5pm/$15, 5pm-midnight/$20, and midnight-9am and all day Sun/$25.

Dixie Color Lab
521 S. Highland, 458-1818. Custom printing and enlarging on a commercial basis. Photo equipment too.

The Fun Shop.
Poplar Plaza, 324-3274. If you're looking for a gag gift or magic trick, this is the place to shop.

Hunt's Photo Supply
3626 New Getwell Rd, 363-0262. The city's best buy in camera equipment.

La Papier Boutique
775 E. Brookhaven Cl, 761-3143. Stationery, paper plates, paper napkins, paper....

Little John's
Overton Square, 725-4003. It's fun and full of unusual items—everything from roller skating derbies to picnic supplies. If you're looking for a unique zany gift, this should be your first stop.

Magazine
43 Union, 526-3420. A petite menagerie of Danskins and Capezios, books, candles, stationery,... in an attractive setting.

Museum Gift Shops. See individual museums.

The Occasion Shop
1726 Poplar, 726-4905. You can find a gift for every occasion in this cluttered small shop. Antique jewelry and beautiful unusual gift wrapping.

Personally Yours Unlimited
772 E. Brookhaven Cl, 683-4586. So many things can be personalized; you'll probably want to ask the staff for help and suggestions. Sells and prints names and initials on everything from bows to luggage tags and, of course, stationery.

A. Schwab*
163 Beale, 523-9782. On Beale for over 100 years. A general store stocked with everything from love potions to piece goods, overalls, top hats, and spiked shoes. The mezzanine floor is a museum display area. Free souvenir postcards for visitors. The slogan: If you can't find it at Schwab's, you're better off without it.

Strings and Things
1492 Union, 278-0500. The music buff will enjoy just looking at this music store started in 1971 by two young musicians. They do custom work for such stars as Jeff Beck, Kiss, and Kenny Loggins and have worked on designing the new Gretsch Committee guitar and a new Aeolian electric piano.

Super D
Branches all over the city. Inexpensive full service drug stores.

RECORDS

Peaches
Park Center, 458-6484. Large selection of records and tapes.

Poplar Tunes
4195 Summer, 324-3855. 4622 Faronia Rd, 346-7172. 308 Poplar (main store), 525-6348. They were here during the creative '50s and '60s and have a super Memphis music section. Excellent selection of records and tapes, and lots of discontinued records. Best of all, you can listen to the demos.

Select-O-Hits Record Shop
605 Chelsea, 523-1190. Run by Johnny, Skip, and Cathy Phillips*, Sam's nephews and niece, the shop specializes in rhythm and blues, jazz, black gospel, and contemporary blues music. Some discontinued oldies.

SPORTING GOODS

All American Inc.
3230 Summer, 324-3783. Team outfits and equipment.

Alpine Sports
1939 Poplar, 722-1972. It's Colorado transplanted — ski equipment and simulated ski slopes for practice.

Breakaway Athletics
1708 Union. 722-8797. Two Boston marathoners opened this store so of course the emphasis is on running equipment.

Bert Dargie Golf Co.
2883 Poplar, 327-1674. Custom made clubs, new and used clubs, repairs, and refinishing. Lessons may be arranged.

Dowdle Sporting Goods Co.
2896 Walnut Grove Rd, 327-7381. H. V. Highsmith, one of the city's finest gunsmiths, works here.

Dunn's Supply Store
Hwy. 57, Grand Junction, Tn, 38039, (901) 764-2193. Dog equipment, boots, spittoons, cookstoves, saddles, raingear, khakis.... Things you can't find anywhere else. Catalogue and world-wide mail order service.

Harwood Arms
903 S. Cooper, 276-7571. Modern and antique, new and used guns.

Ben Howell & Son Saddlery Co.
4447 Summer, 767-2711. Western riding equipment and clothes.

Joyner Sporting Goods
3024 Covington Pike, 382-1490. 4719 Poplar, 685-2843. Large selection of jogging shoes and equipment.

Memphis Bicycle & Motorcycle Co.
2575 Summer, 323-7601. A good place for motorcycle and bike enthusiasts. Equipment sold and repaired.

Memphis Cycle & Supply Co.
421 Monroe, 526-4142. Parts and supplies for all kinds of cycles, bicycles, lawn mowers.... If you like hardware stores, you'll be in heaven here.

Outdoors Inc.
5245 Poplar. 767-6790. Sales people can answer all your questions and provide equipment for canoeing, kayaking, skiing, and backpacking.

Saddles 'n Such
2137 S. Germantown Rd, 754-7452. Expensive English riding equipment.

Sports Arena
2136 S. Germantown Rd, 754-6420. Team outfits and equipment.

Sportsman's One Stop
N. Club Rd, West Memphis, Ark, 735-3395. Tremendous stock of down clothing and sports equipment.

Sportsman's Supermarket
4751 Summer, 761-4433. Full service — every sport is covered.

York Arms Co.
4627 Summer, 683-2401. Whitehaven Plaza, 396-9810. Poplar Plaza, 452-1173. They first opened in 1905 at 162 S. Main Str.

Where To Stay

Opening of the first Holiday Inn in the U.S. at 4941 Summer in 1952.
Spence, Bob, Kem, Betty and Carole Wilson cut the ribbon.

HOTELS/MOTELS

Memphis has been the site of many famous hotels. The Gayoso Hotel* was an early city landmark and the city's finest hotel at the time of the Civil War. In the racetrack and pre-prohibition glory days, the Luehrmann Hotel was famous for its elegance and dining room. Many visitors came by private railroad cars.

In more recent times the Peabody Hotel* (renovated as a luxury hotel and reopened Sept. 1981) was a "must" for city visitors. Football pep rallies were held in the lobby, and trained ducks rode the elevators and swam in the lobby's fountain. The South's elite dined and danced at the Skyway where Maitre'd Alonzo Locke's savoir faire and ability to remember names made him a living legend.

The most recent development in the hotel business put Memphis on the map as the nation's innkeeper. Kemmons Wilson was traveling with his family in the summer of 1951 and realized the need for convenient in-expensive lodging for people traveling by car. The result—Holiday Inns. The first Holiday Inn was built in 1952, and now, under different management, operates as the Royal Oaks-East (4941 Summer). Today Holiday Inn has 1,748 inns worldwide with approximately 300,000 rooms (more than any other hotel/motel chain). There are presently nine Holiday Inns in the Memphis area, with the Holiday Inn-Rivermont their star.

Any historical account of hotels and motels in the city, tragically must include the Lorraine Motel*. It is here that Dr. Martin Luther King Jr. was assassinated in 1968. He had come to Memphis to lead demonstrations in support of a strike by the sanitation workers. He was assassinated on the balcony outside his room which is today a shrine to his memory and work.

Memphis currently has about 8,500 first class rooms. The Convention and Tourist Bureau of Memphis (526-1919) keeps up with additions and subtractions, and has a housing bureau to help convention planners make arrangements. State, regional, national, and international conventions have been booked here.

The following Memphis hotels/motels offer free parking and air conditioning. The chart indicates whether a pool, restaurant, and lounge are on the grounds.

KEY TO PRICES

$ 1 bed, 1 person room rates from $13 to $19; 2 bed, 2 person room rates from $18 to $26.

$$ 1 bed, 1 person rates from $20 to $24; 2 bed, 2 person rates from $23 to $38.

$$$ 1 bed, 1 person rates from $26 to $30; 2 bed, 2 person rates from $29 to $42.

$$$$ 1 bed, 1 person rates from $33 to $46; 2 bed, 2 person rates from $39 to $58.

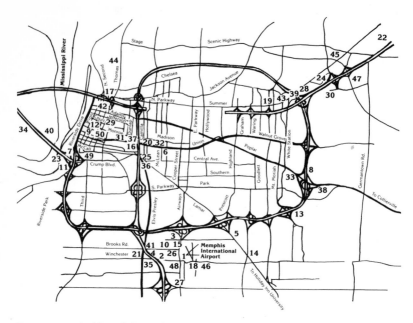

Recommended hotels/motels capable of holding meetings for 200 + are:

MAP NO.	NAME, ADDRESS & PHONE	POOL	RESTAU-RANT	LOUNGE	PRICE
1	**Admiral Benbow Inn-Airport** 2201 Winchester Rd. 345-6251	x	x	x	$$$
2	**Best Western - Executive Plaza Inn** 1471 E. Brooks Rd. 332-3500	x	x	x	$$$
3	**Hilton Inn-Airport** 2240 Democrat Rd. 332-1130	heated indoor	x	x	$$$$
4	**Holiday Inn-Airport** 1441 Brooks Rd. (Brooks Rd. & I-55) 398-9211	x	x	x	$$$
5	**Holiday Inn-Holiday City** 3728 Lamar Ave., (Hwy./78) 363-1300	x	x	x	$$$

MAP NO.	NAME, ADDRESS & PHONE	POOL	RESTAU- RANT	LOUNGE	PRICE
6	**Holiday Inn-** **Overton Square Area** 1837 Union 278-4100	x	x	x	$$$
7	**Holiday Inn-Rivermont** 200 W. Georgia (Riverside Dr. at I-55) 525-0121	x	x	x	$$$$
8	**Hyatt Regency Memphis** 939 Ridge Lake Blvd. (Poplar & I-240) 761-1234	x	x	x	$$$$
9	**Peabody Hotel** 149 Union Ave. 529-4000, 529-4100 (reservations)	x	x	x	$$$$
10	**Quality Inn-Airport** 1400 Springbrook Ave. 332-8980	x	x	x	$$$
11	**Quality Inn-Riverview** 271 W. Alston (at Harahan Bridge) 946-3301		x	x	$$$
12	**Ramada Inn-Convention Center** 160 Union 525-5491	x	x	x	$$$
13	**Ramada Inn-Mt. Moriah** 2490 Mt. Moriah (at I-240) 362-8010	x	x	x	$$$
14	**Ramada Inn-Roadside Hotel** 3896 Lamar (at Getwell) 365-6100	x	x	x	$$$
15	**Rodeway Inn-Airport** 2949 Airways Blvd. 345-1250	x	x	x	$$$
16	**Rodeway Inn-Midtown** 889 Union (Medical Center) 526-8481	x	x	x	$$

MAP NO.	NAME, ADDRESS & PHONE	POOL	RESTAU-RANT	LOUNGE	PRICE
17	**Sheraton Convention Center Hotel** 300 N. 2nd 525-2511	x	x	x	$$$$
18	**Sheraton Inn-Airport** 2411 Winchester 332-2370	x	x	x	$$$$

Additional Memphis hotels/motels:

MAP NO.	NAME, ADDRESS & PHONE	POOL	RESTAU-RANT	LOUNGE	PRICE
19	**Admiral Benbow Inn-East** 4720 Summer Ave. (Hwy. 64, 70, 79) 682-4601	x	x	x	$$
20	**Admiral Benbow Inn-Midtown Motel** 1220 Union 725-0630	x	x	x	$$$
21	**Airport Motor Inn** 3265 Elvis Presley Blvd. 396-0142	x	x	x	$$$
22	**Best Western-Lakeland Inn** 9822 Huff & Puff Rd. (Canada Rd. & I-40) 388-7120	x	x		$$
23	**Best Western-Riverbluff Inn** 340 Illinois Ave. W. (at Harahan Bridge) 948-9005	x	x		$$
24	**Best Western-Welcome Inn** 1541 Sycamore View Rd. (Macon Rd. & I-240) 388-1300	x	x	x	$$$
25	**Coach and Four Motor Lodge** 1318 Lamar (at I-240 N.) 726-5000	indoor (sauna & exercise room)	24 hr.	x	$$

MAP NO.	NAME, ADDRESS & PHONE	POOL	RESTAU-RANT	LOUNGE	PRICE
26	**Day's Inn Motel** 1533 Brooks Rd. E. (at I-55) 345-2470	x	x		$
27	**Day's Inn Motel** 1970 Shelby Dr. E. (at I-55) 332-0222	x	x		$$
28	**Day's Inn Motel** 5301 Summer (at I-40 & I-240) 761-1600	x	x		$
29	**Downtowner Motor Inn** 22 N. 3rd. 525-8363	x	x	x	$$
30	**Holiday Inn-Macon Rd.** 6101 Shelby Oaks Dr. (Macon Rd. & I-40) 388-7050	x	x	x	$$$
31	**Holiday Inn-Medical Center** 969 Madison 522-8300	x	x	x	$$$
32	**Holiday Inn-Midtown** 1262 Union 725-1900	x	x	x	$$
33	**Holiday Inn-Poplar** 5679 Poplar (at I-240) 682-7881	x	x	x	$$$$
34	**Holiday Inn-** **West Memphis, Ark.** Jct. I-40 & I-55 735-6480	x	x	for guests only	$$$
35	**Howard Johnson's** 3280 Elvis Presley Blvd. (1 mi. from Graceland) 345-1425	x	24 hr.		$$$
36	**Lamplighter Motor Inn** 667 S. Bellevue (Lamar exit E. at I-240) 726-1000				$

MAP NO.	NAME, ADDRESS & PHONE	POOL	RESTAU-RANT	LOUNGE	PRICE
37	**La Quinta Motor Inn-Medical Center** 42 S. Camilla (at Union) 526-1050	x	x	x	$$
38	**Quality Inn-East** 5877 Poplar (at I-240) 767-6300	x	x	x	$$$
39	**Ramada Inn-East** 5225 Summer (at I-40, I-240 & 70) 682-7691	x	x	x	$$$
40	**Ramada Inn-of West Memphis, Ark.** 1100 N. Ingram (at I-240, adjacent to Southland Greyhound Park) 735-8600	heated outdoor	x	x	$$
41	**Regal 8 Inn** 1360 Springbrook Ave. (Brooks & 55) 396-3620	x			$
42	**River Place** 100 N. Front 526-0583	x	x		$
43	**Royal Oaks-East** 4941 Summer (Hwy. 64, 70, 79) 683-2411	x	x		$
44	**Royal Oaks-North** 4022 Thomas (Hwy. 51 N.) 357-9565	x	x	x	$
45	**Shelby Motel** 6803 Hwy. 70 386-3311	x	x		$
46	**Sheraton Skyport** (sleeping and meeting rooms only) inside Memphis Airport (near Delta) 345-3220				$$$

MAP NO.	NAME, ADDRESS & PHONE	POOL	RESTAU-RANT	LOUNGE	PRICE
47	**Stuckey's & Carriage Inn Motel** 6790 Raleigh-LaGrange Rd. (Whitten Rd. at I-240) 386-5500		x		$
48	**Travelodge-Airport** 3222 Airways Blvd. 396-9170	x	x	x	$$$
49	**Travelodge-Crump Blvd.** 180 Crump Blvd. E. 942-3291	x	x		$
50	**Travelodge-Downtown** 265 Union Ave. 527-4305	x	x		$$

As seen on the map, most of the city's hotels/motels are clustered around the airport and medical center or at the intersections of I-240 and major arteries in and out of the city.

Today there are only a few downtown hotels/motels; outstanding among them are the Holiday Inn-Rivermont, Peabody Hotel, and Sheraton Convention Center Hotel. In the planning stage is a large convention hotel adjacent to Cook Convention Center*.

For in-town readers—don't forget "get-away-weekends". Many special, reduced rate packages, some even including champagne and a room-service breakfast, are offered by the city's major hotels/motels. What a treat!

Looking for luxurious accommodations for your pet while you're away? Eden Kennel, 7524 Raleigh-LaGrange, is reputed to be the fanciest. Many other good ones are listed in the yellow pages under Kennels.

YMCA & USO ROOMS

The YMCA* and USO offer an inexpensive alternative to hotels/motels. The Mason Branch of the YMCA (3548 Walker, 323-4505) offers rooms for men and women 18 and older for $37.52 per week plus a $15 deposit. The USO (327-4498) operates out of the same building and offers accommodations for 12 military personnel. Rates are $6 per night plus $1 key deposit. Memphis' USO plans social, recreational, and religious entertainment for active duty military personnel in the Arkansas, Mississippi, Tennessee, and Kentucky area. If you've got any questions, just phone them. They're open seven days a week (on F and Sat until midnight).

CAMPING

Tennessee's two parks adjacent to Memphis, T. O. Fuller and Meeman-Shelby, both offer camping:

T. O. Fuller State Park*

U.S. 61 at Memphis / 3269 Boxtown Rd., 38109. 785-3950. T. O. Fuller has 54 year-round camp sites open to the public. These sites are for tents or trailers and include the use of picnic tables, hot showers, modern lavatories and toilets, and a coin-operated laundry room with washers and dryers.

Rates are $6.63 per site for up to four persons, a trailer, and a car. For each extra person over age seven, a 50¢ charge. Maximum stay, two weeks. No reservations accepted. Camper quiet time, 10pm.

The park offers a seasonal swimming pool and snack bar and year-round picnic sites, nature trails, playground, and golf course.

Meeman-Shelby Forest State Park*

U.S. 51 N. / Route 3, Millington 38053 (about 13 miles north of Memphis on the river). 876-5201. Meeman-Shelby offers the public 49 year-round camp sites for tents or trailers.

Picnic tables, hot showers, modern lavoratories and toilets, and a coin-operated laundry room are available. Sites are $6.63 per night for up to four persons. For each extra person over age seven, a 50¢ charge. Maximum stay, two weeks. No reservations accepted. Quiet time, 10pm.

This 12,600 acre park also has five "ultra-modern" cabins for rent March-Dec. The two bedroom, one bath cabins are fully equipped with linens, pots and pans, dishes, silverware, and television. They are heated but also have fireplaces. The cabins rent for $40 per night during the week and $45 per night on weekends. With roll-away beds, they can accommodate six. Reservations accepted. Two night minimum March-June. Seven night minimum, July-Sept. Check-in time, 1pm daily.

Shelby Forest seasonally offers a restaurant, swimming pool, boats for rent, a group camp, snack bars, a stable, a museum, and nature and sports programs for children and adults. Year-round fishing, nature trails, playground, gift shop, boat launching ramps, and back-packing trails.

Memphis also has two public campgrounds, Canada Trace and Lakeland:

Canada Trace Campground
3300 Canada Rd. at I-40. 388-3053. This public campground currently has 76 sites, 35 with water, sewer and electricity, the others with water and electricity only. The campground offers a full-service grocery, laundromat, shower building, modern lavatory facilities, a fishing lake, and swimming pool. Rates per night for two persons, no hook-up/$6.50, with electricity and water/$8, and with electricity, water, and sewerage hook-up/$8.50. For each additional person over age three, a $1 charge. Extra charge, $1.25 to hook up air conditioning. Reservations accepted.

Lakeland Campground
3970 Canada Rd. at I-40. 388-2150. This public campground offers unlimited space for primitive camping and 200 spaces with water, electricity, and sewer hook-ups for trailer camping. Hot water showers, a modern lavatory, a camp store and laundromat on the campground. Rates per night for up to four persons, no hook-up/$5.83, with electricity and water/$6.89, with electricity, water, and sewerage/$7.42. For each additional person over age three, a $1 nightly charge. Overnight campers may swim and fish on the 300-acre lake without additional charge; others must pay $3 per person to fish and $3 per person to swim and picnic.

Useful
Information

Erwin Williamson and Federal Express Corp.

View from the Civic Center south along Mid-America Mall, 1981. Federal Express' airplane and sign are superimposed.

A hodge-podge of information and phone numbers for the tourist and resident.

LINC

If you memorize only one phone number let it be 528-2999. LINC, Library Information Center, is a free human services, recreational, and educational information and referral service. If you want to find a chess club, square dancing group, free meal program for the elderly, day care service, soccer team to join, ... call LINC. Helpful, knowledgeable, concerned,... they're an invaluable service to our community. Open 9am-9pm M-F, 9am-6pm Sat.

EMERGENCY NUMBERS

Most are in operation 24 hours a day, 7 days a week.

Police Department - Memphis - 528-2222 (emergency only).
  Suburban:
    Bartlett - 388-3400.
    Collierville - 853-4777.
    Germantown - 754-7222.
    Millington - 872-3333.
    Shelby County Sheriff - 528-3611.
Fire Department - Memphis - 458-3311.
  Suburban:
    Arlington - 867-2433.
    Bartlett - 386-1333.
    Collierville - 853-4866.
    DeSoto Woods - 393-0100.
    Germantown - 754-1414.
    Horn Lake - 393-7669.
    Millington - 872-3331.
    Pipertown - 853-2195.
    Shelby County - 386-1265.
    Southaven - 393-7441.
    Walls - 781-1414.
Ambulance/Memphis Fire Department - 458-3311.
Ambulance/Shelby County-Medic - 274-3183.
Emergency Medical Service - 523-1313. Serves 9 counties.
Doctor's Exchange - 527-3311. Will make referrals to physicians and
  dentists and contact doctors on call.
Poison Control Center - 528-6048.

Suicide and Crisis Intervention - 274-7477.
Rape Hotline - 274-7477.
Mental Health Information - 272-1111.
Gay Switchboard - 726-GAYY. 7pm-1am daily. Information, referral, and crisis line.
Animal Emergency Center - 323-4563. Open only when veterinarians' offices are closed.
Tn. Highway Patrol - 386-3831. Reports on hazardous road conditions and assistance in emergency and travel situations.
FBI - 525-7373.
U.S. Secret Service - 521-3568.
Memphis Light Gas & Water - 523-0711 from 7:30am-9pm. After hours emergencies: 528-4465.

USEFUL NUMBERS

Correct Time - 526-5261.
Weather - 521-1500. 345-6700 (long range forecasts). 345-6600 (river stages and forecasts).
Telephone Directory Assistance - 1411.
Mayor's Action Center - 528-2500. Phone with your complaints, suggestions, comments, or problems concerning city administration and services. Praise would probably be a welcome relief. Very helpful.
Shelby County Assistance Center - 528-3585. For the county what the Mayor's Action Line is for the city.
City Mayor - 528-2800.
County Mayor - 528-3500.
Shelby County Government "Dial-The-News" - 528-3535. Taped listing of County Mayor's schedule and of county government meetings.
City Council - 528-2786.
Memphis Area Chamber of Commerce - 523-2322. Supplies economic data on the community and works with businesses considering expanding or relocating in the area. Films, slides, and maps available to members.
Germantown Chamber of Commerce - 755-1200.
Millington Chamber of Commerce - 872-1486.
Board of Education - 454-5200.
Health Department - 528-3800.
Memphis/Shelby County Public Library and Information Center - 528-2965. General information about the library. Branches throughout the city with a main branch at Peabody and McLean. The library houses a circulating and reference collection of books, journals, cassette tapes, albums, microfilm, microfiche, musical scores, art reproductions, posters, film, pamphlets, etc. Special programming throughout the

🛺 year includes story hours for children, genealogy workshops, resume instruction, puppet shows, etc. The library is also the home of LINC* (528-2999), the human services, recreation, and educational information and referral service.

U.S. Postal Service - 521-3451 (general information), 521-3336 (zip code information).

MATA* - 523-2521. Bus and schedule information.

Lawyer Referral Services of Memphis/Shelby County Bar Assn. - 527-6002.

Memphis/Shelby County Medical Society - 726-0301. Lists of physicians for newcomers.

Crime Stoppers - 528-CASH. Tipsters phone with information about selected crimes. Rewards for information leading to arrest and indictments.

Better Business Bureau - 272-9641. Handles consumer complaints. Operates a Fact Line (272-9542) with taped bi-weekly messages on consumer problems.

"Commercial Appeal" Action Please - 526-3311. Handles consumer complaints.

Women's Resource Center - 458-1407. Programs, classes, films, ...on subjects of particular interest to women.

The International Group of Memphis - phone LINC (528-2999) for current phone number. They offer group activities, programs, and classes for the city's foreign population.

United Service Organizations, Inc. (USO) - 327-4498. Information, referrals, travel services, recreational programs, and inexpensive lodging for active duty military personnel and their dependents. 10am-10pm Tu-Th, 10am-11:30pm F, 9am-11:30pm Sat, noon-8pm Sun.

Taped Medical Information - 726-7777.

Taped Agricultural Information - 377-2500. Over 400 subjects covered, everything from canning to insect control.

🛺 Taped Children's Stories - 323-KIDS.

Taped Poems and Animal Sounds by J. C. Levy - 278-2370.

Dial-A-Bible Story - 725-1318.

A list of community service numbers is in the front of the phone directory.

TV & RADIO STATIONS

PUBLIC TV STATIONS
WMC-Channel 5 (NBC)
WHBQ-Channel 13 (ABC)
WREC-Channel 3 (CBS)
WPTY-Channel 24
WKNO-Channel 10 (educational channel)

Additional stations available by subscribing to Cablevision (346-9980).

RADIO STATIONS

WHBQ-AM 56 top forty
WREC-AM 60 adult contemporary
WMPS-AM 68 country
KSUD-AM 73 gospel
WMC-AM 79 country
KWAM-AM 990 gospel
WDIA-AM 1070 black soul
WLOK-AM 1340 rhythm & blues/contemporary rock
WTNN-AM 1380 gospel
WWEE-AM 1430 primarily talk shows. Music buffs should tune in to Mrs.
  Sam Phillips' swing era/big band program 2-4pm Sun.
WMQM-AM 1480 gospel
WMSO-AM 1590 gospel
WQOX-FM 88.5 educational programs for children elementary through
  high school age. In conjunction with cable TV channel 30, they also
  broadcast vocational training programs.
WLYX-FM 89 collegiate
WKNO-FM 91 educational
WSMS-FM 92 jazz/blues
WEE-FM 94 easy listening
WHRK-FM 97 disco
WMPS-FM 97.1 disco
WMC-FM 100 rock
KWAM-FM 101 progressive country/black gospel
WZXR-FM 103 album oriented/rock
WEZI-FM 106 easy listening

PUBLICATIONS

NEWSPAPERS

The city's major newspapers, **"The Commercial Appeal"** (morning and Sunday) and the **"Memphis Press-Scimitar"** (afternoon), are both owned by Scripps-Howard. Rates are the same for both papers: 25¢ daily, 75¢ Sun. To subscribe phone 529-2666 or write Circulation, Memphis Publishing Co., 495 Union, 38101.

Monday through Saturday "The Commercial Appeal" runs a daily calendar listing attractions, special performances, and public meetings. On Friday the paper has a special Weekend Living section with feature articles on weekend special events, restaurant and bar reviews, suggested short trips, and a calendar of events. The Sunday Fanfare Section also includes a weekly calendar of events and reviews of current art exhibits.

The "Memphis Press-Scimitar" Thursday edition includes art reviews and a special city-area section with a weekly calendar of club and neighborhood events. Friday's Showcase section has theatre, film and art information plus what to do after work—who's playing where and who's the best bartender.

There are many neighborhood newspaper/newsletters and several special interest publications. Among the latter—**"The Dixie Flyer"**, a free underground local paper, P.O. Box 4074, 38104, 722-8730; the **"Tri-State Defender"**, a black weekly, $15/year, P.O. Box 2065, 38101, 523-1818; **"The Daily News"**, a M-F daily primarily for legal notices, $54/year, 193 Jefferson, 38103, 523-1561. See Shopping for shoppers' newspapers.

OTHER PUBLICATIONS—See individual chapters for additional and topical publications.

"Memphis Magazine"—well-done monthly. If you want to get the most out of the city, it's a must. $15/yearly. Subscription Dept., "Memphis Magazine", P.O. Box 16566, 38116, 345-8000.

"Key"—a bi-weekly guide pamphlet to attractions and entertainment in Memphis. Available free in hotels and motels or by subscription, $12/yearly. "Key Magazine" of Memphis, 3373 Poplar, Suite 306, 38111.

"Kaleidoscope"—Memphis/Shelby County Public Library and Information Center's monthly calendar. The library offers films, children's programs, adult discussion groups and classes, special seminars and workshops, art exhibits, and much more. Pick up free monthly calendar at any branch. It'll keep you in touch.

"Sharing"—a valuable community human services newsletter. $5/yearly. MSU Human Services CO-OP, Public Service and Continuing Education, 011 Richardson Towers, Memphis State University, 38152.

"Summer Survival Kit"—No household should be without one. Free from LINC at the beginning of summer. Pick one up at the library branch nearest you. Gives performance schedules, sports and camp information, and much, much, much more.

Free **county government pamphlets** on services for the elderly, information for the newcomer, services for children, zoning and planning information, ... from the Public Affairs Dept. Assistance Center, 160 N. Main, Rm. 850, 38103, 528-3585.

"Sidetreks 1, 2, & 3"—3 booklets published by "The Commercial Appeal" on short trips outside Memphis. $2.50 each from "The Commercial Appeal", 495 Union Ave., 38101.

"Program Resources and Techniques"—This booklet published annually by the Memphis/Shelby County Public Library and Information Center*, costs $1 and just might be the best buy in town. Lists available speakers and their topics, suggested tours and excursions, a bibliography on public speaking, and tips for a program planner.

"The Memphis/Shelby County Directory of Elected Government Officials"—Put out by the League of Women Voters and available from them (4670 Shady Grove Rd./767-2351) for 10¢ + 18¢ postage. It'll enable you to get in touch with your representatives.

"The Gayoso Street Review"—a Memphis literary magazine. $2.50/copy in local bookstores or $6/yearly for 3 issues. P.O. Box 11736, 38111.

"Raccoon"—Well-respected local poetry journal. $3.95/issue, $7/year for 2 issues. St. Luke's Press, Suite 401, Mid-Memphis Tower, 1407 Union, 38104. 357-5441.

"Center for Southern Folklore Magazine"—a quarterly magazine specializing in folkways in the Mid-South. Subscriptions are $5/year. Center for Southern Folklore*, 1216 Peabody Ave., 726-4205.

ESPECIALLY FOR TRAVELERS & NEWCOMERS

Climate - Temperature: Jan. average high/49°, average low/33°; July average high/90°, average low/72°. Average annual days over 90/65. Average annual days of sunshine/123. Average annual precipitation/49 inches. Average annual days of snow/5.

Convention and Visitors Bureau - 526-1919. Located in the Commerce Title Bldg., 12 S. Main, Suite 107, 38103, the bureau works with local government, business, and community organizations to attract conventions and tourists to Memphis. Runs information booths at the zoo*, Overton Square*, Libertyland*, Graceland*, and Mid-America Mall*.

Tennessee State Information Center - 345-5956. Located on Hwy. 55 between Shelby Dr. and Brooks Rd. Provides free tourist information pamphlets on state's attractions. Open 24 hours a day, daily.

Tourist & Newcomers Information - 458-3385. The Baker family provides this service out of its furniture store at 3980 Park. Free brochures and travel information. They'll serve as guides for groups.

Want to see the sights either individually with a **guide** or on a **tour,** see Transportation/By Bus/Tours & Guides.

Maps—Where to get one? Your best bet for a detailed city road map is one of the city's drugstores or gas stations. About $2.

Touch Me/Information - Just touch the computer screen and information on historical sights, sports and recreation, where to eat or shop, and transportation pops into view free of charge. A space on the shopping and restaurant lists is by paid advertisement. You'll find terminals in Cook Convention Center lobby, (255 N. Main at Exchange), National Bank of Commerce (Mid-America Mall at Monroe), Overton Square* information kiosk (Madison at Cooper), and the Convention and Visitors Bureau's information booth (Elvis Presley Blvd., across from Graceland*). The airport, Holiday Inn-Rivermont, and Mud Island* may have computer terminals in the future.

Rotary Club - 526-1318. Assists foreign students and Rotarians with lodging, transportation, and tourist information. Hours, 9am-5pm M-F.

Travelers' Aid Society - Rm. 1025, 46 N. 3rd, 38103, 525-5466. Open 8:30am-4:30pm M-F, they help travelers in crisis and emergency situations and assist children, senior citizens, or handicapped persons transfering buses or planes. Fee, $5.

Council for International Friendship - Contact LINC (528-2999) for a current phone number. Helps international visitors see Memphis. They'll help plan airport greetings, transportation to professional appointments, interpretive sightseeing tours, and meetings with American host families.

Translators and **foreign language guides** available through the language departments at Memphis State University* (454-2813) and Southwestern* (274-1800).

Active duty **military** personnel see Useful Numbers/USO.

If you're in town and need **courier** service, check the yellow pages under

Messenger Service. One good service is Rabbit Transit (452-0473); they deliver via Volkswagon Rabbits, of course.

Need someone to run an **errand**, do your shopping, or handle the situation for you? Errands of Memphis Inc. (725-7677) and The Butler Did It (726-5920) will do it.

For that special touch, Coopertown Sing-A-Gram will deliver **singing** thank you, birthday, or whatever **notes** for you. Phone 323-9495.

If you need a **secretary**, see Secretarial Services in the yellow pages. Several sound excellent, take 24-hour dictation, and have pick-up and delivery, but "Your Airport Secretary" (345-5965), located at the airport across from the United counter, is probably the most convenient for air travelers.

To send things back to your home office, **express bus and air delivery services** are available. Memphis is the home of Federal Express* (345-3810).

The rain got your hair? See **Beauty Salons** in the yellow pages. A good one, Bermel Coiffures International, 3092 Poplar in Chickasaw Oaks Mall, 454-0234.

You spilled wine on your beaded chiffon gown! There are many good **cleaners** in the city, most with pick-up and delivery service, listed in the yellow pages by locality. Carwile's Custom Cleaners at 2178 Central, 274-3815, will pamper your finest things. Expensive.

The hotel won't allow Fido! Don't despair; there are many fine **kennels** in the area. See Kennels in the yellow pages. The poshest is Eden Kennels, 7524 Raleigh-LaGrange Rd., 754-2060.

You hear there are some restaurants and bars you shouldn't miss, but what about Junior? Check with your hotel/motel for baby **sitting services** or call Baby Sitters Services of Memphis, Inc. (327-4595). Provides home, motel/hotel, or hospital care for children, convalescent and/or elderly, physically and/or mentally handicapped. Fees vary and are on an hourly or daily basis. Office hours, 7am-9pm daily.

Where to worship? **Churches** are listed in the yellow pages by both denomination and locality. Most have an 11am Sunday service. Many churches have day-care, recreational, children's, senior citizen, sports, and counseling services.

You wish Jane still lived next door. You could always borrow her wine glasses, roto-tiller, tables, . . . The next best thing is to rent. See **Rental Service** Stores & Yards in the yellow pages.

Planning a party? See individual Florists and Housewares.../John Simmons Entertains. A child's birthday party? Ask the Sockettes (523-1818) to put on their hour long puppet show. 9am-5pm M-F. $50 per show. Or ask the Story Tellers' League (276-8225) to come tell a tale. No charge. Happy Hands (Park Place Mall, 683-9841) will come to you with a 1½ hour pottery lesson for 20 children or more. Cost, $3.50 per child. Children ages 6 + make three items. Happy Hands fires the creations, and children pick them up at the shop. Other suggestions throughout the book.

If you've moved to Memphis and want to give your time, talents, thoughts, . . . to your community, call the **Volunteer Center** at 452-8655.

The **Newcomers Club** plans monthly activities to help you make new friends and get acquainted with Memphis. Membership dues, $7. LINC has current phone number.

ESPECIALLY FOR THE ELDERLY

Comprehensive services including homemaker services, home health care, a weekly friendly visitor, non-emergency ambulance service, and telephone reassurance calls. For information call:
  Sr. Citizens Services - 726-0211.

Discounts and **special programs** are offered by many private and public institutions. See E&H under individual listings and Arts/Information.

Education - For those 65 + , state college classes are free on a space available basis. See: Colleges & Universities chapter.

Financial & Medical Benefits - For information contact:
  Social Security Administration - 521-1010.
  Medicare - 521-1010.
  Medicaid - 529-7398.
  Chapman Center for the Partially Sighted Elderly, Southern College of Optometry, 1245 Madison, provides various free services for indigent elderly persons who are blind or partially sighted.

General Information
Mayor's Office on Aging - 525-CARE.
County Booklet on Services - 528-3585.
Metropolitan Inter-Faith Assn.'s monthly newspaper, "Mid-South Senior" - P.O. Box 17407, 38117, 527-0208; year's subscription/$4.

Housing - For information call:
Metropolitan Inter-Faith Assn. (MIFA) - 527-0208.
Federal Housing Authority - 521-4201.
Memphis Housing Authority - 523-7620.
Shelby County Housing Authority - 528-3073.

Legal Advice - For information contact:
Legal Services for Senior Citizens - 526-5550.
Lawyer Referral Services - 527-6002.

Meals, at sites throughout the community or delivered to your home:
Metropolitan Inter-Faith Assn. (MIFA) - 527-0208.
Project Memphis Encounters Eating Together - 278-5050.

Recreational Activities - For information about the club or group nearest you:
Sr. Citizens Services - 726-0211.
Josephine K. Lewis Center for Sr. Citizens - 272-7408.
Memphis Park Commission - 454-5750.
Am. Assn. of Retired Persons - 358-0145.

Transportation. See Transportation/ For the Elderly & Handicapped.

ESPECIALLY FOR THE HANDICAPPED

WTTL, West Tn. Talking Library, Suite 113, 2277 Union, 38104, 528-2929, is a radio station for the visually impaired. On the air 6am-9pm daily. Its Memphis Talking Library, daily newspapers, best selling novels, and magazines read over closed circuit to special receivers, is available free to qualified individuals. Write or phone WTTL for an application form.

The **Temple Israel Sisterhood Braille Committee** transcribes into braille for the Memphis City Schools and upon request for others. Contact Mrs. Kopald at 683-8896.

The literature department of the main library at Peabody and McLean has 200+ **talking books** available for the blind and physically handicapped. The Roundtable Bookstore, 557 Erin Dr., 761-0512, also has a good collection of tapes and cassettes for adults and children.

LINC section of the main library at Peabody and McLean has an **MCM telephone communication device** for the hearing impaired.

Interpreting Service for the Deaf, 3548 Walker Ave., 38111, 327-4233, provides interpreters for any hearing impaired person. Fees are based on ability to pay. Hours, 8:30am-5pm M-F. Make appointments in advance.

First Baptist Church **Deaf Ministry**, 200 E. Parkway N., 38112, 454-1131, and East Frayser Church of Christ, 2285 Frayser Blvd., 38127, 357-7444, both have church services for the deaf and provide interpreting services for them. In addition to services at 11am and 7pm Sun. and Sunday School at 9:30am, First Baptist also has captioned films and social events aimed particularly at the hearing impaired. See Downtown Churches for additional religious programs for the handicapped.

Transportation. See Transportation/ For the Elderly & Handicapped.

Parking spaces for the handicapped are indicated by rectangular blue signs with a wheelchair logo. They are designated near the entrances to most public spaces. Special handicapped parking spaces and transportation by golf cart to the field are available on a limited basis at Liberty Bowl Stadium. For information and to make arrangements phone 278-4747.

Worth
The
Drive

A family outing near Raleigh Springs about 1902.

If you feel stuck in a rut, how about a weekend or day excursion? Here are some spots worth the drive. Many are suitable for children. You know your child's interests, so you be the judge.

Mark Hanna and James Cortese's articles in "The Commercial Appeal" Friday Living Section suggest additional tours, routes, restaurants, and places to spend the night. Many of these articles are reprinted in a series of booklets about small vacations, "Sidetreks 1, 2, & 3", available from "The Commercial Appeal" 495 Union, 38101. Include your name, address, telephone number, and $1.25 for "Sidetreks 1" or $2.50 for "Sidetreks 2 or 3". Or buy one in person for $2 at the Memphis Publishing Co. (495 Union), in room 515 of the Memphis Bank and Trust Co. Building (4515 Poplar, next to Goldsmith's Oak Court), or at Seessel's Supermarket (1761 Union).

Considering an Arkansas excursion? Get a copy of the monthly magazine "Arkansas Times". Their office, 500 E. Markham, Suite 110C, Little Rock, 72201, (501) 375-2985.

ARKANSAS

CRATER OF DIAMONDS STATE PARK
About 230 miles from Memphis in southwest Arkansas, two miles southwest of Murfreesboro on State Hwy. 301. Happy hunting! Bring your own hand garden tools; learn what to look for and the history of the field from the 10-minute slide show at the Visitor Center; then dig. Chances are you'll find a bit of diamond, amethyst, opal, agate, jasper, or quartz. The first diamond was found here in 1906 and the last extremely valuable one in 1974, a 16-carat diamond worth $150,000. The 900-acre park with its 78-acre diamond field open to the public 8am-5pm summer, 8:30am-4:30pm winter. Admission to diamond field, adults/$2, children 6-15/$1, and children under 6 with parent/free. Group rates are half price; advance notice required. The visitor center has a restaurant and gift shop. Camping is being developed. For information contact the Superintendent, Route 1, Box 364, Murfreesboro, 71958, (501) 285-3113.

HEBER SPRINGS
Red Apple Inn, Eden Isle, Heber Springs, 72543, (501) 362-3111. Resort inn 150 miles from Memphis. Lodging, an attractive dining room, swimming, tennis, rental sailboats, and golf. Year-round rates for a double are $50+ a day. Many private homes around the lake. Popular for fishing and water sports.

HOT SPRINGS
196 miles from Memphis, a resort and horse racing town. Oaklawn Park

operates a 56 day racing season, Feb-early Apr. Nine to ten events are run daily, the first race at 1:30pm M-F, 1pm Sat. Track closed Sun. Parimutuel betting is legal.

Historic Bathhouse Row has been maintained for bathers and tourists. There are two display springs and many others to bathe in for a fee. The full treatment, including whirlpool and massage, costs about $15. Closed Sun.

There are many hotels, restaurants, and nightspots in Hot Springs. The Arlington Hotel, up on the hill, is the grand old lady. Its Fountain and Venetian Rooms and Bohemia Restaurant are worth visits. Le Mirabelle and Hamilton House, both elegant restaurants, the latter located in a 1930s converted Italian style villa on Lake Hamilton, are highly recommended. Or try the barbecued ribs at McClard's.

National parks and forests, golf courses, tennis, and swimming nearby. Town is served by an airport and buses. For entertainment, racing, and accommodations information call 1-800-643-1570 or write the Hot Springs Chamber of Commerce, Convention Blvd. & Malvern Ave., 71901.

LITTLE ROCK

137 miles southwest of Memphis on I-40. Located on the south bank of the Arkansas River with the foothills of the Ozarks to its west is the state's capital and largest city. It was surveyed in 1821, incorporated in 1831, and chartered as a city in 1836. The State Capitol circa 1912, the War Memorial building (begun in 1833 as the first statehouse), the restored houses of the Quapaw area, and the contemporary Arkansas Art Center all deserve a visit. Shoppers might enjoy browsing in the specialty stores in the Heights.

Hungry? Try Coy's, 11400 Rodney Parham, 224-2000, for steaks. Jacques & Suzanne, 30th floor, 1st National Bldg, 376-6616, offers such exotica as catfish quenelles and chocolate fondue in an elegant European atmosphere. Have lunch Tu-F at La Petite Tea Room, 905 Autumn Rd, in west Little Rock, 225-3696, or try a Sam Peck salad at the Hotel-Motel Sam Peck. The plush Afterthought is a good place for drinks and live entertainment.

Lake Maumelle and Pinnacle Mountain are nearby.

OZARKS

Three different destinations within the Ozark mountains—something for everyone. Fall leaves are usually at their brightest the middle two weeks in Oct. For leaf reports phone toll free 1-800-643-8383 (out of state), 1-800-238-8999 (in state).

EUREKA SPRINGS. Its a long drive, 180 miles from Memphis, to this Victorian town founded in 1879. Built on two mountaintops, with

230 winding streets that never cross each other, the town has 63 springs, artists' and craftsmen's shops lining the main street, and two Victorian hotels: Crescent Hotel on the mountaintop (Eureka Springs, 72632, (501) 253-9766) and the New Orleans on Main Street (Eureka Springs, 72632, (501) 253-8630). The Chamber of Commerce office on Main Street has free walking tour maps pointing out such noteworthy sites as St. Elizabeth's Catholic Church, featured in Ripley's Believe-It-Or-Not as the only church entered through its belfry. Visit Thorncrown Chapel, designed by Fay Jones & Asso., winner of the prestigious 1981 Am. Inst. of Architects' Honor Award. Gray Line offers city and vicinity tours daily during the main tourist season May-Oct. A Passion Play is performed in the town's outdoor amphitheatre nightly at 8:30pm. No performances on M, Th, the 3rd F in May, and the last Sat in Oct. Tickets, $4-5. Group rates available. For reservations or information write Elna M. Smith Foundation, Eureka Springs, 72632 or phone (501) 253-8781. Another major attraction is the nationally recognized War Eagle Crafts Festival each Oct at War Eagle Mill, Rt. 6, Box 293, Rogers, Ark, 72756, (501) 789-2610.

The Kings and War Eagle Rivers are nearby. See North Arkansas Rivers.

Lost Bridge Inn, a remote resort with tennis court, restaurant and fantastic view of Beaver Lake, is nearby on Hwy. 127 between Eureka Springs and Pea Ridge.

OZARK FOLK CENTER. A new development composed of a 1,043 seat music auditorium and a 17-building crafts area, designed as a museum to display the Ozark culture and history. The center is in full operation from Memorial Day weekend through Labor Day with limited operations in May, Sept, and Oct. The craft buildings open at 10am daily. Admission, adults/$2, children 6-15/$1. Musical performances, 8pm nightly, except Sun. Admission, adults/$2, children 6-15/$1. Two shops sell the craftsmen's wares. A fast-food restaurant and dining room operate on the grounds. There is a 60-unit air conditioned inn and a pool. For information write Ozark Folk Center, Mountain View, 72560, (501) 269-3851. For lodge reservations phone (501) 269-3871. Or stay at the circa 1886 Inn near the courthouse in Mountain View. Try a plate lunch at the Rainbow Cafe on the town square. Fifteen miles northwest on Hwy. 14 is Blanchard Springs Cavern. There are geological exhibits and underground tours. Open 9am-4:30pm daily. Adults/$3.50, children 6-12/$1.50, under 6/free, senior citizens/$1.75. For information contact USDA, Forest Service, P.O. Box I, Mountain View, 72560, (501) 757-2211.

NORTH ARKANSAS RIVERS - About a 250 mile drive. Canoeists* find rivers to match their ability. For the advanced: try the Cassatot, Richland Creek-Falling Water Creek (kayaks only), the Hailstone section of the Buffalo near Boxley, the Mulberry, and the Big Piney near Long Pool. For beginners and intermediates: try the Spring River near Hardy (popular annual Memorial Day race), Kings River, War Eagle River, the Caddo, and Cadron Creek. Others: float the one-day whitewater falls section of the Cassatot near Hwy. 4 or the 23-mile two day scenic Buffalo from Ponca to Pruitt. Motels and camping facilities available.

Fishermen love the area's trout fishing. White River Ozark float trips are famous. Boats, guides, and equipment available for day or overnight trips leaving from just below Bull Shoals Dam. Arrangements may be made in advance through Crow-Barnes Resort, Bull Shoals, (501) 445-4242 or through Gaston's White River Resort, Lakeview, Ark, 72642, (501) 431-5202. Both offer cabin/motel lodgings, a swimming pool, tennis courts, and restaurant. Gaston's also has an airstrip, boat dock, and lodge. The season is year-round, but the most interesting and comfortable time to go is March-Nov.

STUTTGART
100 miles from Memphis, Hwy. 79. A duck hunter's* paradise in the rice growing area of Arkansas. The area seems to be the principal migration goal of southward winging mallards and other ducks along the Mississippi Flyway. A duck calling championship contest is held Thanksgiving weekend each year. Deer, wild turkey, and small game abound. Guides are available. Write Stuttgart Chamber of Commerce, P.O. Box 932, 72160, or phone (501) 673-1602 for a list of camps, guides, motels, and rates.

Twenty miles northeast of Stuttgart is a culinary wonder, DeValls Bluff. In this small town there are three true "finds": catfish at Murry's, barbecue at Craig's, and coconut cream pie and chili at Mary's Pie Shop.

WAPANOCCA NATIONAL WILDLIFE REFUGE
25 miles northwest of Memphis, Hwy. 42, P.O. Box 279, Turrell, 72384, (501) 343-2595. Once the area's most famous private hunting club, now a public wildlife preserve. A fantastic spot for nature lovers and fishermen. The 5,485-acre preserve is open in daylight. Boats and motors for rent ($4-$15/day) from the concessionaire daily Apr-Sept, or you may bring your own if motor is less than 10 h.p. Office open 8am-4:30pm M-F. Fishermen, bring your own bait and license. No firearms, except during specially authorized hunts. No picnicking. No camping.

MISSISSIPPI

Many ante-bellum structures still stand. Mary Wallace Crocker's *Historic Architecture in Mississippi* is an excellent guide to them. *White*

Pillars by J. Frazer Smith is a broader architectural study which includes information on both Mississippi and Tennessee.

COLUMBUS
166 miles southeast of Memphis. Birthplace of Tennessee Williams who won the Pulitzer Prize for drama in 1955 for his play "Cat on a Hot Tin Roof". Columbus has more than 100 ante-bellum buildings. Styles range from cottage to mansion, and many are nationally famous. An annual pilgrimage shows several houses to the public each Apr. Incorporate a visit here with stops in Macon, Aberdeen, and Pontotoc which also have pilgrimages.

There are several national motel outlets and restaurants. Steve's, a downtown cafe, has good daily specials and pizza, and Reuben's, on the river, is a good bet for catfish. Or try the Possum Town Depot, a renovated train station serving steaks and seafood. If you're in the mood for shopping, visit the gift shop Lagniappe Ltd.

CORINTH
91 miles east on Hwy. 72. Corinth is famous as the railroad junction for the Memphis & Charleston and the Mobile & Ohio. The nearby Shiloh National Military Park* in Tennessee commemorates the battle for these railroad lines so important during the Civil War. Curlee House, an ante-bellum home in Corinth at 709 Jackson Str., is open 1-3pm M-Sat. There are many local motels, or you can stay at nearby Pickwick State Park* Inn in Tennessee.

Take a short drive out Hwy. 45 or 72 to Hwy. 356 and Jacinto, an 1850s Mississippi boom-town now being restored. The 1854 brick early Federal style courthouse is usually open. If not, you'll find the courthouse custodian nearby, and he'll open it for you.

"THE DELTA"
A land of big farms, big cars, lots of whiskey, and blues music. It legendarily extends from the lobby of the Peabody Hotel* in Memphis south along the Mississippi River to Catfish Row in Vicksburg. Don't go here to see ante-bellum homes; the Delta was plagued by floods until levees were built in the latter part of the 19thc. Wealthy people lived in the adjoining hill lands, only going to the Delta to work. Today there is a certain sophisticated chic about life, literature and art in the small towns here. It is the home of a unique and romanticized lifestyle where southern hospitality abounds, and the sun beats down on cotton and soybean fields stretching as far as the eye can see. The best way to go here is as a guest of a native, but here are some places that will give you a feel for the area even without a host:

BOYLE/CLEVELAND/MERIGOLD - Boyle is 115 miles south of
Memphis on Hwy. 61. The tiny town's Boyle Blvd. has specialty shops

and a tea room, Sweet Olive, that draws lunch crowds from around the state. Open 11:30am-1pm M-Sat. It seats only 34, so phone ahead for reservations (601) 846-1100.

Between Boyle and Cleveland, which is three miles to the north on Hwy. 61, is The Greenhouse. Named for its converted home, the restaurant/bar is open for lunch 11:30am-2:30pm M-F and for dinner 5:30-10pm M-Th & 5:30-11pm F & Sat. The lounge, open 4pm-1am, has live entertainment Th-Sat.

Shoppers might want to stop in Cleveland at the Fireside Shop on Main Street.

Merigold, seven miles farther north on Hwy. 61, is home of the Mc-Carty's pottery studio and Winery Rushing, both open 10am-5pm Tu-Sat. Ask in Merigold for directions.

CLARKSDALE - 75 miles south on U.S. 61. You'll find the Delta Blues Museum on the highway as you enter town. It commemorates the many blues singers and musicians born in the Delta. See: Music. The Museum is in a room of the Myrtle Hall branch of the Carnegie Public Library. Open in winter: 1-6pm Tu-F, 1-8pm M, 11am-4pm Sat; in summer: 1-5:30pm M-F, 1-5pm Sat. Closed Sun year-round. There are album covers, photographs, records for visitors' listening, newspaper and magazine clips, and assorted memorabilia. One of the most interesting exhibits is a map showing the birthplaces of blues greats. Taped video interviews and performances can be seen on a playback TV. A slide show narrated by B. B. King has been assembled by Memphis' Center for Southern Folklore. Occasional live music programs and lectures are sponsored by the museum. $5 T-shirts are for sale.

Downtown Clarksdale is being redeveloped as the Sunflower Mall with gift, book, and clothing stores. Don't miss the Gingerbread House for children's clothes and The Magpie for gifts.

Hungry? Try the Den on Sunflower for steaks and spaghetti, Rest Haven on Hwy. 61 for daily specials with a Lebanese flair, The Warehouse for drinks and daily luncheon specials, Abe's for barbecue, or drive to Kathryn's on Moon Lake*.

GREENVILLE - 150 miles south on Hwy. 61 to Leland, Hwy. 82 to Greenville. Greenville is on the Mississippi River—you get the feel of a rivertown. The population has grown to 40,444, and yet Greenville has maintained its old downtown. The train depot has been converted into the C&G Ltd. restaurant and bar serving lunch and dinner and offering live music at night. Five miles north on the Great River Rd. are the Winterville Indian Mounds. Open to the public, adults/50¢, children/35¢.

Hungry? Dinner at Doe's Eat Place, 502 Nelson, (601) 334-3315, is an unusual treat. You enter through the kitchen to feast on their widely acclaimed tamales, gumbo, and steaks. Tamales are served all day and at dinner, 6:30-10:30pm daily. BYOB. Expensive. Or try the C&G Ltd. depot; the Marina, a barge on the water across the levee serving crab claws and Mexican cornbread; the Venetian Cafe for Italian food; Sherman's Grocery where they serve luncheon specials and sandwiches in the back. Lillo's in Leland, 10 miles east of Greenville, is famous for its pizza and shrimp supreme.

GREENWOOD - 130 miles south on I-55 to Grenada, Hwy. 7 to Greenwood. Old cotton warehouses downtown remind the visitor of a slower way of life. Three rivers flow through town: the Tallahatchie flows west to east and meets the Yalobusha to form the Yazoo which flows east to west—the land is very flat. Cottonlandia, in town on Hwys. 49 and 82 west, is a natural history museum of the area, telling the story of farming from Indian artifacts through cotton's heyday. The museum is free, open 10am-5pm Tu-F, 1-5pm Sat & Sun. Groups are welcome, but phone ahead (601) 453-0925. Florewood, a "living plantation" of 22 buildings, constructed in 1976 on 100 acres of state park, is two miles from town. It is open 9am-5pm Tu-Sat, 1-5pm Sun. Adults/$2.50, school children/ $1.50, pre-school/free.

For dinner try Lusco's, 722 Carrollton, (601) 453-5365, famous throughout the Delta for its atmosphere, pompano, steak, and shrimp. The restaurant opened in 1932 in the back part of a grocery store and hasn't changed much since. You sit in individually partitioned rooms behind faded chintz curtains. Open 5-10:30pm M-Sat. BYOB. Expensive. Or try Giardina's for steaks and seafood; Malouf's Delicatessen or Malouf's Downtown for sandwiches, pizza, and draft beer; Webster's for lunch or cocktails on the patio or beneath ceiling fans.

Carrollton, 14 miles east on Hwy. 82, is a pre-Civil War town chartered in 1833. It was the setting for the movie version of Faulkner's *The Reivers* starring Steve McQueen. The old courthouse, Merrill Store circa 1834 (now being restored), the old jail museum, and several noteworthy cottage style homes are part of the town's charm. There's a pilgrimage each Apr. Malmaison, the much acclaimed home of Greenwood Leflore, chief of the Choctaws, stood nearby until destroyed by fire in 1942.

HOLLYWOOD - 30 miles south on U.S. 61. Frog legs, fried chicken, and steaks are the fare at The Hollywood ((601) 363-1126), once the site of a stagecoach stop, now a roadhouse/restaurant with live music. Dinner is served 6-10:30pm Th-Sat. Beer or BYOB. MC, Visa. Reservations recommended for Sat.

INDIANOLA - 30 miles west of Greenwood on Hwy. 82. The Antique Mall ((601) 887-2522) sells antiques 10am-5pm and serves lunch in the back noon-2pm Tu-Sat. Phone for lunch reservations.

MOON LAKE - About 60 miles south on Hwy. 61 just off Hwy. 49 to Helena, Ark. Lots of cypress trees and good fishing in this cut-off of the

Mississippi River. Several juke joints are on the lake for beer sipping. Try steaks, salad, and onion rings at Kathryn's ((601) 337-2962). BYOB. Phone ahead for reservations.

MOUND BAYOU - About 100 miles south on U.S. 61. An all-black town founded 1886-87 by Isiah T. Montgomery and Benjamin T. Green. The Louisville, New Orleans & Texas Railroad owned one million acres of land here and asked Montgomery, a plantation owner and former slave of Joseph Davis, brother of Jefferson Davis, President of the Confederacy, to set up the town.

VICKSBURG - 225 miles south on the Mississippi River. During the Civil War General Grant's army and Admiral Porter's ironclads finally forced Vicksburg's surrender. The 1,330-acre Civil War National Military Park is a reminder. The old courthouse has been turned into a museum, and two ante-bellum homes are open to the public year-round: McRaven, 1445 Harrison St., and Cedar Grove, 2200 Oak St. Ten more houses are opened for the annual pilgrimage each March. Visit the Waterways Experiment Station on Halls Ferry Rd., used by the Army Engineer Corps in their control of the Mississippi River floodplain, and Biedenharn's Candy Co., said to be the first place in the world to bottle Coca-Cola, now a 3-room museum, open 9am-5pm M-Sat, 1:30-4:30pm Sun; adults/$1, elementary school children/50¢, preschool children/free.

Try the Biscuit Co., Maxwell's, The Old Southern Tea Room, or Tuminello's for dinner. For more information contact the Vicksburg Chamber of Commerce (601) 636-1012. Two ante-bellum homes take overnight guests, Anchuca ((601) 636-4931) and Cedar Grove ((601) 636-1605).

While you're in the area, drive south 25 miles to Port Gibson, the third oldest town in the state, the site of a major Civil War battle in 1863, and now listed in its entirety in the National Register of Historic Places. Many of its homes are open during the March pilgrimage.

GULF COAST
It's a long drive, 360 miles to Gulfport, but the Coast offers fresh seafood and white sand beaches. Gulfport, Pascagoula, Gautier, Ocean Springs, and Biloxi all have ante-bellum homes and spring pilgrimage tours. Highlights are Jefferson Davis' last home Beauvoir in Gulfport and the scenic drive in Pass Christian. Tie this trip in with a visit to New Orleans, Mobile, or points east.

HOLLY SPRINGS
About 40 miles southeast of Memphis on Hwy. 78. Amazingly for a town with a population of 3,000 in 1860 and 8,000 in 1970, it has produced 13 generals, one admiral, six U.S. Senators, ten U.S. Congressmen, and 18

judges. The area was occupied by Chickasaw Indians until the 1830s and most of the larger houses were not built until 1850-60. Locally made brick and ironwork are seen in buildings throughout the South. An annual pilgrimage is held the end of Apr.

JACKSON
220 miles south on I-55. Jackson has been the state capital since 1822. Much of the city was burned by Gen. Wm. Sherman's troups in 1863, but the old Capitol, the Governor's Mansion, and the new Capitol are worth a look.

Hungry? The Old Tyme Delicatessen and Le Fleur's are favorite eating spots in north Jackson. Nearby are Sundancer, a restaurant/nightspot with a South American flavor and Wild Bill's Cadillac, an urban cowboy nightspot. Dennery's, off the interstate near the Coliseum, and the small Mayflower Cafe on Capitol Str. offer good seafood. Crechales on Hwy. 80W looks like a truck stop but serves good steaks and seafood. The Silver Platter is a small, downtown French restaurant open for lunch and dinner. George Street Grocery Restaurant & Lounge is a favorite downtown watering hole and restaurant.

Drive north around the Ross Barnett Reservoir and stop for a catfish dinner at Cock of the Walk. Canton, 20 miles to the north, draws crowds from around the state to their annual flea market each Oct. The town's old courthouse, homes, and churches are worth a glance.

If you're heading south on #49, try the "lazy Susan" lunch (11am-2pm daily) or dinner (6-7:30pm M-Sat) at Mendenhall's Round Table. They've been operating since 1915 in this Victorian hotel.

NATCHEZ
It's a long trip, 331 miles south on the Mississippi River, but some of the most photographed houses in America are here. There are three homes possibly dating to the British period (1763-1779), examples of architecture from the Spanish period (1779-1798), and many ante-bellum mansions. Several are open year-round, but it is best to visit during the March or Oct pilgrimages. For information contact: the Chamber of Commerce (P.O. Box 725, Natchez, 39120, (601) 445-4611) the Natchez Pilgrimage (P.O. Box 347, Natchez, 39120, toll free 1-800-647-6742), or the Natchez Deluxe Tour Headquarters (211 N. Pearl Str., P.O. Box 1585, Natchez, 38120, toll free 1-800-647-6768). The latter will provide free maps and information on restaurants, points of interest, and where to stay. The Chamber has printed a free walking tour map/brochure.

The riverboat dock area of Natchez, Under the Hill, once popular for gambling and prostitution, is now the home of a popular catfish restaurant, Cock of the Walk, and the lounge, Under-the-Hill Club. For dinner in a historic setting try the Carriage House of Stanton Hall or the Post House in King's Tavern. The Ramada Inn on the river bluff offers a beautiful view and good luncheon buffet.

Plans are underway to restore the illustrious Eola Hotel. There are many motels/hotels. Overnight accommodations are also available in such historic homes as Dixie, Texada, The Burn, Monmouth, Linden, and Elgin Plantation. For information and reservations contact The Room Committee, P.O. Box 347, Natchez, 39120, (601) 446-6631.

OXFORD

80 miles south on I-55 and Hwy. 6. Life here centers around the University of Mississippi which opened its doors in 1848. The only building then was the Lyceum, today administrative offices. The town was incorporated in 1837, but the courthouse and much of the square were burned by Union forces in 1864.

William Faulkner, chronicler/creator of Yoknapatawpha County and recipient of the Nobel Prize in 1949 and the Pulitzer Prize for fiction in 1955 for "A Fable", put Oxford on the literary map. In 1930 he bought Rowan Oak, an ante-bellum house built by Col. Robt. Shegog, and lived there until his death in 1962. The home ((601) 234-3284) is open 10am-noon & 2-4pm M-F, 10am-noon Sat. Closed Sun. Admission, free. Guides answer questions and give tours. The Center for the Study of Southern Culture ((601) 232-5993) operates a reading room filled with Faulkner memorabilia in Barnard Observatory. Open 8am-5pm M-F. Each Aug the center sponsors a week-long public Faulkner conference.

Faulkner and L.Q.C. Lamar, lawyer, congressman, Secretary of the Interior under Pres. Cleveland, and U.S. Supreme Court Justice from 1888 to 1893, are buried beneath the cedars and large magnolia in St. Peter's Cemetery. Lamar's cottage-style circa 1856 house and Ammadelle, an Italianate house used for scenes in "Home from the Hills" starring Robert Mitchum, are often included in the mid-Apr. pilgrimage.

Two other spots to visit: St. Peter's Episcopal Church, founded 1851, located at the corner of Jackson and South 9th Str. (Faulkner attended services here) and University Museum on University Ave., open 10am-4pm Tu-Sat, 1-4pm Sun. (It houses a little bit of everything — Theora Hamblett paintings to costumed fleas.)

The Gumbo Co. on the square does justice to its name and also offers other Louisiana fare. Right off the square is The Gin, a nightclub in a converted cotton gin, and The Warehouse for hamburgers and beer. There are several good motels or you can spend the night on campus in one of Alumni House's 50 rooms ((601) 234-2331).

PHILADELPHIA

About 190 miles southeast of Memphis on Hwys. 16, 15, 19. State office election years are busiest, but each year, for a week at the end of July or first of Aug., about 12,000 people, including politicos from across the state, flock to the Neshoba County Fair. The fair has been a forum for

Mississippi politicians since it began in 1889. All U.S. senators and congressmen since the days of H. D. Money, and all Mississippi governors since A. J. McLaurin (1896-1900), have spoken here. For in-between-speech-time, there are exhibits, carnival rides and games, harness racing, band concerts, a beauty contest, flea market, art show, cakewalk, dances, and lots of visiting among friends. About 500 private cabins are on the fairgrounds.

Also near Philadelphia is a reservation where the Choctaw Indians have reorganized their tribal government. Their ancestors met near here in 1830 and, under coercion, accepted the Treaty of Dancing Rabbit Creek making their land holdings, about one quarter of the state, part of the U.S. The treaty dissolved the Choctaw tribal government and forced 19,000 Choctaws to move to Indian territory in Oklahoma. It was agreed that Indians who wanted to stay in Mississippi would be given state citizenship and a parcel of farmland. Those who left made the infamous five month journey over the "Trail of Tears". About 1,200 Indians chose to remain. White settlers forced their retreat to this swampy area of east-central Mississippi.

RESERVOIR LAKES

These lakes were "engineer made" in the 1940s as part of the effort to control flooding. They are wildlife refuges and no hunting is permitted. Rates and regulations are standard throughout Mississippi parks.

Cabin rates range from $20-$30 based on style and accommodations. They may be reserved in advance. A $15 deposit is required for 2-7 nights, $30 for 8-14 nights. During in-season, May to mid-Sept, the minimum stay is three nights and the maximum two weeks. During off-season, mid-Sept to Apr., the cabins may be rented for a minimum of two nights and a maximum of one month. Check-in time is 3pm; check-out, 11am. Cabins are designed for four people and are furnished and equipped for housekeeping.

Group camps are rented to a minimum of 25 people for one night and three meals during off-season; to a minimum of 40 people for two nights and six meals during in-season. A night's lodging is $3.25. Each meal is $3.25.

Campground rates are: primitive/$3.50, with electrical hook-ups/$6, with electrical, water, and sewerage hook-ups/$6.50, senior citizens/$4.

Boats are rented with life preservers. Rates: fishing boats $5/day or $3.50/½ day, paddle boats $3/hour, sail boats $5/hour or $15/day, and canoes $3/hour or $12/day. Boat launching is $3/day or $50/season.

Lake swimming rates, adults/$1 and children/50¢. Pool swimming, adults/$1.25, children/75¢. Groups may rent swimming areas after hours, first hour/$50, each additional hour/$25.

Roller skates rent for $1.50 per person. Skating reservations are possible for groups.

Miniature golf, 75¢ per person per game.

Tennis courts 1½ hours for $2.

Bicycle rental, for single bikes/$2 an hour, for tandem bikes/$2.50 an hour or $10 a day.

Groups may arrange to rent picnic, lodge, and meeting space.

ARKABUTLA LAKE - 40 miles south on I-55, west of Hernando on Hwy. 304, in Arkabutla State Park, P.O. Box 24, Arkabutla, 38602, (601) 562-4385. It's muddy, but marvelous for fishing. A lot of Memphis' sailors can be found here. There are 138 camping sites with facilities and a primitive camp.

SARDIS LAKE - 50 miles south on I-55, east of Sardis on Hwy. 315, in John Kyle State Park, P.O. Box 115, Sardis, 38666, (601) 487-1345. Probably the most popular of the four lakes, Sardis has excellent fishing and a sandy shore. The park has a lodge with two large rooms for meetings, catering service for private parties, a swimming pool, four lighted tennis courts, a recreation building, fishing boats, group camp facilities for 128 persons, 200 camping pads, ten duplex cabins (five with and five without fireplaces). The Panola Pilgrimage each spring is raising money to restore the Heflin House, circa 1858, in nearby Sardis.

ENID LAKE - 72 miles south on I-55: Yocona Ridge State Park, Rt. 1, Oakland, 38948, (601) 623-7356. Excellent crappie fishing and a comfortable visitors center with fireplace, veranda, and catfish restaurant (closed M) are the highlights here. The park has four modern duplex chalet style cabins, 250 camping pads, and fishing boats for rent.

GRENADA LAKE - 102 miles south on I-55, east of Grenada on Hwy. 8; Hugh White State Park, Grenada, 38901, (601) 226-4934. There are four motel rooms in the park headquarters, 20 brick cottages, 200 camping pads, a marina, and the Lake Shore Lodge Restaurant open 4-10pm Tu-Sun (good food, reasonable prices, BYOB). The lake is good for water sports and fishing. You might want to try Guy's Fish House, a family all-u-can-eat catfish restaurant, 30 miles away in Vaiden.

TUPELO

103 miles southeast of Memphis on Hwy. 78. Elvis Presley's* birthplace. The white wood two-room shotgun house Elvis was born in has been turned into a museum, open 10am-5pm M-Sat, 2-5pm Sun. Admission, 50¢. An Elvis memorial chapel, open the same hours, was designed by Leroy McCarty and built in 1979.

Hungry? Try Johnnie's Drive-In on E. Main Str. near the Elvis museum and chapel for good lean barbecue or Finney's Sandwiches and Sodas on W. Main Str. For steaks try Gloster 205 or Jefferson Place. For Greek dishes and pizza, Vanelli's Pizzeria, 712 S. Gloster.

TENNESSEE

COVINGTON, HENNING, DURHAMVILLE, and RIPLEY
35-50 miles north of Memphis.

Covington is 35 miles north of Memphis on U.S. 51. Tennessee Gins, Inc. ((901) 476-7842), built here in 1973 and one of the three largest automated gins in the U.S., begins ginning in mid-Sept and continues through Nov. Visitors are welcome, but no groups and no tours. Covington is also noted for a walking horse show in June, sky diving competition in May, and barbecue festival in Aug. For information contact the Covington Chamber of Commerce (901) 476-9727.

Ten miles to the north on Hwy. 87, just off 51, is the tiny town of Henning, famous as the birthplace of Alex Haley, author of *Roots*. You can drive by the graveyard where Chicken George was buried, the old CME Church, and the Haley home. No motels, but Ripley and Covington offer several.

A few miles to the east of Henning is Durhamville. Durhamville Methodist Church was built before 1847 and is still in use. Except for its four front columns, the church is typical of the frame clapboard construction of its time.

Six miles north on U.S. 51 is Ripley. Several manufacturers are here; it's fun to shop in the outlet stores. One of the best is Ance K, manufacturer of high quality children's clothes.

DUDE RANCHES
Spring Creek Dude Ranch, north of Grand Junction on Hwy. 18, is a 2,000-acre ranch with Sat night entertainment, an animal breeding farm, rental housing, and limited campsites. Features horseback riding, cookouts, and hayrides. For information phone (901) 527-5421 or 764-2921.

Loretta Lynn's Dude Ranch, on Hwy. 46 in Hurricane Mills, off I-40 near Dickson, is a 3,500-acre working ranch. Hurricane Creek Mill which operated 1896-1930 as a gristmill now houses the Loretta Lynn Museum. The ranch has a general store, swimming pool, children's petting zoo, hiking trails, country music, square dancing, horseback riding, and hayrides. For information write or phone (615) 296-7700.

JACKSON
70 miles northeast of Memphis on I-40. Tennessee's appellate courts, including the state Supreme Court, meet in the courthouse here to adjudicate matters arising in the western part of the state.

Jackson was home of the legendary railroad/folk hero Casey Jones*. He is buried in Mt. Calvary Cemetery here and his home, Casey Jones Home & Railroad Museum, (901) 668-1222, is the focal point of a commercial development, Casey Jones Village, Hwy. 45 Bypass & I-40. Open 9am-5pm M-Sat, 1-5pm Sun. Ages 13+/$2, 6-12/$1, under 6/free. The Carl Perkins* Museum, in this same development, recognizes the town's country/rockabilly music star. Open 9am-9pm M-Sat, 1-5pm Sun. Adults/$1, children 6-12/50¢, under 6/free. The Casey Jones Motel here has several cabooses converted into hotel rooms. The Old Country Store serves BLD 6am-10pm M-Sat.

Highland Park School (901) 424-0149, on Forrest Ave., is a log cabin school museum with original school supplies on display. Open, Th afternoons and selected Sun afternoons. Vann Gardens, a 12-acre private garden on Country Club Lane, is also open to the public and is lovely in early spring. The town's Art Deco bus station is worth a glance.

KNOXVILLE & THE SMOKIES
Northeast corner of the state. If you're wistful for the mountains, Knoxville, Gatlinburg, and the Smokies are about eight hours to the northeast via I-40. On the way you might want to stop in Cookeville, home of the new five-state $5-million Appalachian Crafts Center.

LA GRANGE and GRAND JUNCTION
50 miles east on Hwy. 57. A refined town when Memphis was still malaria infested and swampy, La Grange today is registered as a National Historical Village. Founded in 1819, it boasts ante-bellum homes, gardens, and churches, many of which are opened each Oct for the town's Harvest Festival Tour.

Take Hwy. 18 to Buford Ellington Rd. and nearby Ames Plantation in Grand Junction, the home each Feb for the National Field Trial Championship. The bird dogs draw a world-wide audience of hunters* to the 18,500-acre site and the circa 1847 manor house. Groups may arrange tours year-round. For information phone (901) 764-2124.

If you're hungry, Lewis' in Moscow serves good barbecue and breakfasts. BLD 6am-10pm Tu-Sun.

MASON
About 25 miles northeast of Memphis off I-40 on Hwys. 70 & 79. Some people say Bozo's Cafe ((901) 294-3400) in this small town serves the best barbecue in the world. Open 10:30am-9pm M-Sat. No alcohol or beer sold or allowed on the premises. No credit cards.

SOUTHERN MIDDLE TENNESSEE

CHATTANOOGA - about 380 miles away, via I-40 to Nashville then I-24 to Chattanooga. See Rock City (open 8:30am-7pm daily; adults/ $4.75, children 6-12/$2.75, under 6/free), Cravens House, Point Park, Lookout Mountain (ride the incline), the site of the Battle of

Chickamauga, Confederate and National Cemeteries, ... Chattanooga is the fourth largest city in Tennessee.

Besides its many tourist attractions and beautiful homes, the city boasts two good hotels: the elegant renovated Read House and The Chattanooga Choo-Choo Hilton. The latter has train cars converted to rooms, an indoor swimming pool, tennis courts, and ice skating. It is part of a shopping/restaurant area developed within the old train station. Or you might want to stay in the quaint Chanticleer Lodge on Lookout Mountain.

Hungry? At The Gazebo you can dine in jail cells, in the basement, or by the fireplace in an old courthouse room reassembled here. Or try The Walden Club, The Brass Register, The Green Room at Read House, or any of the restaurants in the Choo-Choo.

For expert kayakers or rafters — the Ocoee River is about an hour's drive east of Chattanooga. Six rafting companies offer guided trips.

LYNCHBURG - Hwys. 50 & 55 between Tullahoma and Fayetteville. Home of the world famous Jack Daniel Distillery (NRHP), producer of Tennessee "sippin" whiskey since 1866. Free guided tours start from Bethel House (8am-3:30pm daily). In the town proper, see the 1884 courthouse, old jail, Farmer's Bank, and general store. The Lynchburg Ladies' Handiwork Store sells handmade quilts and afghans. Try lunch at the marble soda fountain in the Lynchburg Drug Store or a "midday dinner" at Salmon Hotel. Fayetteville and Shelbyville are the nearest places for hotel/motel rooms.

MONTEAGLE - about 70 miles northwest of Chattanooga on Hwy. 64. One of only four chatauquas in existence in the U.S. today, Monteagle Sunday School Assembly first held its summer religious and cultural programs in 1883. People stayed in tents then, but today privately owned rustic rambling houses cover the hilly assembly grounds, about 70 miles northwest of Chattanooga on Hwy. 64. Daily programs during the season, late June-mid Aug, run the gamut from bridge lessons, lectures on Saul Bellow, nightly movies, swimming, and hiking to twilight prayers. For information on the program or house rental, contact The Assembly, Monteagle, 37356, (615) 924-2286. About eight miles west on Hwy. 64 is Sewanee, home of the University of the South, a Gothic-style residential college. Each summer in early Aug, Sewanee and Monteagle sponsor an arts and crafts fair.

NASHVILLE
Visit the state's capital, a four hour drive northeast on I-40. There's the Grand Ole Opry and Opryland, the Ryman Auditorium, Parthenon, historic homes, colleges, Cheekwood and Tennessee State Museums, and the Iroquois Steeplechase each May.

Before the Revolutionary War, settlers ventured into Tennessee and by 1780 there were log cabins in the middle Tennessee/Nashville area. As prosperity came, settlers emulated east coast settlements and built such homes as Andrew Jackson's Hermitage (NRHP) circa 1831. Other period buildings include: Belmont Mansion circa 1850 (Belmont Blvd. (615) 383-7001; open 10am-2:30pm F & Sat; adults/$1.50, students 5-12/50¢, under 5/free), Belle Meade Mansion circa 1853 (US 70S, (615) 352-7350; open 9am-5pm M-Sat, 1-5pm Sun; adults/$2.50, students 13-18/$2.00, children 6-12/$1, under 6 with parent/free), and William Strickland's State Capitol (NRHP) circa 1845 (Charlotte Ave. in downtown Nashville; open 8am-4:30pm M-F, tours 9am-4pm M-F, 9:30am-4pm Sat & Sun; free).

Memphians might be particularly interested in the homes of Memphis' founders: Andrew Jackson's Hermitage (NRHP) (12 miles east of Nashville off US 70N; open 8am-6pm daily June 1 -Labor Day, 9am-5pm daily Sept-May; adults/$2.50, children 6-13/75¢, under 6/free), John Overton's Travelers Rest (six miles south of Nashville off Hwy. 31; open 9am-4pm M-Sat, 1-4pm Sun; adults/$1, children 12-18/50¢, under 12/25¢), and Gen. James Winchester's Cragfont (off Hwy. 25, five miles east of Gallatin; open 10am-5pm Tu-Sat, 1-6pm Sun, Apr. 15-Nov 1; adults/$1.50, children 12-18/75¢, under 12/25¢).

J. Frazer Smith in his book *White Pillars* mentions many other middle Tennessee sites for architecture buffs including homes in Lebanon, Clarksville, Gallatin, Hendersonville, Franklin, Springhill, Columbia, Murfreesboro, and Pulaski.

The first floor of Tennessee's executive mansion, Far Hills (882 S. Curtiswood Lane, (615) 383-5401), is open free to the public 9-11am Tu & Th. Reservations are required for groups of five or more. No groups under 12 years of age allowed. The house was built between 1929 and 1931 by Mr. and Mrs. W. Ridley Wills and was bought by the state in 1949. The home is furnished with antiques and works of art by Tennesseans. The dining room chair seats were needlepointed by Memphis volunteers.

For music lovers the Grand Ole Opry ((615) 889-3060) and Opryland are a must. Performances, summer: 3, 6:30, & 9:30pm F & Sat, 2pm Sun; fall and spring: 7:30pm F, 3, 6:30 & 9:30pm Sat; winter: 7:30pm F, 6:30 & 9:30pm Sat. Reserved tickets ($7/evening, $5/matinees) should be ordered six months in advance from Grand Ole Opry Tickets, 2808 Opryland Dr, 37214. General admission tickets ($6/evening, $4/matinees) go on sale Tu for the following weekend. They cannot be ordered by mail. The Grand Ole Opry offers daily Nashville tours, special tours, and guides. For information write or call Grand Ole Opry Tours, 2810 Opryland Dr, Nashville 37214, (615) 889-9490.

Country music can also be heard at many local bars and nightspots, among them, Wind in the Willows, 2205 State Str. 320-9154, and

Bluegrass Inn, 1914 Broadway, 320-0624. One of the best spots for progressive country and pop is the Exit-In, 2208 Elliston Place, 327-2784.

The city offers a wide selection of hotel/motels. One of the newest and nicest is the downtown Hyatt Regency across from the Capitol. Also downtown is the renovated Hermitage Hotel. If you're going to a Vanderbilt basketball game or seminar, the Holiday Inn-Vanderbilt is near the campus. Or you might want to stay at Opryland in the Opryland Hotel or Holiday Inn.

Hungry? There's an increasingly wide choice: The Gerst House (228 Woodland St, 256-9760) offers authentic German food; Julian's (2412 W. End Ave., 327-2412) and Arthur's (Belle Meade Shopping Center, W. End Ave., 383-8841) are both good French restaurants open only for dinner M-Sat; Jimmy Kelly's (4310 Harding Rd., 292-3090) serves excellent steaks in a converted house; Satsuma (417 Union Str., 256-5211) sadly open only for lunch, serves marvelous fresh breads and home cooked specials; Loveless Motel (south of town on Hwy. 100, 646-9700) offers fried chicken and homemade blackberry jam.

The Nashville Area Chamber of Commerce, 161 N. 4th Ave., 37219, (615) 259-3900, puts out a yearly magazine, "Visitor's Guide", available for $2 per copy from Plus Media, 230 Great Circle Rd., 37228, (615) 259-4600.

TENNESSEE STATE PARKS

There are many within middle and western Tennessee offering relatively inexpensive camping facilities and often cabin or lodge facilities. Rates and regulations are standard throughout the state parks.

Inn rates are: single (1 person) $25, double (2 persons) $32, and suites $50-$75. Charge of $5 for each additional person. Children under 12 free when accompanied by a parent. Baby cribs, free. Check out time, 1pm. No pets allowed.

Cabin rates vary according to architectural style and accommodations provided. They are graded AAA, AA, and A with respective rates of $40, $30 and $20. AAA and AA cabins are completely equipped including linens and cooking and eating utensils. Cabins classified A may not have kitchen facilities, but all other accommodations are provided. Cabins must be reserved for a minimum of two nights and from June through Aug for a minimum of a week (M-M). They're popular so make your plans well ahead.

Group camps rent on a weekly basis June-Aug and as short-term camps during the spring and fall. The camps charge $1 per person per day except Meeman-Shelby which charges $2 per person per day.

Campground rates are $4-$6 depending upon site characteristics. Primitive camping, 50¢ per person. Campsites, half-price for senior citizens. No advance reservations accepted. Maximum stay, two weeks. One car permitted per family at a campsite.

Bike rentals, $1.25 per hour.

Personally owned boats permitted only on large lakes. Boat rental rates: non-powered boats, $2/hour; fishing boats with trolling motors, $6/½ day, $10/day; fishing boats with outboard motors, $18/day.

In addition to state fishing licenses, park permits are required for fishing on park-owned and operated lakes. Fee, $1 for everyone over 16. Senior citizens free. TVA and U.S. Army Corps of Engineers lakes offer free fishing.

Rates at lifeguarded lakes and swimming beaches are $1/person and at pools $1.25/person.

Golf courses at state resort parks charge $6/18-holes, $3/9 holes. T. O. Fuller charges $5/18 holes, $2.50/9 holes. Golf carts are $4.50/9 holes and there is a daily $1.50 charge for privately owned golf carts. Those who play often may want to purchase an annual statewide permit for $200, senior citizens/$100. Senior citizens may play free on non-holiday M.

For a current rate schedule or more information contact the Tn. Dept. of Conservation, Division of State Parks, 2611 West End Ave, Nashville, 37203, (615) 741-3251.

The parks are great for a vacation and a good place to stay while seeing the rest of the state.

CHICKASAW STATE PARK · Hwy. 100, Henderson, 38340, (901) 989-5141. 11,215 acres; paths for nature buffs; two lakes with facilities for swimming, boating, fishing; picnicking; recreation lodge; 100-seat restaurant; 12 air conditioned cabins ($20-25); 75 camping sites; group camp.

DAVID CROCKETT STATE PARK · U.S. 64, Lawrenceburg, 38464, (615) 762-9408. Located on banks of Shoal Creek where Crockett operated a powder mill, grist mill, and distillery. Crockett lived in nearby Lawrenceburg from 1817 to 1822 while he served in the Tennessee legislature. Olympic swimming pool; facilities for fishing, boating, picnicking; lighted tennis courts; play areas; bike rentals; primitive scout camping area and 100 tent and trailer sites; 200-seat year-round restaurant.

FORT PILLOW STATE PARK · Hwy. 87, P.O. Box 73, Henning, 38041, (901) 738-5466. The French built a temporary stronghold, Fort Prudhomme, here in 1682. Later the Confederate army chose the site as a prime offensive location, built a fort, and named it after Gen. Gideon J. Pillow. Remains of the earthworks are still present. A 10-mile historic hiking trail, primitive campsites, and a lake for fishing and boating are in the 1,646-acre park.

Visit **MEEMAN-SHELBY FOREST STATE PARK*** or **T. O. FULLER
STATE PARK*** right here in our own backyard.

MONTGOMERY BELL STATE PARK - U.S. 70, P.O. Box 684, Burns,
37029, (615) 797-3101. Picnic areas; horseback riding; swimming; fishing; boating; hiking trails; rolling hills; modern cabins ($25); an inn with
rooms ($15+); 110 camping sites; a group camp; restaurant. Of special
historic note is Laurel Furnace, the iron manufacturing operation of
Montgomery Bell who is credited with forging the cannon balls used by
Andrew Jackson at the Battle of New Orleans. The park was also the
birthplace of Cumberland Presbyterian Church.

NATCHEZ TRACE STATE PARK & FOREST - Off I-40, Wildersville,
38388, (901) 968-3742. This 43,000-acre park, named for the famed
Nashville to Natchez, Miss. trail, is the largest of Tennessee's state parks.
The Natchez Trace, probably established by Indians 8,000 years ago,
served as a major route during the 18th and 19th centuries as the South
was settled. Today it is under the jurisdiction of the National Park Service, and both Tennessee and Mississippi have state parks along it. This
Tennessee park lies halfway between Memphis and Nashville and includes four lakes, a swimming beach, facilities for fishing and boating,
picnicking sites, playgrounds, a grocery store, and a recreation building.
There is a 20-unit modern resort inn ($14+) and restaurant complex,
cabins ($22), a group lodge, and camping areas.

NATHAN BEDFORD FORREST STATE PARK - Off U.S. 70, Eva,
38333, (901) 584-6356. Eight miles east of Camden on the shores of
Kentucky Lake, this park marks the site where in 1864 Gen. Forrest's*
cavalry corps made a stand against the Union navy. There is an overlook
on Pilot Knob, once the Confederate observation post. Across the lake is
the site of the Battle of Johnsonville where Forrest destroyed the Union
supply depot. Many trenches and redoubts can be seen. Park facilities include picnic areas with shelters, 50 camping sites, hiking trails, pavilion,
and playground.

PARIS LANDING STATE RESORT PARK - U.S. 79, Buchanan,
38222, (901) 642-4311. This modern park is located on 158,300-acre
Kentucky Lake. It has a full-service marina, an 18-hole golf course and
pro shop, two swimming pools, picnic areas, hiking trails, camp store,
lighted tennis courts, outdoor game area, 80 campsites, and a 100-room
modern inn and dining room complex. The inn is open for duck hunters
in the winter.

PICKWICK LANDING STATE RESORT PARK and SHILOH - 100
miles east of Memphis on Hwy. 57, Pickwick Dam, 38365, (901)

689-3135. Recently acquired from TVA, this lakeside park includes an ultra-modern resort inn with restaurant, swimming pool overlooking the lake, and tennis courts. There are modern cabins, a full-service marina with dry boat storage, fishing, boating, 50 tent and trailer campsites, playgrounds, picnic areas, a swimming beach, boat launching area, and an 18-hole golf course. Be sure to see the 7,700-foot long hydro-electric dam. If you're in a boat you may want to go through the locks for a first hand view.

Dining out? Try Hammer's Homestead, a converted house serving good steaks, Bill Bellis' Botel across the dam for catfish, or the Catfish Hotel near Shiloh for marvelous catfish, hush puppies, onion rings, and chicken.

History buffs will want to make a 15 mile side trip to Shiloh National Military Park on Hwy. 22, site of one of the bloodiest battles of the Civil War. Some historians say it was here the South lost its chance to win the war. Gen. Albert S. Johnson saw that the Union army was about to attack Corinth and take control of the junction of two major Southern rails, the east-west Memphis & Charleston and the north-south Mobile & Ohio. On Apr. 6, 1862, Gen Johnson led the Confederate army in a preventive attack on the Union forces of Gen. U.S. Grant. About 100,000 men fought here with 23,741 casualties, about 13,000 Union and about 11,000 Confederate. The Union army eventually captured the rails and Corinth and successfully cut off the western part of the Confederacy. The 3,772-acre park has a visitor center with Civil War relics and a 20 minute filmed explanation of the battle.

REELFOOT LAKE STATE RESORT PARK · Hwy. 21, Tiptonville, 38079, (901) 253-7756. The park is on Reelfoot Lake, created by the New Madrid earthquakes of 1811-12. The lake is 18 miles long, 2½ miles wide, and a mysterious world of cypress trees and giant lily pads. The fishing is fantastic. Boats specially designed for the shallow water and lily pads may be rented for $6, $8, or $10 per day. Many bald eagles, the national emblem, winter here and scenic eagle and waterfowl boat tours (long and short) are operated daily Apr-Oct. A 3½ hr. boat excursion leaves from the Ellington Hall Museum at 9am daily. Rates, adults/$3, children under 12/$2. A $1 per person short cruise is also available. An ultra-modern resort inn and restaurant are built out over the lake. There are also cabins, a recreation hall, 75 camping sites, a camp store, and auditorium. Nearby is an all-weather 3,500-foot lighted air strip with intercom attendant.

Side trips might include a detour via Hwy. 105 to Rutherford and the Davy Crockett* House. The two-room reconstructed log cabin was the last home of the famous Tennessee humorist, bear hunter, hero of the Creek Indian War (1813-14), state legislator, U.S. Congressman for three terms, and martyr in the cause of Texas independence. Crockett was born near the town of Limestone in east Tennessee in 1786, moved to the Rutherford Fork of the Obion River in west Tennessee in 1823, and left Tennessee for Texas in 1835. The cabin, built on the Rutherford school grounds, contains furniture, tools, and utensils from the early 19thc. Open, 10am-5pm Tu-Sun, June-Aug. Adults/25¢, children/10¢.

Calendar of Annual Events

Memphis Cotton Carnival Assn.

1946 Cotton Carnival parade, Queen Phoebe Cook (Mrs. John Lowber Welsh, Jr.), King R. Vance Norfleet.

Alan Copeland

B. B. King performing at the Beale Street Music Festival in 1978. Memphis-in-May.

JANUARY

It's cold in January, and everyone seems to be staying inside, taking it easy and recuperating from the Christmas season.

College basketball* is packing the gymnasiums, and the rinks at Libertyland* and the Mall of Memphis* are offering everyone a chance to **ice skate***.

Dates to Remember: Jan 1/New Year's Day, Jan 15/Tributes to Dr. Martin Luther King, Jr.

FEBRUARY

Black History is celebrated this month with special exhibits and programs around the city. The main library, 1850 Peabody, 528-2952, can give you information on what's happening.

Grace St. Luke's Episcopal Church, 1720 Peabody, 272-7425, sponsors a **Festival of Arts in Religion.**

The Al Chymia **Shrine Circus, Holiday on Ice,** and **"Jazz Week"** at Memphis State University offer entertainment to all.

This month is a heyday for sports enthusiasts. The **U.S. National Indoor Tennis* Championships** brings all-star professionals to the Racquet Club. The **National Field Trials** are held for 10 days at Ames Plantation in Grand Junction, Tn.* The **Mid-South Sport, Boat, Travel & Vacation Show** is at the Coliseum. **College basketball*** continues its season, **Mid-South Pro Boxing*** matches are at Cook Convention Center, and a **Golden Gloves Competition** is at the Memphis & Shelby County Boxing Arena at the Fairgrounds. The Park Commission's amateur **adult basketball tournaments** are also this month.

Dates to Remember: Feb 12/Abraham Lincoln's birthday, 3rd M/George Washington's birthday celebration, Ash Wednesday, Chinese New Year, Feb 14/St. Valentine's Day.

MARCH

It's spring and all the house and garden tours, bazaars and auctions begin. St. George's Day School, (754-5141) sponsors its annual **Home Tour & Country Store. Pilgrimage tours** get underway in Mississippi. The **Baron Hirsch Food Bazaar,** the **Humane Society Art Auction,** the **Playhouse-On-The-Square*** **Original Art Auction,** and the **Jr. Mid-South Exhibition** at Brooks Memorial Art Gallery* all combine to make this a busy month.

The **Miss Memphis Pageant**, a preliminary to Miss Tennessee and Miss America, is held at the Orpheum.

Many of the city's Irish and non-Irish join in the **Irish Eyes of Memphis Pub Crawl and Walking Parade** on St. Patrick's Day.

Spring cleaning might get you in the mood for the **Memphis Antique Show and Sale** which brings 34 prestigious antique dealers and speakers here to benefit the Madonna Circle's charities. Or perhaps you're more in the mood for fresh new ideas. A $5 ticket allows you to attend Southwestern At Memphis'* provocative symposium, **Dilemma.** Nationally recognized speakers participate. Memphis State University* sponsors a **New Music Festival.** Free concerts in MSU's Harris Auditorium show 20thc. trends.

It's time to get outdoors. **Libertyland*** opens for weekends; MSU holds their **Invitational Outdoor Track Meet; college baseball*** begins its season.

Indoors **college basketball*** and **Mid-South Pro Boxing*** continue. The Park Commission* sponsored **youth basketball tournaments** are this month.

Dates to Remember: Mar 17/St. Patrick's Day, Easter see: April.

APRIL

Easter usually falls in this month, and most churches have special services to celebrate. The Pink Palace* celebrates Easter with a wildflower show, egg hunt, puppet show, animal display, and games on the grounds. Many clubs, community centers, and churches hold Easter egg hunts, and some neighborhoods have their own Easter parades.

Festivals, house tours, and other charitable fund-raisers continue. **Memphis Heritage*** holds its annual **Picnic** on the grounds of the National Ornamental Metal Museum*. Annunciation Greek Orthodox Church, 573 Highland, holds its **Annual Greek Bazaar,** a foodfest of Hellenic specialties. **WEVL**, a community radio station, holds a **Street Festival** on Mid-America Mall. Opera Memphis* holds its elegant **Opera Ball.** Memphis State University* plans special events and shows its campus to the city on **Community Day.** The Whitehaven Community Assn. sponsors the **Whitehaven* Spring Festival.** Harding Academy produces its **Annual International Goodwill Pageant**, and Brooks Art Gallery* begins its **Fun for the Family Days** with workshops, films, clowns, and play. And don't fail to wander through the fabulous **spring-**

time gardens at Dixon Gallery and Gardens* and Memphis Botanical Garden and Goldsmith Civic Garden Center*.

Chicks begin their professional baseball* schedule. Organized **runs** and **college tennis*** also start. The River City Sailing* Assn. holds its **April Fool's Regatta** at Enid Lake*, Miss. **The National Inter-Collegiate Racquetball* Tournament** is held at the Racquet Club. **Mid-South Boxing***, and **college baseball*** continue. Park Commission* sponsored **adult softball begins.**

Dates to Remember: Palm Sunday, Good Friday, Easter Sunday, last Sun night/Daylight Savings Time goes into effect (spring forward, fall back; you'll lose an hour's sleep.).

MAY

The whole month is one big celebration — **Memphis in May** — an extravaganza of carnivals and events built around Memphis' music, visual and performing arts, sports, barbecue, and river. Each year a foreign country is honored. Special events fill each week. For information contact Memphis in May International Festival, Commerce Title Bldg., 12 S. Main, Suite 1224, 38103, 525-4611.

An **International Festival,** the first weekend, salutes the year's honored country. An art exchange, musical entertainment, ethnic foods, and **10-Kilometer and 2-Mile Fun Runs** are all part.

Pork fanciers and chefs come from far and near for the **International Barbecue Contest** the second weekend of May. There's open air cooking, the **Annual Fiddlers Convention,** and rock music in Tom Lee Park*.

The **Beale Street* Music Festival** pays tribute to the birthplace of the blues*. Local, national, and international stars come to Beale Street and Handy Park to sing, strut, and pay homage.

Hot air balloon races fill the city's eastern skies during **Balloonfest,** the third weekend of the month at Shelby Farms Equestrian Center.

The **Fine Arts Festival & Sunset Symphony** in Tom Lee Park* is Memphis in May's grand finale. The city's performing arts* groups give demonstrations, and the Memphis Symphony Orchestra* offers a free pops concert under the stars on the bank of the Mississippi.

Other Memphis in May events include: the **Kiwanis Wolf River Street Fair,** arts, crafts, food, music and games, operated by the Boys Club on Mid-America Mall; Southwestern's **Renaissance Festival** where jugglers, jousters, gypsies and knights cavort and perform; the **Overton Park Funfest,** a day of games; a **Country Fair on the Square** in Collierville; the **May Home Tour** sponsored by the Memphis Chapter of the Assn. for Preservation of Tennessee Antiquities.

Cotton Carnival is usually celebrated the last week in May with parades, krewe events, parties, a fair, air show, music festival, fireworks,.... The carnival dates back to the early 1800s when it was called the Mystic Society of Memphi. In 1872 it became the Memphis Mardi Gras. Thugs and bandits took advantage of the masked balls, and in 1881 the celebration was discontinued. As an attempt to stimulate the cotton industry* during the depression years, the festivities were resumed in 1931 under the name Memphis Cotton Carnival. The festival has been an annual occurrence since then. For information contact the Memphis Cotton Carnival Assn., 1060 Early Maxwell Blvd., 278-0243.

And if that weren't enough activities to fill a year, Old Engine 4501 comes out of retirement for the annual **Sentimental Journey*** round-trip to Corinth, Miss. and the **Metropolitan Opera*** plans its annual visit to Memphis — all in May.

May 1 is Law Day and each year the Shelby County Bar Assn. sponsors **Law Week.** Lawyers give tours of the Justice Center, including the courthouse* (527-3573 for reservations), and man a Phon-A-Thon to answer the public's legal questions. Tours of the Law Center and Correctional Facilities at the Millington Naval Air Station* are also offered. U.S. Naturalization ceremonies are held in the Auditorium.

Lots is going on in the sports area too. A free **annual rugby* tournament** sponsored by Jack Daniels at the Overton Park Soccer Field draws teams from as far away as Florida. MSU hosts the **AIAW Region 11 Tennis* Tournament,** and the **Ely & Walker/Kodel Tennis Tournament** is played at the Racquet Club. Professional and college **baseball*** continue. Park Commission* sponsored **youth baseball** and **softball** start and city **tennis* tournaments** begin.

Dates to Remember: May 1/Law Day, 2nd Sun/Mother's Day, 3rd Sat/ Armed Forces Day, last M/Memorial Day.

JUNE

School is out — get your free copy of "Summer Survival Kit" from the library. It's a must! It describes what's going on in Memphis for kids and adults. The dates, times, ages included, cost, ... for everything from day camps to concerts.

The Memphis Park Commission* and Shelby County Conservation Board* gear up for another full summer. Day camps are open, swimming pools are filled, playgrounds are busy, and tennis lessons are underway. Adults and children are flexing unused winter muscles.

The Library* has a full schedule of films*, reading programs, and story hours for children.

🐦 The **Red Balloon Players*** are in the parks, and **Children's Theatre*** is performing. **Ringling Bros. & Barnum & Bailey Circus** is coming to the Coliseum, and **Libertyland*** opens for the summer on a daily basis.

🐦 Most summertime* activities are for the whole family and the free outdoor **Arts in the Park** concerts are certainly no exception. Memphis Little Symphony offers an annual **Symphony in the Park** in Court Square, and the Blues Foundation sponsors daily **Blues Concerts** in Handy Park. The annual **Beale Street Landing Antique Show & Oyster Bar** is also this month.

June is a major month sportswise in Memphis. The **Danny Thomas Memphis Golf* Classic** brings the top PGA players to Colonial Country Club for a tournament benefitting St. Jude Children's Research Hospital*.

The **Germantown Charity Horse* Show** draws riders from around the country to the Germantown Horse Show Arena.

🐦 The dogs are running at **Southland Greyhound Park***, and the **Chicks*** are playing baseball. The **Mid-South Junior Fishing Rodeo** is scheduled for children in Audubon Park.

Dates to Remember: June 14/Flag Day, 3rd Sun/Father's Day.

JULY

All the summertime* activities in June continue, plus a few additions. The **Pink Palace*** begins **summer courses** for ages 4+. The 🐦 **Downtown Dream Machine*** brings outdoor theatre to Confederate Park, and **Otrabanda,** a floating arts festival, docks at the foot of Monroe for two days. **Memphis Zoo* Day** has special activities to benefit the zoo and the Cancer Society. Fireworks displays around town, lots of people eating watermelon, and the annual **4th of July Picnic & Carnival** at St. Peter's Home for Children are part of the Independence Day celebration.

The **Memphis Hunter-Jumper Classic** brings horseback* riders from around the nation to the Shelby County Equestrian Center for four days. Tennis'* future greats are at the Racquet Club as it hosts the **Girls 18 Clay Court National Championships.** The **Chicks*** are playing, the **greyhounds** running, and **pro-boxing*** continues. Park Commission* sponsored **baseball** and **softball tournaments** are underway.

Political buffs, consider a drive to the **Neshoba County Fair** in Philadelphia, Miss.* the end of this month.

Dates to Remember: July 4/Independence Day, July 14/Bastille Day.

AUGUST

Memphis pays homage to Elvis Presley*. The **Memphis Music*** **Festival** at Cook Convention Center includes music, films, entertainment, lectures, and a memorial service for Elvis. Memphis State University sponsors **Salute to Memphis Music,** a look at the city's blues roots and Elvis — free seminars, lectures, films, and concerts. The latter is a must for music* history buffs! While you're in the mood, why not ride out to Graceland*?

Summertime* activities continue. Chucalissa* adds its **Choctaw Pow-Wow,** a day of Indian games and festivities.

Dog racing*, pro-boxing*, and **Chicks' baseball*** continue.

Date to Remember: Aug 16/Elvis' death.

SEPTEMBER

Labor Day starts the month off with a bang. The Schlitz sponsored **Memphis Music Heritage Festival,** held on Mid-America Mall, packs the first weekend this month with continuous music by nationally known and local stars. It's free! Four stages plus concessions for crafts, food, and beer. The **Annual Memphis Boys' Town Labor Day Weekend Carnival,** 7400 Memphis-Arlington Rd., is also this weekend.

The **Mid-South Fair** brings blue grass and country music, livestock, dairy, and food judging, arts and crafts competitions,... to the Fairgrounds* for ten days. There's a rodeo in the Coliseum. Admission to the Fair and Libertyland*, adults/$2.50, children (ages 4-11)/$1, under 4/free; special promotional days such as school and senior citizen days/50¢; to park on grounds/$2. Libertyland sells ride tickets to fair goers for 30¢ a ticket or $3 for a book of 12 tickets. Rides range from one ticket for kiddie rides to five for "super" rides. For Fair information phone 274-8800.

Drive out east for the **Germantown Festival,** a two-day country celebration with carnivals, arts and craft displays, music, food, and flea market sales.

The city's performing arts groups are all gearing up for a new season. Subscribe now. For information on these groups see the **Arts** chapter. Brooks Memorial Art Gallery* brings in a big-name entertainer this month for its annual black-tie-dinner fundraiser, **Brooks 400 Gala.**

Fashion shows abound showing us what we need in our winter wardrobes, and **Double Take,** a four-day sale of "gently worn" men's, women's, and children's clothing is sponsored by the Memphis Section of the National Council of Jewish Women at Cook Convention Center. "Hotty Toddy, Gosh A Mighty! Who ...." Back to school time and old **college football*** rivalries are heating up. It may already be too late to get tickets to some games. **College volleyball*** season begins, **pro-boxing*** continues, and there's **Mid-South Wrestling*** at the Coliseum. You haven't been out to see the **Chicks*** yet? Shame on you!

Dates to Remember: 1st M/Labor Day, Rosh Hashanah, Yom Kippur.

OCTOBER

The weather is usually fantastic this month, and everyone is outside. The **Pink Palace*** leads a **field trip** to Wapanocca National Wildlife Refuge* to observe birds, and the newspapers sponsor a free **Funfest** of new games in Overton Park. The **Octoberfest** livens up Mid-America Mall with outdoor music, food, beer, and crafts.

The **Pink Palace* Crafts Fair** is a highlight this month. It draws nationally recognized artists who demonstrate and sell their wares. There is also food, entertainment, and working exhibits. Admission: tickets in advance, adults/$1.75, children/75¢; tickets at the gate, adults/$2.50, children/$1.

There are two big out-of-town draws this month. The **War Eagle Crafts Festival** draws craftsmen from throughout the region to Eureka Springs, Ark.* for a huge and fascinating fair. Fifty miles east of Memphis, La Grange, Tn.* welcomes visitors for its **Harvest Festival Tour** of 19thc. homes and churches. Tickets, available through Goldsmith's ticket offices.

Start your Christmas shopping early at the crafts fairs and at the library's **Friendly Book Sale.** Subsidium's **Christmas Carousel of Shoppes** portends the coming event, bringing booths from specialty stores around the country to the Hyatt Regency; proceeds benefit Memphis Oral School for the Deaf. St. George's Episcopal Church, 8250 Hwy. 72, sponsors its **Antiques Arcade,** three days of exhibition and sale.

Planning a big night out on the town? One of the city's most fashionable events is the **Memphis Symphony Ball.** Tickets available through the symphony* office. Friends of the Library sponsors its **Dine With the Authors** dinner at the Hyatt Regency. And don't forget to attend a pep rally and **college football*** game. Park Commission* sponsored **adult basketball** begins.

Spooks and goblins appear for **Halloween.** There are puppet shows at the Library, puppet shows, pumpkin carving, horror flicks and a costume contest at the Pink Palace*, and a carving contest on Court Square*. Both the Orpheum* and Lyceum Film Theatre offer scary films*. There are several haunted houses around town for daring visitors, and the community centers* have Halloween parties.

Dates to Remember: 2nd M/Columbus Day, Oct 31/Halloween, last Sun night/Return to Central Standard Time (pick up that hour's sleep you lost in Apr).

NOVEMBER

Christmas bazaars are a great place to shop. Your dollars are doing double duty — a gift for a friend and a gift to charity. St. Patrick's Catholic Church*, the Memphis Humane Society, and Le Bonheur* through the Collierville Twigs are some of the beneficiaries this month. If you're shopping for the unusual—a glider ride for two, "hot tubbing", or a lawyer to change your name—the **ACLU Adventure Auction** at Playhouse-on-the-Square is for you. This is also the month for the Mid-South Arts & Crafts Show/Sale in Cook Convention Center; admission, adults/$2, children/$1.

Lots of dancing and Greek food and wine are part of **Greek Night** sponsored by Annunciation Greek Orthodox Church at the Cook Convention Center.

College football*, college soccer*, pro-boxing*, and **wrestling*** are in action. **College basketball*** and Park Commission* sponsored **youth basketball** start.

Dates to Remember: 1st Tu after 1st M/Election Day, Nov 11/Veterans Day, 4th Th/Thanksgiving Day.

DECEMBER

"'Tis the season…" and jolly it is — filled with Christmas events and shopping.

The **Christmas Parade** and the **city's tree lighting** on Mid-America Mall are signs that the Christmas season is officially here.

Overton Square* is filled with street vendors, pony rides, puppet shows, ice skaters, and costumed carolers, all part of the annual **A Dickens' Christmas.**

Florists decorate the Fontaine House* and baked goods stock the bazaar in the Assn. for Preservation of Tennessee Antiquities' **Home for Christmas.**

The **Magevney* Open House** delights with Christmas decorations, cards and instrumental music of the period.

Twenty-one community organizations decorate twenty-one trees at the Hyatt Regency for **Trees of Christmas**. Ornaments are auctioned.

The "children's only" shop at the Maternal Welfare League's **Children's Christmas House** is a big draw. Adults are excluded from this particular room, and the prices are right. Another marvelous place to do your Christmas shopping is at the **Memphis Academy of Arts* Christmas Bazaar and Sale.**

Memphis Ballet* and Memphis Symphony Orchestra* perform the perennial favorite **"The Nutcracker Suite".** Libertyland* opens specially for the season with ice skating, rides, music and dance shows, and hand-carved miniature village scenes. Theatre Memphis* presents **"A Christmas Carol".** There are special planetarium shows at the Pink Palace* and at Craigmont Planetarium* about the **Star of Bethlehem. Children's Theatre*** is active, and there are numerous **Christmas concerts** and choir performances. The Pink Palace* has a **party for animals** to celebrate the season and a **puppet show** version of **"A Christmas Carol".**

If you're in charge of **decorations** at your house, don't forget the Christmas **workshops** at Goldsmith's Civic Garden Center* and at Dixon Gallery and Gardens*. You'll get some new ideas.

The National Cotton Council **Maid of Cotton Contest** brings beautiful girls to the city from around the country for the finals this month.

The **Liberty Bowl*,** an after season battle between top ranking college football teams at the Coliseum, is a highlight of the sports calendar. **College basketball*** and **pro-boxing*** are active. The **Corporate Tennis Classic** is at Wimbleton Racquet Club.

Merry Christmas! Happy New Year!

Dates to Remember: Dec 3/Hanukkah, Dec 25/Christmas, Dec 31/New Year's Eve.

CALENDARS

Many organizations print excellent calendars. Check these for more specific information:

Convention and Visitors Bureau of Memphis* Calendar - printed in three-month segments. 12 S. Main, Suite 107, 38103, 526-1919.

Memphis Magazine* Calendar - included in the monthly magazine. Subscription, $15 per year. Towery Publishing Co., 1535 E. Brooks Rd., P.O. Box 16566, 38116, 345-8000.

The Commercial Appeal* Calendars - Daily and Friday Living Section weekly calendars. 25¢ daily, 75¢ Sun. 495 Union. 529-2372.

The Memphis Press-Scimitar* Calendar - Thursday City-Area Section club and neighborhood events calendar. 25¢ daily. 495 Union. 529-2522.

Library Information Center (LINC*) Calendar - Two-year calendar of community events and benefits to help groups schedule without conflicts. Compiled in conjunction with the Junior League of Memphis, Inc. 528-2999.

Kaleidoscope - monthly calendar of what's happening at city libraries. Memphis/Shelby County Public Library and Information Center*. Pick up a free copy at any branch.

Sharing - monthly newsletter of social service information. Subscription, $5 per year. Human Services CO-OP, 011 Richardson Towers, Memphis State University, 38152, 454-2021.

Key Magazine - commercial calendar available free in motels and hotels around the city. Office, 3373 Poplar. 458-3912.

Several art groups, museums, and the botanical gardens have **newsletters** describing their programs and special events. These are mailed to "support group" members. Membership fees are reasonable, tax deductible, and a good way to support what you like in your community. See individual listings.

INDEX

The Memphis Guide
Redbird Press
P.O. Box 11441
Memphis, Tn. 38111

Please send _____ copies of *The Memphis Guide* at $7.95 per copy (postage & handling included) to:

Name _____

Address _____

City_____ State_____ Zip_____

Enclosed is _____ in check or money order to cover cost.
Please gift wrap _____.
For deliveries in Tennessee add 42¢ sales tax.

The Memphis Guide
Redbird Press
P.O. Box 11441
Memphis, Tn. 38111

Please send _____ copies of *The Memphis Guide* at $7.95 per copy (postage & handling included) to:

Name _____

Address _____

City_____ State_____ Zip_____

Enclosed is _____ in check or money order to cover cost.
Please gift wrap _____.
For deliveries in Tennessee add 42¢ sales tax.

The Memphis Guide
Redbird Press
P.O. Box 11441
Memphis, Tn. 38111

Please send _____ copies of *The Memphis Guide* at $7.95 per copy (postage & handling included) to:

Name _____

Address _____

City_____ State_____ Zip_____

Enclosed is _____ in check or money order to cover cost.
Please gift wrap _____.
For deliveries in Tennessee add 42¢ sales tax.

CUT ALONG DOTTED LINE